The New Map of (1911-1914)

The Story of the Recent European Diplomatic Crises and Wars and of Europe's Present Catastrophe

Herbert Adams Gibbons

Alpha Editions

This edition published in 2022

ISBN: 9789356712508

Design and Setting By

Alpha Editions

awww.alphaedis.com

Email - info@alphaedis.com

Contents

Map—The Balkan Peninsula in 1914

FOREWORD

On a July day in 1908, two American students, who had chosen to spend the first days of their honeymoon in digging the musty pamphleteers of the *Ligue* out of the Bodleian Library, were walking along the High Street in Oxford, when their attention was arrested by the cry of a newsboy. An ha'penny invested in a London newspaper gave them the news that Niazi bey had taken to the Macedonian highlands, and that a revolution was threatening to overthrow the absolutist *régime* of Abdul Hamid. The sixteenth century was forgotten in the absorbing and compelling interest of the twentieth.

Two weeks later the students were entering the harbour of Smyrna on a French steamer which was bringing back to constitutional Turkey the Young Turk exiles, including Prince Sabaheddine effendi of the Royal Ottoman House. From that day to this, the path of the two Americans, whose knowledge of history heretofore had been gained only in libraries, has led them through massacres in Asia Minor and Syria, and through mobilizations and wars in Constantinople, Bulgaria, Macedonia, Greece, and Albania, back westward to Austria-Hungary, {x} Italy, and France, following the trail of blood and fire from its origin in the Eastern question to the great European conflagration.

On the forty-fourth anniversary of Sedan, when German aëroplanes were flying over Paris, and the distant thunder of cannon near Meaux could be heard, this book was begun in the Bibliothèque Nationale by one of the students, while the other yielded to the more pressing call of Red Cross work. It is hoped that there is nothing that will offend in what is written here. At this time of tension, of racial rivalry, of mutual recrimination, the writer does not expect that his judgments will pass without protest and criticism. But he claims for them the lack of bias which, under the circumstances, only an American—of this generation at least—dare impute to himself.

The changes that are bringing about a new map of Europe have come within the intimate personal experience of the writer.

If foot-notes are rare, it is because sources are so numerous and so accessible. Much is what the writer saw himself, or heard from actors in the great tragedy, when events were fresh in their memory. The books of the colours, published by the Ministries of Foreign Affairs of the countries interested, have been consulted for the negotiations of diplomats. From day to day through these years, material has been gathered from newspapers, especially the Paris *Temps*, the London *Times*, the Vienna *Freie Press*, the

Constantinople *Orient*, and other journals of the Ottoman capital. {xi} The writer has used his own correspondence to the New York *Herald*, the New York *Independent*, and the Philadelphia *Telegraph*. For accuracy of dates, indebtedness is acknowledged to the admirable British *Annual Register*.

I am indebted to my friends, Alexander Souter, Litt.D., Professor of Humanity in Aberdeen University, and Mrs. Souter, for reading the proofs of this book and seeing it through the press in England. In the United States, the same kind office has been performed by my brother, Henry Johns Gibbons, Esq., of Philadelphia.

As this book goes to press for the third American edition, I wish to express my thanks to readers in Great Britain, America, France, Germany, and Australia for suggestions and corrections, and in particular to Baron Shaw of Dunfermline, to whom I owe the idea of the map that has been added to face the title-page.

PARIS, July, 1915.

CHAPTER I
GERMANY IN ALSACE AND LORRAINE

The war of 1870 added to the German Confederation Alsace and a large portion of Lorraine, both of which the Germans had always considered theirs historically and by the blood of the inhabitants. In annexing Alsace and Lorraine, the thought of Bismarck and von Moltke was not only to bring back into the German Confederation territories which had formerly been a part of it, but also to secure the newly formed Germany against the possibility of French invasion in the future. For this it was necessary to have undisputed possession of the valley of the Rhine and the crests of the Vosges.

From the academic and military point of view, the German thesis was not indefensible. But those who imposed upon a conquered people the Treaty of Frankfort forgot to take into account the sentiments of the population of the annexed territory. Germany annexed land. That was possible by the right of the strongest. She tried for over forty years to annex the population, but never succeeded. The makers of modern Germany were not alarmed at the persistent refusal of the Alsatians to become loyal German subjects. They knew that this would take time. They looked forward to the dying out of the party of protest when the next generation grew up,—a generation educated in German schools and formed in the German mould by the discipline of military service.

That there was still an Alsace-Lorraine "question" after forty years is a sad commentary either on the justice of the annexation of Alsace-Lorraine by Germany or on the ability of Germany to assimilate that territory which she felt was historically, geographically, and racially a part of the Teutonic Empire. In 1887, when "protesting deputies" were returned to the *Reichstag* in overwhelming numbers, despite the governmental weapons of intimidation, disenfranchisement, and North German immigration, Bismarck was face to face with the one great failure of his career. He consoled himself with the firm belief that all would be changed when the second generation, which knew nothing of France and to which the war was only a memory, peopled the unhappy provinces.

But that second generation came. Those who participated in the war of 1870, or who suffered by it, were few and far between. The hotheads and extreme francophiles left the country long ago, and their place was taken by immigrants who were supposed to be loyal sons of the Vaterland. Those of the younger indigenous brood, whose parents had brought them up as irreconcilables, ran away to serve in the French foreign legion, or went into exile, and became naturalized Frenchmen before their time of military service arrived. And yet the unrest continued. Strasbourg, Metz, Mulhouse, and Colmar were centres of political agitation, which an autocratic government and Berlin police methods were powerless to suppress.

The year 1910 marked the beginning of a new period of violent protest against Prussian rule. Not since 1888 was there such a continuous agitation and such a continuous persecution. The days when the Prussian police forbade the use of the French language on tombstones were revived, and the number of petty police persecutions recorded in the local press was equalled only by the number of public demonstrations on the part of the people, whose hatred of everything Prussian once more came to a fever-heat.

Let me cite a few incidents which I have taken haphazard from the journals of Strasbourg and Metz during the first seven months of 1910. The *Turnverein* of Robertsau held a gymnastic exhibition in which two French societies, those of Belfort and Giromagny, were invited to participate. The police refused to allow the French societies to march to the hall in procession, as was their custom, or to display their flags. Their two presidents were threatened with arrest. A similar incident was reported from Colmar. At Noisseville and Wissembourg the fortieth annual commemoration services held by the French veterans were considered treasonable, and they were informed that they would never again be allowed to hold services in the cemetery. At Mulhouse the French veterans were insulted by the police and not allowed to display their flags even in the room where they held their banquet. At the college of Thann a young boy of twelve, who curiously enough was the son of a notorious German immigrant, whistled the *Marseillaise* and was locked up in a cell for this offence. The conferring of the cross of the Legion of Honour on Abbé Faller, at Mars-la-Tour, created such an outburst of feeling that the German ambassador at Paris was instructed to request the French Government to refrain from decorating Alsatians. A volunteer of Mulhouse was reprimanded and refused advancement in the army because he used his mother-tongue in a private conversation. On July 1st, twenty-one border communes of Lorraine were added to those in which German had been made the official language. On July 25th, for the first time in the history of the University of Strasbourg, a professor was hissed out of his lecture room. He had said that the Prussians could speak better French than the Alsatians. The most serious demonstration which has occurred in Metz since the annexation, took place on Sunday evening, January 8, 1910, when the police broke up forcibly a concert given by a local society. The newspapers of Metz claimed that this was a private gathering, to which individual invitations had been sent, and was neither public nor political. The police invaded the hall, and requested the audience to disband. When the presiding officer refused, he and the leader of the orchestra were arrested. The audience, after a lively tussle, was expelled from the hall. Immediately a demonstration was planned to be held around the statue of General Ney. A large crowd paraded the city, singing the *Sambre-et-Meuse* and the *Marseillaise*. When the police found themselves powerless to stop the procession without bloodshed, they were compelled to call out the troops to clear the streets with fixed bayonets.

These incidents demonstrated the fact that French ideals, French culture, and the French language had been kept alive, and were still the inspiration of the unceasing—and successful—protest of nearly two million people against the Prussian domination. The effervescence was undoubtedly as strong in Alsace-Lorraine "forty years after" as it had been on the morrow of the annexation. But its francophile character was not necessarily the expression of desire for reunion with France. The inhabitants of the "lost provinces" had always been, racially and linguistically, as much German as French. Now that the unexpected has happened, and reunion with France seems probable, many Alsatians are claiming that this has been the unfailing goal of their agitation. But it is not true. It would be a lamentable distortion of fact if any such record were to get into a serious history of the period in which we live.

The political ideal of the Alsatians has been self-government. Their agitation has not been for separation *from* the German Confederation, but for a place *in* the German Confederation. A great number of the immigrants who were sent to "germanize" Alsace and Lorraine came to side with the indigenous element in their political demands. If the question of France and things French entered into the struggle, and became the heart of it, two reasons for this can be pointed out: France stood for the realization of the ideals of democracy to the descendants of the Strasbourg heroes of 1793; and the endeavour to stamp out the traces of the former nationality of the inhabitants of the provinces was carried on in a manner so typically and so foolishly Prussian that it kept alive the fire instead of extinguishing it. Persecution never fails to defeat its own ends. For human nature is keen to cherish that which is difficult or dangerous to enjoy.

To understand the Alsace-Lorraine question, from the internal German point of view, it is necessary to explain the political status of these provinces after the conquest, and their relationship to the Empire, in order to show that their continued unrest and unhappiness were not due to a ceaseless and stubborn protest against the Treaty of Frankfort.

When the German Empire was constituted, in 1872, it comprehended twenty-five distinct sovereign kingdoms, duchies, principalities, and free cities, and in a subordinate position, the territory ceded by France, which was made a *Reichsland,* owned in common by the twenty-five confederated sovereignties. The King of Prussia was made Emperor of the Confederation, and given extensive executive powers. Two assemblies were created to legislate for matters affecting the country as a whole. The *Bundesrath* is an advisory executive body as well as an upper legislative assembly. *It is composed of delegates of the sovereigns of the confederated states.* The lower imperial house, or *Reichstag,* is a popular assembly, whose members are returned by general elections throughout the Empire. In their internal affairs the confederated states are autonomous, and have their own local Parliaments. This scheme, fraught with dangers and seemingly unsurmountable difficulties, has survived; and, thanks to the predominance of Prussia and the genius of two great emperors, the seemingly heterogeneous mass has been moulded into a strong and powerful Empire.

In such an Empire, however, there never has been any place for Alsace-Lorraine. The conquered territory was not a national entity. It had no sovereign, and could not enter into the confederacy on an equal footing with the other twenty-five states. The Germans did not dare, at the time, to give the new member a sovereign, nor could they conjointly undertake its assimilation. Prussia, not willing to risk the strengthening of a south German state by the addition of a million and a half to its population, took upon herself what was the logical task of Baden or Wurtemberg or Bavaria.

So Alsace-Lorraine was an anomaly under the scheme of the organization of the German Empire. During forty years the *Reichsland* was without representation in the *Bundesrath,* and had thus had no real voice in the management of imperial affairs. By excluding the "reconquered brethren" from representation in the *Bundesrath,* Germany failed to win the loyalty of her new subjects. Where petty states with a tithe of her population and wealth have helped in shaping the destinies of the nation, the *Reichsland* had to feel the humiliation of "taxation without representation." It was useless to point out to the Alsatians that they had their vote in the *Reichstag.* For the *Bundesrath* is the power in Germany.

Nor did Alsace-Lorraine have real autonomy in internal affairs. The executive power was vested in a *Statthalter,* appointed by the Emperor, and supported by a foreign bureaucracy and a foreign police force. Before the Constitution of 1911, there was a local Parliament, called the *Landesausschuss,* which amounted to nothing, as the imperial Parliament had the privilege of initiating and enacting for the *Reichsland* any law it saw fit. Then, too, the delegates to the *Landesausschuss* were chosen by such a complicated form of suffrage that they represented the *Statthalter* rather than the people. And the *Statthalter* represented the Emperor!

In the first decade after the annexation, Prussian brutality and an unseemly haste to impose military service upon the conquered people led to an emigration of all who could afford to go, or who, even at the expense of material interest, were too high-spirited to allow their children to grow up as Germans. This emigration was welcomed and made easy, just as Austria-Hungary encouraged the emigration of Moslems from Bosnia and Herzegovina. For it enabled Bismarck to introduce a strong Prussian and Westphalian element into the *Reichsland* by settling immigrants on the vacant properties. But most of these immigrants, instead of prussianizing Alsace, have become Alsatians themselves. Some of the most insistent opponents of the Government, some of the most intractable among the agitators, have been those early immigrants or their children. This is quite natural, when we consider that they have cast their lot definitely with the country, and are just as much interested in its welfare as the indigenous element.

The revival of the agitation against Prussian Government in 1910 was a movement for autonomy on internal affairs, and for representation in the *Bundesrath*. The Alsatians wanted to be on a footing of constitutional equality with the other German States. One marvels at the Prussian mentality which could not see—either with the Poles or with the Alsatians—that fair play and justice would have solved the problems and put an end to the agitation which has been, during these past few years especially, a menace on the east and west to the existence of the Empire.

Something had to be done in the *Reichsland*. The anomalous position of almost two million German subjects, fighting for their political rights, and forming a compact mass upon the borders of France, was a question which compelled the interest of German statesmen, not only on account of its international aspect, but also because of the growing German public sentiment for social and political justice. The *Reichstag* was full of champions of the claims of the Alsatians,—champions who were not personally interested either in Alsace-Lorraine or in the influence of the agitation in the *Reichsland* upon France, but who looked upon the Alsace-Lorraine question as a wrong to twentieth-century civilization.

On March 14, 1910, Chancellor von Bethmann-Hollweg announced to the *Reichstag* that the Government was preparing a constitution for Alsace-Lorraine which would give the autonomy so long and so vigorously demanded. But he had in his mind, not a real solution of the question, but some sort of a compromise, which would satisfy the confederated states, and mollify the agitators of the *Reichsland, but at the same time preserve the*

Prussian domination in Alsace-Lorraine. In June, Herr Delbrück, Secretary of State for the Interior, was sent to Strasbourg to confer with the local authorities and representatives of the people concerning the projected constitution. It was during this visit that the Alsatians were disillusioned. A dinner, now famous or notorious, whichever you like, was given by the *Statthalter,* to which representative (!) members of the *Landesausschuss* were invited. At this dinner the real leaders of the country, such as Wetterlé, Preiss, Blumenthal, Weber, Bucher, and Theodor,—the very men who had made the demand for autonomy so insistent that the Government could no longer refuse to entertain it—were conspicuous by their absence. Those bidden to confer with Herr Delbrück in no way represented, but were on the other hand hostile to, the wishes of the people.

We cannot go into the involved story of the fight in the *Reichstag* over the new Constitution. The Delbrück project was approved by the *Bundesrath* on December 16, 1910, and debated in the following spring session of the *Reichstag.* Despite the warnings of the deputies from the *Reichsland,* and the brilliant opposition of the Socialists, the Constitution given to Alsace-Lorraine, on May 31st, was a pure farce. In no sense was it what the people of the *Reichsland* had wanted, although representation in the *Bundesrath* was seemingly given to them. The new Constitution preserved the united sovereignty of the confederated states, and its delegation to the Emperor, who still had the power to appoint and recall at will the *Statthalter,* and to initiate legislation in local matters. A *Landtag* took the place of the *Landesausschuss.* The Upper Chamber of the *Landtag* consists of thirty-six members, representing the religious confessions, the University and other bodies, the supreme court of Colmar, and the municipalities and chambers of commerce of Strasbourg, Mulhouse, Metz, and Colmar, to the number of eighteen; *and the other eighteen chosen by the Emperor.* The Lower Chamber has sixty members, elected by direct universal suffrage, with secret ballot. Electors over thirty-five possess two votes, and over forty-five three votes.

By forcing this Constitution upon Alsace-Lorraine, the interests of Prussia and of the House of Hohenzollern were considered to the detriment of the interests of the German Empire. A glorious opportunity for reconciliation and assimilation was lost. The Emperor would not listen to the admission of Alsace-Lorraine to the *Bundesrath* in the only logical way, by the creation of a new dynasty or a republican form of government, so that the Alsatian votes would represent a *sovereign* state. Prussia in her dealings with Alsace-Lorraine, has always been afraid, on the one hand, of the addition of *Bundesrath* votes to the seventeen of Bavaria, Saxony, Baden, and Wurtemberg, and on the other hand, of the repercussion upon her internal suffrage and other problems with the Socialists.

Since 1911, the eyes of many Alsatians have been directed once more towards France as the only—if forlorn—hope of justice and peace. What words could be found strong enough to condemn the suicidal folly of the German statesmen who allowed the disappointment over the Constitution to be followed by a series of incidents which have been like rubbing salt into a raw wound?

The first *Landtag*, in conformity to the Constitution of 1911, was elected in October. It brought into life a new political party, called "The National Union," led by Blumenthal, Wetterlé, and Preiss, who united for the purpose of demanding what the Constitution had not given them—the autonomy of Alsace and Lorraine. This party was badly beaten in this first election. But its defeat was not really a defeat for the principles of autonomy, as the German press stated at the time. The membership of the new *Landtag* was composed, in majority, of men who had been supporters of the demand for autonomy, but who had not joined the new party for reasons of local politics. Herr Delbrück had given universal suffrage (a privilege the Prussian electorate had never been able to gain in spite of its reiterated demands) to the *Reichsland* in the hope that the Socialists would prevent the Nationalists from controlling the Alsatian *Landtag*. Many Socialists, however, during the elections at Colmar and elsewhere, did not hesitate to cry in French, "*Vive la France! A bas la Prusse!*"

The Prussian expectations were bitterly deceived. The Landtag promptly showed that it was merely the Landesausschuss under another name. The nationalist struggle was revived; the same old questions came up again. The Government's appropriation "for purposes of state" was reduced one-third, and it was provided that the *Landtag* receive communication of the purposes for which the money was spent. The *Statthalter's* expenses were cut in half, and a bill, which had always been approved in previous years, providing for the payment of the expense of the Emperor's hunting trips in the *Reichsland*, failed to pass.

In the spring of 1912, the Prussians showed their disapproval of the actions of the new *Landtag* by withdrawing the orders for locomotives for the Prussian railways from the old Alsatian factory of Grafenstaden near Strasbourg. This was done absolutely without any provocation, and aroused a violent denunciation, not only among the purely German employés of the factory and in the newspapers, but also in the *Landtag*, which adopted an order of the day condemning most severely the attitude of the Imperial Government towards Alsace-Lorraine, of which this boycott measure was a petty and mean illustration.

The indignation was at its height when Emperor Wilhelm arrived in Strasbourg on May 13th. Instead of acting in a tactful manner and promising to set right this wrong done to the industrial life of Strasbourg, the Emperor addressed the following words to the Mayor:

"Listen. Up to here you have known only the good side of me; it is possible that you will learn the other side of me. Things cannot continue as they are: if this situation lasts, we shall suppress your Constitution and annex you to Prussia."

This typically Prussian speech, which in a few lines reveals the hopelessly unsuccessful tactics of the German Government towards the peoples whom it has tried to assimilate the world over, only served to increase the indignation of the inhabitants of the *Reichsland*; in fact, the repercussion throughout all Germany was very serious.

The arbitrary threat of the Emperor was badly received in the other federated states, whose newspapers pointed out that he had exceeded his authority. It gave the Socialists an opportunity to attack Emperor Wilhelm on the floor of the *Reichstag*. Four days after this threat was made, an orator of the Socialist party declared

"We salute the imperial words as the confession, full of weight and coming from a competent source, that annexation to Prussia is the heaviest punishment that one can threaten to impose upon a people for its resistance against Germany. It is a punishment like hard labour in the penitentiary with loss of civil rights."

This speech caused the Chancellor to leave the room with all the Ministry. On May 22d, the attack upon Emperor Wilhelm for his words at Strasbourg was renewed by another deputy, who declared that if such a thing had happened in England, "the English would shut up such a King at Balmoral or find for him some peaceful castle, such as that of Stemberg or the Villa Allatini at Salonika."

The answer of the *Landtag* to Emperor Wilhelm's threat was the passing of two unanimous votes: one demanding that hereafter the Constitution could not be modified except by the law of the country and not by the law of the Empire, and the other demanding for Alsace-Lorraine a national flag.

One could easily fill many pages with illustrations of senseless persecutions, most of them of the pettiest character, but some more serious in nature, which Alsace and Lorraine have had to endure since the granting of the Constitution. Newspapers, illustrated journals, clubs and organizations of all kinds have been annoyed constantly by police interference. Their editors, artists, and managers have been brought frequently into court. Zislin and Hansi, celebrated caricaturists, have found themselves provoked to bolder and bolder defiances by successive condemnations, and have endured imprisonment as well as fines. Hansi was sentenced to a year's imprisonment by the High Court of Leipsic only a month before the present war broke out, and chose exile rather than a Prussian fortress.

The greatest effort during the past few years has been made in the schools to influence the minds of the growing generation against the "*souvenir de France*" and to impress upon the Alsatians what good fortune had come to them to be born German citizens.

Among the boys, the influence of this teaching has been such that over twenty-two thousand fled from home during the period of 1900-1913 to enlist in the Foreign Legion of the French Army. The campaign of the German newspapers in Alsace-Lorraine, and, in fact, throughout Germany, was redoubled in 1911. Parents were warned of the horrible treatment accorded to the poor boys who were misguided enough to throw away their citizenship, and go to be killed in Africa under the French flag. The result of this campaign was that the Foreign Legion received a larger number of Alsatians in 1912 than had enlisted during a single year since 1871!

Among the girls, the German educational system flattered itself that it could completely change the sentiments of a child, especially in the boarding-schools. Last year the Empress of Germany visited a girls' school near Metz, which is one of the best German schools in the *Reichsland*. As she was leaving, she told the children that she wanted to give them something. What did they want? The answer was not sweets or cake, but that they might be taught a little French!

Since 1910, the German war budget has carried successively larger items for the strengthening of forts and the building of barracks in Metz, Colmar, Mulhouse, Strasbourg, Neuf-Brisach, Bischwiller, Wissembourg, Mohrange, Sarrebourg, Sarreguemines, Saarbruck, Thionville, Molsheim, and Saverne. The former French provinces have been flooded with garrisons, and have been treated just as they were treated forty years ago. The insufferable spirit of militarism, and the arrogance of the Prussian officers in Alsatian towns, have served to turn against the Empire many thousands whom another policy might have won. For it must be remembered that by no means all the inhabitants of the *Reichsland* have been by birth and by home training French sympathizers. Instead of crushing out the "*souvenir de France*," the Prussian civil and military officials have caused it to be born in many a soul which was by nature German.

The most notorious instance of military arrogance occurred in the autumn of 1913 in Saverne. Lieutenant von Forstner, who was passing in review cases of discipline, had before him a soldier who had stabbed an Alsatian, and had been sentenced to two months' imprisonment. "Two months on account of an Alsatian blackguard!" he cried. "I would have given you ten marks for your trouble." The story spread, and the town, tired of the attitude of its garrison, began in turn to show its contempt for the Kaiser's soldiers. Windows in von Forstner's house were broken. Every time officers or soldiers appeared on the streets they were hooted. Saverne was put under martial law. Threats were made to fire upon the citizens. One day Lieutenant von Forstner struck a lame shoemaker across the forehead with his sword. The affair had gone so far that public sentiment in Germany demanded some action. Instead of adequately punishing von Forstner and other officers, who had so maddened the civil population against them, the German military authorities gave the guilty officers nominal sentences, and withdrew the garrison.

All these events had a tremendous repercussion in France. It is impossible to exaggerate the ill-feeling aroused on both sides of the Rhine, in Germany, in Alsace-Lorraine, and in France by the persecutions in the *Reichsland*. Only one who knows intimately the French can appreciate their feeling—or share it—over the Zislin and Hansi trials, the Saverne affair, the suppression of the *Souvenir Français*, the *Lorraine Sportive* and other organizations, and the campaign against the Foreign Legion. It has given the French soldiers in the present war something to fight for which is as sacred to them as the defence of French soil. The power of this sentiment is indicated by the invasion of Alsace, the battle of Altkirk, and the occupation of Mulhouse at the beginning of August. The French could not be held back from this wild dash. Strategy was powerless in the face of the sentiment of a *national* army.

The Alsatian leaders themselves have seen the peril to the peace of Europe of the German attitude towards their country. They did not want France drawn into a war for their liberation. They were alarmed over the possibility of this, and desired it to be understood that their agitation had nothing international in it. The attitude of all the anti-Prussian parties may be summed up in the words of Herr Wolff, leader of the Government Liberal party, who declared that "all the inhabitants of the *Reichsland* had as their political ambition was only the elevation of Alsace-Lorraine to the rank of an independent and federated state, like the other twenty-five component parts of the German Empire." Their sincerity and their desire to preserve peace is proved by the motion presented by the leaders of four of the political groups in the *Reichsland*, which was voted on May 6, 1912, without discussion, by the *Landtag*:

"The Chamber invites the *Statthalter* to instruct the representatives of Alsace-Lorraine in the *Bundesrath* to use all the force they possess against the idea of a war between Germany and France, and to influence the

Bundesrath to examine the ways which might possibly lead to a *rapprochement* between France and Germany, which *rapprochement* will furnish the means of putting an end to the race of armaments."

The mismanagement of the *Reichsland* has done more than prevent the harmonious union of the former French provinces with Germany. It has had an effect, the influence of which cannot be exaggerated, upon nourishing the hopes of revenge of France, and the resentment against the amputation of 1870. On neither side of the Vosges has the wound healed. The same folly which has kept alive a Polish question in eastern Prussia for one hundred and twenty-five years, has not failed to make impossible the prussianizing of Alsace and Lorraine. The Prussian has never understood how to win the confidence of others. There has been no Rome in his political vision. As for conceptions of toleration, of kindness, and of love, they are non-existent in Prussian officialdom. Nietzsche revealed the character of the Prussian in his development of the idea of the *übermensch*. The ideal of perfect manhood is the imposition of one will on another will by force. Mercy and pity, according to Nietzsche, were signs of weakness, the symbols of the slave.

Under the circumstances, then, we are compelled after forty-five years to revise our estimate of Bismarck's sagacity. His genius was limited by the narrow horizon of his own age. He did not see that the future Germany needed other things that France could give far more than she needed Alsace and Lorraine. In posterity, Bismarck would have had a greater place had he, in the last minutes of the transactions at Versailles, given back Alsace and Lorraine to France, waived the war indemnity, and asked in return Algeria or other French colonies.

But would it have been different under Germany in the French colonies? A Herrero, employed in the Johannesburg mines, wrote his brother in German South-West Africa: "The country of the English is truly a good country. Even if your superior is present, he doesn't strike you, and if he strikes you and goes thus beyond legal limits, he is punished like anyone else."

CHAPTER II
THE "WELTPOLITIK" OF GERMANY

When the transrhenane provinces of the old German Empire were added to France in the eighteenth century, the assimilation of these territories was a far different proposition from their refusion into the mould of a new German Empire in 1871. In the first place, the old German Empire was a mediæval institution which, in the evolution of modern Europe, was decaying. Alsace and Lorraine were not taken away from a political organism of which they were a vital part. The ties severed were purely dynastic. In the second place, the consciousness of national life was awakened in Alsace and Lorraine during the time that they were under French rule, and because they shared in the great movement of the birth of democracy following the French Revolution.

France, then, by the Treaty of Frankfort, believed that she had been robbed of a portion of her national territory. The people of the annexed provinces, as was clearly shown by the statement of their representatives at Bordeaux, did not desire to enter the German Confederation.

Germany failed to do the only thing that could possibly have made her new territories an integral part of the new Empire, *i.e.* to place Alsace-Lorraine upon a footing of equality with the other states of the Confederation, and make their entry that of an autonomous sovereign state. Consequently, neither in France nor in the *Reichsland* was the Treaty of Frankfort accepted as a permanent change in the map of Europe. Germany has always been compelled, in her international politics, to count upon the possibility of France making an attempt to win back the lost provinces. She has sought to form alliances to strengthen her own position in Europe, and to keep France weak. France, the continued object of German hostility, has found herself compelled to ally herself with Russia, with whom she has never had anything in common, and to compound her colonial rivalries in Africa with her hereditary enemy, Great Britain. This is the first cause of the unrest in Europe that has culminated in a general European war.

The second cause is the *Weltpolitik* of Germany which has brought the German Empire into conflict with Great Britain and France outside of Europe, and with Russia in Europe.

On the map of Europe, Russia, Great Britain, and France are, in 1914, practically what they were in 1815. The changes, logical and in accordance with the spirit of centralization of the nineteenth century, have transformed middle and south-eastern Europe. The changes in south-eastern Europe have been effected at the expense of the Ottoman Empire, and have been a gradual development throughout the century, from the outbreak of the Greek revolution in 1822 to the Treaty of London in 1913. In middle Europe, during the twelve years between 1859 and 1871, the three Powers whose national unity, racially as well as politically, was already achieved at the time of the Congress of Vienna, were brought face to face with three new Powers, united Germany, united Italy, and the Dual Monarchy of Austria-Hungary.

The nineteenth century has been called the age of European colonization. Europe began to follow its commerce with other continents by the imposition of its civilization and its political system upon weaker races. Checked by the rising republic of the United States from encroaching upon the liberties of the peoples of North and South America, there have been no acquisitions of territory by European nations in the western continents since the Congress of Vienna. European expansion directed itself towards Africa, Asia, and the islands of the oceans. There was no Oriental nation strong enough to promulgate a Monroe Doctrine.

In extra-European activities, Great Britain, France, and Russia were the pioneers. That they succeeded during the nineteenth century in placing under their flag the choicest portions of Africa and the backward nations of Asia, was due neither to the superior enterprise and energy, nor to the greater foresight, of the Anglo-Saxon, French, and Russian nations. They had achieved their national unity, and they were geographically in a position to take advantage of the great opportunities which were opening to the world for colonization since the development of the steamship and the telegraph.

But the other three Powers of Europe came late upon the scene. It has only been within the last quarter of a century that Germany and Italy have been in the position to look for overseas possessions. It has only been within the last quarter of a century that Austria, finding her union with Hungary a durable one, has been able to think of looking beyond her limits to play a part, as other nations had long been doing, in the history of the outside world.

By every force of circumstances, the three new States—threatened by their neighbours, who had looked with jealous, though powerless, eyes upon their consolidation—were brought together into a defensive alliance. The Powers of the Triple Alliance drifted into a union of common general aims and ambitions, if not of particular interests, against their three more fortunate rivals, who had been annexing the best portions of the Asiatic and African continents while they were struggling with internal problems.

Oceans of ink have been wasted upon polemics against the peace-disturbing character of the Triple Alliance. Especially has Germany and her growing *Weltpolitik* been subject to criticism, continuous and untiring, on the part of the British and French press. But the question after all is a very simple one: the three newer Powers of Europe have not been willing to be content with an application in practical world politics of the principle that "to him that hath shall be given." Germany and Italy, transformed under modern economic conditions into industrial states, have been looking for outside markets, and they have wanted to enjoy those markets in regions of the globe either actually under their flag or subjected to their political influence. In other words, they have wanted their share in the division of Africa and Asia into spheres under the control of European nations.

Is a logical and legitimate ambition to play a part in the world's politics in proportion to one's population, one's wealth, one's industrial and maritime activity, necessarily a menace to the world's peace? It has always been, and I suppose always will be, in the nature of those who have, to look with alarm upon the efforts of those who have not, to possess something. Thus capital, irrespective of epoch or nationality or of religion, has raised the cry of alarm when it has seen the tendency for betterment, for education, for the development of ideals and a sense of justice on the part of labour. In just the same way, Russia with her great path across the northern half of Asia and her new and steadily growing empire in the Caucasus and central Asia; France with the greater part of northern and central Africa, and an important corner of Asia under her flag; and Great Britain with her vast territories in every portion of the globe, raised the cry of "Wolf, Wolf!" when the Powers of the Triple Alliance began to look with envious eye upon the rich colonies of their neighbours, and to pick up by clever diplomacy—and brutal force, if you wish—a few crumbs of what was still left for themselves.

The result of these alarming ambitions of the Triple Alliance has been the coming together of Russia, France, and England, hereditary enemies in former days but now friends and allies, in the maintenance of the colonial "trust."

The great cry of the Triple Entente is the maintenance of the European equilibrium. For this they have reason. Europe could know no lasting peace under Teutonic aggression. But is there not also to the account of the Triple Entente some blame for the unrest in Europe and for the great catastrophe which has come upon the world? For while their policy has been the maintenance of the European equilibrium, it has been coupled with the maintenance of an extra-European balance of power wholly in their favour.

The sense of justice, of historical proportion, and the logic of economic evolution make one sympathize, in abstract principle, not only with the *Weltpolitik* of Germany, but also with Austria-Hungary's desire for an outlet to the sea, and with Italy's longing to have in the Mediterranean the position which history and geography indicated ought to be, and might again be, hers.

But sympathy in abstract principle is quite another thing from sympathy in fact. In order to appreciate the *Weltpolitik* of Germany, and be able to form an intelligent opinion in regard to it—*for it is the most vital and burning problem in the world to-day*—we must consider it from the point of view of its *full significance in practice* in the history of the world.

Bismarck posed as the disinterested "honest courtier" of Europe in the Congress of Berlin. The declaration he had made, that the whole question of the Orient "was not worth the finger bone of a Pomeranian grenadier," was corroborated by his actions during the sessions of the Congress. We have striking illustrations of this in the memoirs of Karatheodory pasha, who recorded from day to day, during the memorable sessions of the Congress, his astonishment at the indifference which Bismarck displayed to the nationalities of the Balkans, and to the complications which might arise in Europe from their rivalries.

Bismarck did not see how vital was to be the Balkan question with the future of the nation he had built. Nor did he see the intimate relationship between the economic progress of united Germany and the question of colonies. One searches in vain the speeches and writings of the Iron Chancellor for any reference to the importance of the two problems, in seeking the solution of which the fabric of his building is threatened with destruction.

Perhaps it is easy for us, in looking backwards, to point out the lack of foresight which was shown by Bismarck in regard to the future of Germany. Forty-five years later, we are able to pass in review the unforeseen developments of international politics and the amazing economic evolution of contemporary Europe. Perhaps it is unreasonable to expect that much attention and thought should have been given by the maker of modern Germany to the possible sphere that Germany might be called upon to play in the world outside of Europe.

For we must remember that the new Germany, after the Franco-Prussian War, was wholly in an experimental stage, and that the duty at hand was the immediate consolidation of the various states into a political and economic fabric. There was enough to demand all the attention and all the genius of Bismarck and his co-workers in solving these problems. Cordial relationship with Austria had to be reëstablished. The dynasties of the south German kingdoms and of the lesser potentates, whose names still remained legion in spite of the *Reichsdeputationshauptschluss* of 1803, had to be carefully handled. There were four definite internal problems which confronted Bismarck: the relationship of the empire to the Catholic Church; the reconciliation of the different peoples into a harmonious whole; the establishment of representative government without giving the strong socialistic elements the upper hand; and the development of the economic wealth of Germany.

There was little time to think of Germany's place in the world's politics. In foreign affairs, it was considered that the exigencies of the moment could be met by adopting a policy of conciliation towards both Russia and Austria, and the winning of the friendship of Italy. The *Kulturkampf*, the creation of the *Bundesrath* under Prussian hegemony, and the formation of the Triple Alliance and the events connected with them, are important in an analysis of Germany's international politics. Unfortunately we cannot bring them into the scope of this book. We can mention only the various factors that have been directly responsible for giving birth to what is called the *Weltpolitik*.

These factors are the belief of the German people in the superiority of their race and its world-civilizing mission; their connotation of the word "German"; the consciousness of their military strength being disproportionate to their political influence; the rapid increase of the population and the development of the industrial and commercial prosperity of the empire; and the realization of the necessity of a strong navy, with naval bases and coaling-stations in all parts of the world, for the adequate protection of commerce.

The belief of the German people in the superiority of their race and its world-civilizing mission is a sober fact. It pervades every class of society from the Kaiser down to the workingman. It is heralded from the pulpit, taught in the schools, and is a scientific statement in the work of many of Germany's leading scholars. The anthropologist Woltmann said that "the German is the superior type of the species *homo sapiens*, from the physical as well as the intellectual point of view." Wirth declared that "the world owes its civilization to Germany alone" and that "the time is near when the earth must inevitably be conquered by the Germans." The scientific book—a serious one—in which these statements occur was so popular that it sold five editions in three years! Paulsen remarked that "humanity is aware of, and admires, the German omnipresence." Hartmann taught that the European family is divided into two races, male and female, of which the first, of course, was exclusively German, while the second included Latins, Celts, and Slavs. "Marriage is inevitable." Goethe expressed in *Faust* the opinion that the work of the Germans was to make the habitable world worth living in, while Schiller boasted, "Our language shall reign over the whole world," and that "the German day lasts until the end of time." Schiller also prophesied that "two empires shall perish in east and west, I tell you, and it is only the Lutheran faith which shall remain." Fichte, one hundred years ago, exhorted the Germans to be "German patriots, and we shall not cease to be cosmopolitan." Heine believed that "not only Alsace and Lorraine, but all France shall be ours."

To show the German state of mind towards those whom they have not hesitated to provoke to arms, the remarkable teaching of Hummel's book, which is used in the German primary schools, is a convincing illustration. Frenchmen are monkeys, and the best and strongest elements in the French race asserted to be German by blood. The Russians are slaves, as their name implies. Treitschke's opinion of the British is that "among them love of money has killed all sentiment of honour and all distinction of just and unjust. Their setting sun is our aurora." One of the leading newspapers of Germany recently said: "The army of the first line of which Germany will dispose from the first day of the mobilization will be sufficient to crush France, even if we must detach a part of it against England. If England enters the war, it will be the end of the British Empire, for England is a colossus with feet of clay."

The Kaiser has been the spokesman of the nation in heralding publicly the belief in the superiority of the German people, and its world mission. It was at the twenty-fifth anniversary of the founding of the Empire that the scope of the *Weltpolitik* was announced by Wilhelm II. He said:

"The German Empire has become a world empire (*ein Weltreich*). Everywhere, in the most distant lands, are established thousands and thousands of our compatriots. German science, German activity, the defenders of the German ideal pass the ocean. By thousands of millions we count the wealth that Germany transports across the seas. It is your duty, gentlemen, to aid me to establish strong bonds between our Empire of Europe and this greater German Empire (*dieses grössere Deutsche Reich*) ... May our German Fatherland become one day so powerful that, as one formerly used to say, *Civis romanus sum*, one may in the future need only to say, *Ich bin ein deutscher Burger.*"

At Aix-la-Chapelle, on June 20, 1902, he revealed his ambition in one sentence, "*It is to the empire of the world that the German genius aspires.*" Just before leaving for the visit to Tangier in 1905—the visit which was really the beginning of one of the great issues of the present war—he said at Bremen: "If later one must speak in history of a universal domination by the Hohenzollern, of a universal German empire, this domination must not be established by military conquest.... *God has called us to civilize the world: we are the missionaries of human progress.*" This idea was developed further at Münster, on September 1, 1907, when the Kaiser proclaimed: "The German people will be the block of granite on which our Lord will be able to elevate and achieve the civilization of the world!"

This attitude of mind is as common among the disciples of those wonderful leaders who founded the international movement for the solidarity of interests of labour, as it is among the aristocratic and intellectual elements of the nation. The German Socialist has proclaimed the brotherhood of man, and the common antagonism of the wage-earners of the world against their capitalistic oppressors. But, for all his preaching, the German Socialist is first of all a German. He has come to believe that the mission of Socialism will be best fulfilled through the triumph of Germanism. This belief is sincere. It is a far cry from Karl Marx to the militant—or rather militarist—German Socialist, bearing arms gladly upon the battlefields of Europe to-day, because he is inspired by the thought that the triumph of the army in which he fights will aid the cause of Socialism.[1]

> [1] While the *Landtage* of the German states are mostly controlled by Conservative elements, owing to restricted suffrage, the *Reichstag* is one of the most intelligently democratic legislative bodies in the world. Its social legislation is surpassed by that of no other country. During thirty years the Socialist vote in Germany has increased one thousand per cent. It now represents one-third of the total electorate. But the Socialists are to a man behind the war.

There is a striking analogy between the German Socialist of the present generation and the Jacobins of 1793. The heralders of *Liberté, Egalité et Fraternité* fought for the spread of the principles of the Revolution through God's chosen instruments, the armies of France, and were carried away by their enthusiasm until they became the facile agents for saddling Europe with the tyranny of Napoleon. Love for humanity was turned into blood-lust, and fighting for freedom into seeking for booty and glory. Are the profound thinkers of the German universities, and the visionaries of the workingmen's forums following to-day the same path? Does the propagation of an ideal lead inevitably to a blind fanaticism, where the dreamer becomes in his own imagination a chosen instrument of God to shed blood?

There is undoubtedly an intellectual and idealistic basis to German militarism and to German arrogance.

Their connotation of the word "German" has led the Germans to look upon territories outside of their political confines as historically and racially, hence rightfully, virtually, and eventually theirs. A geography now in its two hundred and forty-fifth edition in the public schools (Daniel's *Leitfaden der Geographie*) states that "Germany is the heart of Europe. Around it extend Austria, Switzerland, Belgium, Luxemburg, and Holland, which were all formerly part of the same state, and are peopled entirely or in the majority by Germans."

When German children have been for the past generation deliberately taught as a matter of fact—not as an academic or debatable question—that *Deutschland* ought to be more than it is, we can understand how the neutrality of their smaller neighbours seems to the Germans a negligible consideration. No wonder the soldiers who ran up against an implacable enemy at Liège, Namur, and Charleroi thought there must be a mistake somewhere, and were more angered against the opposition of those whom they regarded as their brothers of blood than they later showed themselves against the French. No wonder that the sentiment of the whole German nation is for the retention of Belgium, their path to the sea. It was formerly German. Its inhabitants are German. Let it become German once more!

But to the Germans there are other and equally important elements belonging to their nation outside of the states upon the confines of the empire. These are the German emigrants and German colonists in all portions of the world. In recent years there has come to the front more than ever the theory that *German nationality cannot be lost by foreign residence or by transference of allegiance to another State: once a German, always a German.*

Convincing proof of this is found in the new citizenship law, sanctioned with practical unanimity by the *Reichstag* and *Bundesrath*, which went into effect on January 1, 1914. According to Article XIII of this law, "a former German who has not taken up his residence in Germany may on application be naturalized." This applies also *to one who is descended from a former German, or who has been adopted as the child of such*! According to Article XIV, any former German who holds a position in the German Empire in any part of the world, in the service of a German religious society or of a German school, is looked upon as a German citizen "by assumption." Any foreigner holding such a position may be naturalized without having a legal residence in Germany. The most interesting provision of all is in Article XXV, section 2 of which says: "Citizenship is not lost by one who before acquiring foreign citizenship has secured on application the written consent of the competent authorities of his home state to retain his citizenship."

Germany allows anyone of German blood to become a German citizen, even if he has never seen Germany and has no intention of taking up his residence there; and Germans, who have emigrated to other countries, secure the amazing opportunity to acquire foreign citizenship without losing their German citizenship.

The result of this law, since the war broke out, has been to place a natural and justifiable suspicion upon all Germans living in the countries of the enemies of Germany. It is impossible to overestimate the peril from the secret ill-will and espionage of Germans residing in the countries that are at war with Germany. There are undoubtedly many thousands of cases where Germans have been honest and sincere in their change of allegiance, but how are the nations where they have become naturalized to be sure of this? A legal means has been given to these naturalized Germans to retain, *without the knowledge of the nation where their oath of allegiance has been received in good faith*, citizenship in Germany.

German emigration and colonization societies, and many seemingly purely religious organizations for "the propagation of the faith in foreign lands," have been untiring in their efforts to preserve in the minds of Germans who have left the Fatherland the principle, "once a German always a German." The Catholic as well as the Lutheran Church has lent itself to this effort. Wherever there are Germans, one finds the German church, the German school, the *Zeitung*, the *Bierhalle*, and the *Turnverein*. The Deutschtum is sacred to the Germans. One cannot but have the deepest respect for the pride of Germans in their ancestry, in their language, in their church, and in the preservation of traditional customs. There is no better blood in the world than German blood, and one who has it in his veins may well be proud of it: for it is an inheritance which is distinctly to a man's intellectual and physical advantage. But, in recent years, the effort has been made to confuse *Deutschtum* with *Deutschland*. Here lies a great danger. We may admire and reverence all that has come to us from Germany. But the world cannot look on impassively at a propaganda which is leading to *Deutschland über alles!*

When we take the megalomania of the Germans, their ambition to fulfil their world mission, their belief in their peculiar fitness to fulfil that mission, and their idea of the German character of the neighbouring states, and contrast the dream with the reality, we see how they must feel, *especially as they are conscious of the fact that they dispose of a military strength disproportionate to their position in mondial politics*. Great Britain, with one-third less population, "the colossus with the feet of clay," owns a good fourth of the whole world; France, the nation of "monkeys," which was easily crushed in 1870, holds sway over untold millions of acres and natives in Africa and Asia; while Russia, the nation of "slaves," has a half of Europe and Asia.

The most civilized people in the world, with a world mission to fulfil, is dispossessed by its rivals of inferior races *and of inferior military strength*! The thinking German is by the very nature of things a militarist.

But even if the *logic* of the *Weltpolitik*, under the force of circumstances, did not push the German of every class and category to the belief that Germany must solve her great problems of the present day by force of arms, especially since her military strength is so much greater than that of her rivals, the nature of the German would make him lean towards force as the decisive argument in the question of extending his influence. For from the beginning of history the *German* has been a *war man*. He has asserted himself by force. He has proved less amenable to the refining and softening influences of Christianity and civilization than any other European race. He has worshipped force, and relied wholly upon force to dominate those with whom he has come into contact. The leopard cannot change his spots. So it is as natural for the German of the twentieth century to use the sword as an argument as it was for the German of the tenth century, or, indeed, of the first century. We cannot too strongly insist upon this fatal tendency of the German to subordinate natural, moral, legal, and technical rights to the supremacy of brute force. There is no conception of what is called "moral suasion" in the German mind. Although some of the greatest thinkers of the world have been and are to-day Germans, yet the German nation has never come to the realization that the pen may be mightier than the sword. Give the German a pen, and he will hold the world in admiration of his intellect. Give him a piano or a violin, and he will hold the world in adoration of his soul. But give him a sword, and he will hold the world in abhorrence of his force. For there never was an *übermensch* who was not a devil. Else he would be God.

But the *Weltpolitik* has had other and more tangible and substantial causes than the three we have been considering. It is not wholly the result of the German idea that Germany can impose her will upon the world and has the right to do so. The power of Germany comes from the fact that her people have been workers as well as dreamers. *The rapid increase of the population and development of the industrial and commercial prosperity of the empire* have given the Germans a wholly justifiable economic foundation for their *Weltpolitik*.

United Germany, after the successful war of 1870, began the greatest era of industrial growth and prosperity that has ever been known in the history of the world. Not even the United States, with all its annual immigration and opening up of new fields and territories, has been able to show an industrial growth comparable to that of Germany during the past forty years. In this old central Europe cities have grown almost over night.

Railways have been laid down, one after the other, until the whole empire is a network of steel. Mines and factories have sprung into being as miraculously as if it had been by the rubbing of Aladdin's lamp. The population has increased more than half in forty years.

It was as her population and her productive power increased far more quickly and far beyond that of her neighbours, that Germany began to look out into the extra-European world for markets. She had reached the point when her productivity, in manufacturing lines, had exceeded her power of consumption. Where find markets for the goods? German merchants, and not Prussian militarists, began to spread abroad in Germany the idea that there was a world equilibrium, as important to the future of the nations of Europe as was the European equilibrium. Germany, looking out over the world, saw that the prosperity of Great Britain was due to her trade, and that the security and volume of this trade were due to her colonies.

Who does not remember the remarkable stamp issued by the Dominion of Canada to celebrate the Jubilee of Queen Victoria? On the mercatorial projection of the world, the British possessions were given in red. One could not find any corner of the globe where there were not ports to which British ships in transit could go, and friendly markets for British commerce. The Germans began to compare their industries with those of Great Britain. Their population was larger than that of the great colonial power, and was increasing more rapidly. Their industries were growing apace. For their excess population, emigration to a foreign country meant annual loss of energetic and capable compatriots. Commerce had to meet unfair competition in every part of the world. Outside of the Baltic and North Seas, there was no place that a German ship could touch over which the German flag waved.

It was not militarism or chauvinism or megalomania, but the natural desire of a people who found themselves becoming prosperous to put secure and solid foundations under that prosperity, that made the Germans seek for colonies and launch forth upon the *Weltpolitik*.

The first instance of the awakening on the part of the German people to a sense that there was something which interested them outside of Europe, was the annexation by Great Britain in 1874 of the Fiji Islands, with which German traders had just begun, at great risk and painstaking efforts, to build up a business. This was the time when the Government was engaged in its struggles with the Church and socialism, and when the working of the *Reichstag* and the *Bundesrath* was still in an experimental stage. Nothing could be done. *But there began to be a feeling among Germans that in the future Germany ought to be consulted concerning the further extension of the sovereignty of a European nation over any part of the world then unoccupied or still independent.* But Germany was not in a position either to translate this sentiment into a vigorous foreign policy, or to begin to seize her share of the world by taking the portions which Great Britain and Russia and France had still left vacant.

German trade, still in its infancy, received cruel setbacks by the British occupation of Cyprus in 1878 and of Egypt in 1883, the French occupation of Tunis in 1881, and the Russian and British dealings with central Asia and Afghanistan. The sentiment of the educated and moneyed classes in Germany began to impose upon the Government the necessity of entering the colonial field. The action in Egypt and in Tunis brought about the beginning of German colonization. Bismarck had just finished successfully his critical struggle with the socialists. The decks were cleared for action. In 1882, a Bremen trader, Herr Lüdritz, by treaties with the native chiefs, gained the Bay of Angra-Pequena on the west coast of Africa. For two years no attention was paid to this treaty, which was a purely private commercial affair. In 1884, shortly after the occupation of Egypt, a dispute arose between the British authorities at Cape Town and Herr Lüdritz. Bismarck saw that he must act, or the old story of extension of British sovereignty would be repeated. He telegraphed to the German Consul at Cape Town that the Imperial Government had annexed the coast and *hinterland* from the Orange River to Cape Frio.

Other annexations in Africa and the Pacific followed in the years 1884-1886. In Africa, the German flag was hoisted over the east coast of the continent, north of Cape Delgado and the river Rovuma, and in Kamerun and Togo on the Gulf of Guinea. In the Pacific, Kaiser Wilhelm's Land was formed of a portion of New Guinea, with some adjacent islands, and the Bismarck Archipelago, the Solomon Islands, and the Marshall Islands were gathered in. Since those early years of feverish activity, there have been no new acquisitions in Africa, other than the portion of French Congo ceded in 1912 as "compensation" for the French protectorate of Morocco. In the Pacific, in 1899, after the American conquest of the Philippines, the Caroline, Pelew, and Marianne groups and two of the Samoan Islands were added.

In China, Germany believed that she had the right to expect to gain a position equal to that of Great Britain at Hongkong and Shanghai, of France at Tonkin, and Russia in Manchuria. She believed that it was just as necessary for her to have a fortified port to serve as a naval base for her fleet as it was for the other Powers, and that by a possession of territory which could be called her own she would be best able to get her share of the commerce of the Far East. From 1895 to 1897, Germany examined carefully all the possible places which would serve best for the establishment of a naval and commercial base. At the beginning of 1897, after naval and commercial missions had made their reports, a technical mission was sent out whose membership included the famous Franzius, the creator of Kiel. This mission reported in favour of Kiau-Chau on the peninsula of Shantung in north China.

When negotiations were opened with the Chinese, the answer of the Chinese Government was to send soldiers to guard the bay! The Kaiser, in a visit to the Czar at Peterhof in the summer of 1897, secured Russian "benevolent neutrality." The murder of two missionaries in the interior of the province, on November 1st of the same year, gave Germany her chance. Three German war vessels landed troops on the peninsula, and seized Kiau-Chau and Tsing-Tau. After five months of tortuous negotiations, a treaty was concluded between Germany and China on March 6, 1899. Kiau-Chau with adjacent territory was leased to Germany for ninety-nine years. To German capital and German commerce were given the right of preference for every industrial enterprise on the peninsula, the concession for the immediate construction of a railway, and the exclusive right to mining along the line of the railway. Thus the greater part of the province of Shantung passed under the economic influence of Germany.

The entry of Japan into the war of 1914 is due to her desire to remedy a great injustice which has been done to Japanese commerce in the province of Shantung by the German occupation, to her fear of this naval base opposite her coast (just as she feared Port Arthur), and probably to the intention of occupying the Marianne Islands, the Marshall Islands, and the Eastern and Western Carolines, in order that the Japanese navy may have important bases in a possible future conflict with the United States.

When Germany leased Kiau-Chau, she declared solemnly that the port of Tsing-Tau would be an open port, *ein frei Hafen für allen Nationen.* But Japanese trade competition soon caused her to go back on her word. She conceived a clever scheme in 1906, by which the Chinese customs duties were allowed to be collected within the Protectorate in return for an annual sum of twenty per cent. upon the entire customs receipts of the Tsing-Tau district. In this way, she is more than recompensed for the generosity displayed in allowing German goods to be subject to the Chinese customs. She reimburses herself at the expense of the Japanese! Berlin could not have been astonished at the ultimatum of August 15th from Tokio.

There has always been much opposition in Germany to the colonization policy of the Government, the dissatisfaction over the poor success of the attempts at African colonization led Chancellor Caprivi to state that the worst blow an enemy could give him was to force upon him more territories in Africa! The Germans never got on well with the negroes. Their colonists, for the most part too poor to finance properly agricultural schemes, lived by trading. Like all whites, they cheated the natives and bullied them into giving up their lands. In South-West Africa, a formidable uprising of the Herreros resulted in the massacre of all the Germans except the missionaries and the colonists who had established themselves there before the German occupation. The suppression of this rebellion took more than a year, and cost Germany an appalling sum in money and many lives. But it cost the natives more. Two thirds of the nation of the Herreros were massacred: while only six or seven thousand were in arms, the German official report stated that forty thousand were killed. The Germans confiscated all the lands of the natives.

In 1906, after twenty-one years of German rule, there were in South-West Africa sixteen thousand prisoners of war out of a total native population of thirty-one thousand. All the natives lived in concentration camps, and were forced to work for the Government. In commenting upon the Herrero campaign, Pastor Frenssen, one of the most brilliant writers of modern Germany, put in the mouth of the hero of his colonial novel the following words: "God has given us the victory because we were the most noble race, and the most filled with initiative. That is not saying much, when we compare ourselves with this race of negroes; but we must act in such a way as to become better and more active than all the other people of the world. It is to the most noble, to the most firm that the world belongs. Such is the justice of God."

German opposition has been bitter also against the occupation of Kiau-Chau. For traders have claimed that the *political* presence of Germany on the Shantung peninsula and the dealings of the German diplomats with the Pekin court had so prejudiced the Chinese against everything German that it was harder to do business with them than before the leasehold was granted. They actually advocated the withdrawal of the protectorate for the good of German commerce!

But German pride was at stake in Africa after the Herrero rebellion. And in China, Kiau-Chau was too valuable a naval base to give up. In 1907, a ministry of colonies was added to the Imperial Cabinet. Since then the colonial realm has been considered an integral part of the Empire.

At every point of this colonial development, Germany found herself confronted with open opposition and secret intrigue. The principal strategic value of south-west Africa was taken away by the British possession of Walfisch Bay, and of east Africa by the protectorate consented to by the Sultan of Zanzibar to the British Crown. Togoland and Kamerun are hemmed in by French and British possession of the *hinterland*. The Pacific islands are mostly "left-overs," or of minor importance. In spite of the unpromising character of these colonies, the commerce of Germany with them increased from 1908 to 1912 five hundred per cent., and the commerce with China through Kiau-Chau from 1902 to 1912 nearly a thousand per cent.

And yet, in comparison to her energies and her willingness—let us leave till later the question of ability and fitness—Germany has had little opportunity to exercise a colonial administration on a large scale. She must seek to extend her political influence over new territories. Where and how? That has been the question. Most promising of all appeared the succession to the Portuguese colonies, for the sharing of which Great Britain declared her willingness to meet Germany halfway. An accord was made in 1898, against the eventuality of Portugal selling her colonies. But since the Republic was proclaimed in Portugal, there has been little hope that her new Government would consider itself strong enough to part with the heritage of several centuries.

For the increase of her colonial empire, Germany has felt little hope. So she has tried to secure commercial privileges in various parts of the world, through which political control might eventually come. We have already spoken of her effort in China. Separate chapters treat of her efforts in the three Moslem countries, Morocco, Persia, and Turkey, and show how in each case she has found herself checkmated by the intrigues and accords of the three rich colonial Powers.

Long before the political union of the German States in Europe was accomplished, there were German aspirations in regard to the New World, when Pan-Germanists dreamed of forming states in North and South America.

These enthusiasts did not see that the Civil War had so brought together the various elements of the United States, the most prominent and most loyal of which was the German element, that any hope of a separatist movement in the United States was chimerical. As late as 1885, however, the third edition of Roscher's *Kolonien, Kolonialpolitik und Auswanderung* stated that "it would be a great step forward, if the German immigrants to North America would be willing to concentrate themselves in one of the states, and transform it into a German state." For different reasons Wisconsin would appear to be most particularly indicated.

As early as 1849, the Germans commenced to organize emigration to Brazil through a private society of Hamburg (*Hamburger Kolonisationverein*), which bought from the Prince de Joinville, brother-in-law of Dom Pedro, vast territories in the state of Santa Catharina. There the German colonization in Brazil began. It soon extended to the neighbouring states of Paraná and Rio Grande do Sul. There are now about three hundred and fifty thousand Germans, forming two per cent. of the population. In no district are they more than fifteen per cent. However, in Rio Grande, there is a territory of two hundred kilometres in which the German language is almost wholly spoken; and a chain of German colonies binds Sao Leopoldo to Santa Cruz.

Among the Pan-Germanists, the three states of southern Brazil have been regarded as a zone particularly reserved for German expansion. The colonial congress of 1902 at Berlin expressed a formal desire that hereafter German emigration be directed towards the south of Brazil. An amendment to include Argentina was rejected. The decree of Prussia, forbidding emigration to Brazil, was revoked in 1896 in so far as it was a question of the three states of Paraná, Santa Catharina, and Rio Grande do Sul.

It has not been very many years since diplomatic incidents arose between Brazil and Germany over fancied German violation of Brazilian territory by the arrest of sailors on shore. But Germany has not entertained serious hope of getting a foothold in South America. Brazil has increased greatly in strength, and there is to-day in South America a tacit alliance between Argentina, Brazil, and Chile to support the American Monroe Doctrine. Germany found, when she was trying to buy a West India island from Denmark, that she had to reckon not only with Washington, but also with Buenos Ayres, Rio, and Santiago.

Finding herself so thoroughly hemmed in on all sides, in the New World and in the Old World, by alliances and accords directed against her overseas political expansion, modern Germany has repeated the history of the Jews. Deprived of some senses, one develops extraordinarily others. Deprived of civil and social rights for centuries, the Jews developed the business sense until to-day their wealth and influence in the business world are far beyond the proportionate numbers of their race. Deprived of the opportunity to administer and develop vast overseas territories, the Germans have turned to intensive military development at home and extensive commercial development abroad, until to-day they are the foremost military Power in Europe, and are threatening British commercial supremacy in every part of the globe.

The German counterpart of the British and French and Russian elements that are directing the destinies of vast colonies and protectorates is investing its energy in business. During the past generation, the German campaign for the markets of the world has been carried on by the brightest and best minds in Germany. There have been three phases to this campaign: manufacturing the goods, selling the goods, and carrying the goods. German manufactures have increased so greatly in volume and scope since the accession of the present Emperor that there is hardly a line of merchandise which is not offered in the markets of the world by German firms.

Articles "made in Germany" may not be as well made as those of other countries. But their price is more attractive, and they have driven other goods from many fields. One sees this right in Europe in the markets of Germany's competitors and enemies. Since the present war began, French and British patriots are hard put to it sometimes when they find that article after article which they have been accustomed to buy is German. In my home in Paris, the elevator is German, electrical fixtures are German, the range in my kitchen is German, the best lamps for lighting are German. I have discovered these things in the past month through endeavouring to have them repaired. Interest led me to investigate other articles in daily use. My cutlery is German, my silverware is German, the chairs in my dining-room are German, the mirror in my bathroom is German, some of my food products are German, and practically all the patented drugs and some of the toilet preparations are German.

All these things have been purchased in the Paris markets, without the slightest leaning towards, or preference for, articles coming from the Fatherland. I was not aware of the fact that I was buying German things. They sold themselves,—the old combination of appearance, convenience, and price, which will sell anything.

That I am unconsciously using German manufactured articles is largely due to the genius of the salesman. It is a great mistake to believe that salesmanship is primarily the art of selling the goods of the house you represent. That has been the British idea. It is today exploded. Is it because the same type as the Britisher who is devoting his brains and energy to solving the problems of inferior people in different parts of the world is among the Germans devoting his energies to German commerce in those same places, that the Germans have found the fine art of salesmanship to be quite a different thing? It is studying the desires of the people to whom you intend to sell, finding out what they want to buy, and persuading your house at home to make and export those articles. From the Parisian and the Londoner, and the New Yorker down to the naked savage, the Germans know what is wanted, and they supply it. If the British university man is enjoying a position of authority and of fascinating perplexity in some colony, and feels that he has a share in shaping the destinies of the world, the German university man is not without his revenge. Deprived of one sense, has he not developed another—and a more practical one?

The young German, brought up in an overpopulated country, unable to enter a civil service which will keep him under his own flag—and remember how intensely patriotic he is, this young German, just as patriotic as the young Frenchman or the young Britisher,—must leave home. He is not of the class from which come the voluntary emigrants. His ties are all in Germany: his love—and his move—all for Germany. So he becomes a German resident abroad, in close connection with the Fatherland, and always working for the interests of the Fatherland. He goes to England or to France, where he studies carefully and methodically, as if he were to write a thesis on it (and he often does), the business methods of and the business opportunities among the people where he is dwelling. He is giving his life to put *Deutschland über alles* in business right in the heart of the rival nation, *and he is succeeding*. During October, 1914, when they tried to arrest in the larger cities of England the German and Austrian subjects they had to stop—there was not room in the jails for all of them! And in many places business was paralyzed.

In carrying the products of steadily increasing volume to steadily growing markets, Germany has been sensible enough to make those markets pay for the cost of transport. Up to the very selling price, all the money goes to Germany. The process is simple: from German factories, by German ships, through German salesmen, to German firms, in every part of the world—beginning with London and Paris.

Germany's merchant marine has kept pace with the development of her industry. Essen may be the expression of one side of modern Germany, which is said to have caused the European war. But one is more logical in believing that Hamburg and Bremen and the Kiel Canal have done more to bring on this war than the products of Krupp. During the last twenty-five years the tonnage of Germany's merchant marine has increased two hundred and fifty per cent., a quarter of which *has been in the last five years, from 1908-1913*. There are six times as many steamships flying the German flag as when Wilhelm II mounted the throne. In merchant ships, Germany stands today second only to Great Britain. The larger portion of her merchant marine is directed by great corporations. The struggle against Great Britain and France for the freight carrying of outside nations has been most bitter—and most successful. *Before the present war, there was no part of the world in which the German flag was not carried by ships less than ten years old.*

With the exception of Kiau-Chau, the colonies of Germany have never been of much practical value, except as possible coaling and wireless stations for the German fleet. But here also the opposition of her rivals has minimized their value. Walfisch Bay and Zanzibar have, as we have already said, lessened the strategical value of the two large colonies on either side of the African continent. In the division of the Portuguese colonies agreed to by Great Britain, it was "the mistress of the seas" who was to have the strategic places—not part of them, but all of them, the Cape Verde Islands, Madeira, and the Azores.

As Germany's commerce and shipping have so rapidly developed, the seeking for opportunities to extend her political sovereignty outside of Europe has not been so much an outlook for industrial enterprise as the imperative necessity of finding naval bases and coaling stations in different parts of the world for the adequate protection of commerce. The development of the German navy has been the logical complement of the development of the German merchant marine. Germany's astonishing naval program has kept pace with the astonishing growth of the great Hamburg and Bremen lines. Germany has had exactly the same argument for the increase of her navy as has had Great Britain. Justification for the money expended on the British navy is that Great Britain needs the navy to protect her commerce, upon which the life of the nation is dependent, and to guarantee her food-supplies. The industrial evolution of Germany has brought about for her practically the same economic conditions as in Great Britain. In addition to the dependence of her prosperity upon the power of her navy to protect her commerce, Germany has felt that she must keep the sea open for the sake of guaranteeing uninterrupted food-supplies for her industrial population. It must not be forgotten that Germany is flanked on east and west by hereditary enemies, and has come to look to the sea as the direction from which her food supplies would come in case of war.

This last factor of the *Weltpolitik*, the creation of a strong navy, must not be looked upon either as a provocation to Great Britain or as a menace to the equilibrium of the world. If it has brought Germany inevitably into conflict with Great Britain, it is because the navy is the safeguard of commerce. The *Weltpolitik* is essentially a *Handelspolitik*. The present tremendous conflict between Great Britain and Germany is the result of commercial rivalry. It is more a question of the pocket-book than of the sacredness of treaties, if we are looking for the cause rather than the occasion of the war. It has come in spite of honest efforts to bring Great Britain and Germany together.

Lord Haldane, in February, 1912, made a trip to Berlin to bring about a general understanding between the two nations. But while there was much discussion of the question of the Bagdad Railway, Persian and Chinese affairs, Walfisch Bay, and the division of Africa, nothing came of it. On March 18th, Mr. Churchill said to the House of Commons: "If Germany adds two ships in the next six years, we shall have to add four; if Germany adds three, we shall have to add six. Whatever reduction is made in the German naval program will probably be followed here by a corresponding naval reduction. The Germans will not get ahead of us, no matter what increase they make; they will not lose, no matter what decrease they make." This was as far as Great Britain could go.

In the spring of 1912, the British fleet was concentrated in the North Sea, and an accord was made with France for common defensive action in the North Sea and the Mediterranean Sea. At the same time, during M. Poincaré's trip to Petrograd, an accord was signed between France and Russia for common naval action in time of war.

The Pan-Germanic movement in recent years has not been a tool of the Government, but rather a party, including other parties, banded together more than once to oppose the German Government in an honourable attempt to preserve peace with the neighbours in the west.

It is a tremendous mistake—and a mistake which has been continuously made in the French, British, and American press since the beginning of the war—to consider the *Weltpolitik* as an expression of the sentiments of the German Emperor and his officials. Since it was forced upon Bismarck against his will, Pan-Germanism has been a power against which the Emperor William II has had to strive frequently throughout his reign. For it has never hesitated to force him into paths and into positions which were perilous to the theory of monarchical authority. The Kaiser has resented the pressure of public opinion in directing the affairs of the Empire. Pan-Germanism has been a striking example of democracy, endeavouring to have a say in governmental policies. The Naval and Army Leagues, the German Colonial Society, and the Pan-Germanic Society are private groups, irresponsible from the standpoint of the Government. They have declared the governmental programs for an increase in armaments insufficient, and have bitterly denounced and attacked them from the point of view exactly opposite to that of the Socialists. The Pan-Germanic Society refused to recognize the treaty concluded between Germany and France after the Agadir incident. Said Herr Klaas at the Hanover Conference on April 15, 1912: "We persist in considering Morocco as the country which will become in the future, let us hope the near future, the colony for German emigration." The same intractable spirit was shown in Dr. Pohl's address at the Erfurt Congress in September, 1912.

We hear much about the Kaiser and the military party precipitating war. A review of the German newspapers during the past few years will convince any fair-minded reader that German public opinion, standing constantly behind the Pan-Germanists, has frequently made the German Foreign Office act with a much higher hand in international questions than it would have acted if left to itself, and that German public opinion, from highest classes to lowest, is for this war to the bitter finish. *It is the war of the people, intelligently and deliberately willed by them.* The statement that a revolution in Germany, led by the democracy to dethrone the Kaiser or to get him out of the clutches of the military party, would put an end to the war, is foolish and pernicious. For it leads us to false hopes. It would be much nearer the truth to say that if the Kaiser had not consented to this war, he would have endangered his throne.

The principle of the *Weltpolitik*, imposed upon European diplomacy by the German nation in the assembling of the Conference of Algeciras, was that no State should be allowed to disturb the existing political and territorial *status quo* of any country still free, in any part of the world, without the consent of the other Powers. This *Weltpolitik* would have the natural effect, according to Karl Lamprecht, in his *Zur Jüngsten Deutschen Vergangenheit*, of endangering a universal and pitiless competition among the seven Great Powers in which the weakest would eventually be eliminated.

CHAPTER III
THE "BAGDADBAHN"

In the development of her *Weltpolitik*, the most formidable, the most feasible, and the most successful conception of modern Germany has been the economic penetration of Asiatic Turkey. She may have failed in Africa and in China. But there can be no doubt about the successful beginning, and the rich promise for the future, of German enterprises in the Ottoman Empire.

The countries of sunshine have always exercised a peculiar fascination over the German. His literature is filled with the Mediterranean and with Islam. From his northern climate he has looked southward and eastward back towards the cradle of his race, and in imagination has lived over again the Crusades. As long as Italy was under Teutonic political influence, the path to the Mediterranean was easy. United Italy and United Germany were born at the same time. But while the birth of Italy threatened to close eventually the trade route to the Mediterranean to Germany, the necessity of a trade route to the south became more vital than ever to the new German Confederation from the sequences of the union.

When her political consolidation was completed and her industrial era commenced, Germany began to look around the world for a place to expand. There were still three independent Mohammedan nations— Morocco, Persia, and Turkey. In Morocco she found another cause for conflict with France than Alsace-Lorraine. In Persia and Turkey, she faced the bitter rivalry of Russia and Great Britain.

The rapid decline of the Ottoman Empire, and the fact that its sovereign was Khalif of the Moslem world, led German statesmen to believe that Constantinople was the best place in the world to centre the efforts of their diplomacy in the development of the *Weltpolitik*. Through allying herself with the Khalif, *Germany would find herself able to strike eventually at the British occupation of India and Egypt, and the French occupation of Algeria and Tunis, not only by joining the interests of Pan-Islamism and Pan-Germanism, but also by winning a place in Morocco opposite Gibraltar, a place in Asia Minor opposite Egypt, and a place in Mesopotamia opposite India.*

The certainty of economic success helped to make the political effort worth while, even if it came to nothing. For Asia Minor and Mesopotamia are countries that have been among the most fertile and prosperous in the whole world. They could be so again. The present backward condition of Asia Minor and Mesopotamia is due to the fact that these countries have had no chance to live since they came under Ottoman control, much less to develop their resources proportionately to other nations. The natives have been exploited by the Turkish officials and by foreign holders of concessions. Frequently concessions have been sought to stop, not to further, development. If there have been climatic changes to account for lack of fertility in Asia Minor, this is largely due to deforestation. Ibn Batutah, the famous Moorish traveller of the first half of the fourteenth century, and Shehabeddin of Damascus, his contemporary, have left glowing accounts of the fertility and prosperity of regions of Asia Minor, now hopelessly arid, as they existed on the eve of the foundation of the Ottoman Empire. Not only have all the trees been cut down, but the roots have been torn up for fuel! One frequently sees in the markets of Anatolian towns the roots of trees for sale. The treatment of trees is typical of everything else. The country has had no chance. In Mesopotamia, the new irrigation schemes are not innovations of the twentieth century, but the revival of methods of culture in vogue thousands of years before Christ.

The Romans and Byzantines improved their inheritance. The Osmanlis ruined it.

In addition to sunshine and romance, political advantages, and prospects of making money, another influence has attracted the Germans to the Ottoman Empire. There is a certain affinity between German and Osmanli. The Germans have sympathy with the spirit of Islam, *as they conceive it to be interpreted* in the Turk. They admire the *yassak* of the Turk, which is the counterpart of their *verboten*. The von Moltke who later led Prussia to her great victories had at the beginning of his career an intimate knowledge of the Turkish army. He admired intensely the blind and passive obedience of the Turk to authority, his imperturbability under misfortune and his fortitude in facing hardship and danger. "Theirs not to reason why: theirs but to do and die" is a spirit which German and Turk understand, and show, far better than Briton, with all due respect to Tennyson. A Briton may obey, but he questions all the same, and after the crisis is over he demands a reckoning. Authority, to the Anglo-Saxon, rests in the body politic, of which each individual is an integral—and ineffaceable—part.

The Turkish military and official cast is like that of the Germans in three things: authority rests in superiors unaccountable to those whom they command; the origin of authority is force upholding tradition; and the sparing of human life and human suffering is a consideration that must not be entertained when it is a question of advancing a political or military end. I have seen both at work, and have seen the work of both; so I have the right to make this statement. For all that, I have German and Turkish friends, and deep affection for them, and deep admiration for many traits of character of both nations. The trouble is that the people of Germany and the people of Turkey allow their official and military castes to do what their own instincts would not permit them to do. The passivity of the Turk is natural: it is his religion, his background, and his climate. The passivity of the German is inexcusable. He will not exorcise the devil out of his own race. It must be done for him.

In 1888, a group of German financiers, backed by the Deutsche Bank, which was to have so powerful a future in Turkey, asked for the concession of a railway line from Ismidt to Angora. The construction of this line was followed by concessions for extension from Angora to Cæsarea and for a *branch* from the Ismidt-Angora line going south-west from Eski Sheir to Konia. The extension to Cæsarea was never made. That was not the direction in which the Germans wanted to go. The Eski Sheir-Konia spur became the main line. The Berlin-Bagdad-Bassorah "all rail route" was born. The Germans began to dream of connecting the Baltic with the Persian Gulf. The Balkan Peninsula was to revert to Austria-Hungary, and Asia Minor and Mesopotamia to Germany. The south Slavs and the populations of the Ottoman Empire would be dispossessed (the philosopher Haeckel actually prophesied this in a speech in 1905 before the Geographical Society of Jena). Russia would be cut off from the Mediterranean. This was the Pan-Germanist conception of the *Bagdadbahn*.

From the moment the first railway concession was granted to Germans in Asia Minor, which coincided with the year of his accession, Wilhelm II has been heart and soul with the development of German interests in the Ottoman Empire. His first move in foreign politics was to visit Sultan Abdul Hamid in 1889, when he was throwing off the yoke of Bismarck. This visit was the beginning of an intimate connection between Wilhelmstrasse and the Sublime Porte which has never been interrupted— excepting for a very brief period at the beginning of the First Balkan War. The friendship between the Sultan and the Kaiser was not in the least disturbed by the Armenian massacres. The hecatombs of Asia Minor passed without a protest. In fact, five days after the great massacre of August, 1896, in Constantinople, where Turkish soldiers shot down their fellow-citizens under the eyes of the Sultan and of the foreign ambassadors, Wilhelm II sent to Abdul Hamid for his birthday a family photograph of himself with the Empress and his children.

In 1898, the Kaiser made his second voyage to Constantinople. This voyage was followed by the concession extending the railway from Konia to the Persian Gulf. It was the beginning of the *Bagdadbahn* in the official and narrower sense. After this visit of the Kaiser to Abdul Hamid, the pilgrimage was continued to the Holy Land. At Baalbek, there is a stone of typically German taste, set in the wall of the great temple, to commemorate the visit of the man who dreamed he would one day be master of the modern world. If this inscription seems a sacrilege, what name have we for the large gap in the walls of Jerusalem made for his triumphal entry to the Holy City? The great Protestant German Church, whose corner-stone was laid by his father in 1869, was solemnly inaugurated by the Kaiser. As solemnly, he handed over to Catholic Germans the title to land for a hospital and religious establishment on the road to Bethlehem. Still solemnly, at a banquet in his honour in Damascus, he turned to the Turkish Vali, and declared: "Say to the three hundred million Moslems of the world that I am their friend." To prove his sincerity he went out to put a wreath upon the tomb of Saladin.

Wilhelm II at Damascus is reminiscent of Napoleon at Cairo. Egypt and Syria and Mesopotamia have always cast a spell over men who have dreamed of world empires; and Islam, as a unifying force for conquest, has appealed to the imagination of others before the present German Kaiser. I have used the word "imagination" intentionally. There never has been any solidarity in the religion of Mohammed; there is none now; there never will be. The idea of community of aims and community of interests is totally lacking in the Mohammedan mind. Solidarity is built upon the foundation of sacrifice of self for others. It is a virtue not taught in the Koran, nor ever developed by any Mohammedan civilizations. The failure of all political organisms of Mohammedan origin to endure and to become strong has been due to the fact that Mohammedans have never felt the necessity of giving themselves for the common weal. The virility of a nation is in the virile service of those who love it. If there is no willingness to serve, no incentive to love, how can a nation live and be strong?

The revelation of Germany's ambition by the granting of the concession from Konia to the Persian Gulf, and the application of the German financiers for a *firman* constituting the Bagdad Railway Company, led to international intrigues and negotiations for a share in the construction of the line through Mesopotamia. It would be wearisome and profitless to follow the various phases of the Bagdad question. Germany did not oppose international participation in the concession. The expense of crossing the Taurus and the dubious financial returns from the desert sections influenced the Germans to welcome the financial support of others in an undertaking that they would have found great difficulty in financing entirely by their own capital. The *Bagdadbahn* concession was granted in 1899: the *firman* constituting the company followed in 1903.

Russia did not realize the danger of German influence at Constantinople, and of the eventualities of the German "pacific penetration" in Asia Minor. She adjusted the Macedonian question with Emperor Franz Josef in order to have a free hand in Manchuria, and she made no opposition to the German ambitions. She needed the friendly neutrality of Germany in her approaching struggle with Japan. Once the struggle was begun, Russia found herself actually dependent upon the goodwill of Germany. It was not the time for Petrograd to fish in the troubled waters of the Golden Horn.

The situation was different with Great Britain. The menace of the German approach to the Persian Gulf was brought to the British Foreign Office just long enough before the Boer crisis became acute for a decision to be made. Germany had sent engineers along the proposed route of her railway. She had neglected to send diplomatic agents!

The proposed—in fact the only feasible—terminus on the Persian Gulf was at Koweit. Like the Sultan of Muscat, the Sheik of Koweit was practically independent of Turkey. While showing deference to the Sultan as Khalif, Sheik Mobarek resisted every effort of the Vali of Bassorah to exercise even the semblance of authority over his small domain. In 1899, Colonel Meade, the British resident of the Persian Gulf, signed with Mobarek a secret convention which assured to him "special protection," *if he would make no cession of territory without the knowledge and consent of the British Government.* The following year, a German mission, headed by the Kaiser's Consul General at Constantinople, arrived in Koweit to arrange the concession for the terminus of the *Bagdadbahn.* They were too late. The door to the Persian Gulf was shut in the face of Germany.

Wilhelm II set into motion the Sultan. The Sublime Porte suddenly remembered that Koweit was Ottoman territory, and began to display great interest in forcing the Sheik to recognize the fact. A Turkish vessel appeared at Koweit in 1901. But British warships and British bluejackets upheld the *independence* of Koweit! Since the Constitution of 1908, all the efforts of the Young Turks at Koweit have been fruitless. Germany remains blocked.

British opposition to the German schemes was not limited to the prevention of an outlet of the *Bagdadbahn* at Koweit. In 1798, the East India Company established a resident at Bagdad to spy upon and endeavour to frustrate the influence of the French, just beginning to penetrate towards India through the ambition of Napoleon to inherit the empire of Alexander. Since that time, British interests have not failed to be well looked after in Lower Mesopotamia. After the Lynch Brothers, in 1860, obtained the right of navigating on the Euphrates, the development of their steamship lines gradually gave Great Britain the bulk of the commerce of the whole region, in the Persian as well as the Ottoman *hinterland* of the Gulf. In 1895, German commerce in the port of Bushir was non-existent, while British commerce surpassed twelve million francs yearly. In 1905, the market was shared about equally between Great Britain and Germany. In 1906, the Hamburg-American Line established a service to Bassorah. British merchants began to raise the cry that if the *Bagdadbahn* appeared the Germans would soon have not only the markets of Mesopotamia but also that of Kermanshah. The Lynch Company declared that the *Bagdadbahn* would ruin their river service, and their representations were listened to at London, despite the absurdity of their contention. The Lynches were negotiating with Berlin also. This mixture of politics and commerce in Mesopotamia is a sordid story, which does not improve in the telling.

The revolution of 1908 did not injure the German influence at Constantinople as much as has been popularly supposed. The Germans succeeded during the first troubled year in keeping in with both sides through the genius of Baron Marschall von Bieberstein, in spite of the Bosnia-Herzegovina affair. Germany was fortunately out of the Cretan and Macedonian muddles, in which her rivals were hopelessly entangled. Mahmud Shevket pasha was always under German influence, and the Germans had Enver bey, "hero of liberty," in training at Berlin. German influence at Constantinople succeeded also in withstanding the strain of the Tripolitan War, although it grew increasingly embarrassing as the months passed to be Turkey's best friend and at the same time the ally of Italy! During the first disastrous period of the war of the Balkan Allies against Turkey, it seemed for the time that the enemies of Germany controlled the Sublime Porte. But the revolver of Enver bey in the *coup d'état* of January, 1913, brought once more the control of Turkish affairs into hands friendly to Germany. They have remained there ever since.

Germany strengthened her railway scheme, and her hold on the territories through which it was to pass, by the accord with Russia at Potsdam in 1910.

The last clever attack of British diplomacy on the *Bagdadbahn* was successfully met. In tracing the extension of the railway beyond Adana, it was suggested to the Department of Public Works that the cost of construction would be greatly reduced and the usefulness of the line increased, if it passed by the Mediterranean littoral around the head of the Gulf of Alexandretta. Then the control of the railway would have been at the mercy of the British fleet. When the "revised" plans went from the

Ministry of Public Works to the Ministry of War, it was not hard for the German agents to persuade the General Staff to restore the original route inland across the Amanus, following the old plan agreed upon in the time of Abdul Hamid. More than that, the Germans secured concessions for a branch line from Aleppo to the Mediterranean at Alexandretta, and for the construction of a port at Alexandretta. The *Bagdadbahn* was to have a Mediterranean terminus at a fortified port, and Germany was to have her naval base in the north-east corner of the Mediterranean, eight hours from Cyprus and thirty-six hours from the Suez Canal! This was the revenge for Koweit.

A month before the Servian ultimatum, Germany had contracted to grant a loan to Bulgaria, one of the conditions of which was that Germany be allowed to build a railway to the Ægean across the Rhodope Mountains to Porto Laghos, and to construct a port there, six hours from the mouth of the Dardanelles. There was a panic in Petrograd.

The events in Turkey since the opening of the war are too recent history and as yet too little understood to dwell upon. But the reception accorded to the *Goeben* and *Breslau* at the Dardanelles, their present[1] anomalous position in "closed waters" in defiance of all treaties, the abolition of the foreign post-offices, the unilateral decision to abrogate the capitulations— all these straws show in which direction the wind is blowing on the Bosphorus. A successful termination of the German campaign in France, which at this writing seems most improbable (in spite of the fact that the Germans are at Compiègne and their aëroplanes pay us daily visits), would certainly draw Turkey into the war—and to her ruin.[2]

[1] October, 1914.

[2] This chapter was written before the sudden and astonishing acts of war by Turkey in sinking a Russian ship and bombarding Russian Black Sea ports on October 29, 1914.

On the other hand, the German reliance upon embarrassing the French and British in their Moslem colonies through posing as the defenders of Islam and Islam's Khalif has not been well-founded. On the battlefield of France, thousands of followers of Mohammed from Africa and Asia are fighting loyally under the flags of the Allies. The Kaiser, for all his dreams and hopes, has not succeeded in getting a single Mohammedan to draw his sword for the combined causes of Pan-Germanism and Pan-Islamism. Have the three hundred million Moslems forgotten the declaration of Damascus?

In seeking for the causes of the present conflict, it is impossible to neglect Germany in the Ottoman Empire. As one looks up at Pera from the Bosphorus, the most imposing building on the hill is the German Embassy. It dominates Constantinople. There has been woven the web that has resulted in putting Germany in the place of Great Britain to prevent the Russian advance to the Dardanelles, in putting Germany in the place of Russia to threaten the British occupation of India and the trade route to India, and in putting Germany in the place of Great Britain as the stubborn opponent of the completion of the African Empire of France. The most conspicuous thread of the web is the *Bagdadbahn*. In the intrigues of Constantinople, we see develop the political evolution of the past generation, and the series of events that made inevitable the European war of 1914.

CHAPTER IV
ALGECIRAS AND AGADIR

In 1904, an accord was made between Great Britain and France in regard to colonial policy in northern Africa. Great Britain recognized the "special" interests of France in Morocco in exchange for French recognition of Great Britain's "special" interests in Egypt. There was a promise to defend each other in the protection of these interests, but no actual agreement to carry this defence beyond the exercise of diplomatic pressure. The accord was a secret one. Its exact terms were not known until the incident of Agadir made necessary its publication in November, 1911.

But that there was an accord was known to all the world. Germany, who had long been looking with alarm upon the extension of French influence in Morocco, found in 1905 a favourable moment for protest. Russia had suffered humiliation and defeat in her war with Japan. Neither in a military nor a financial way was she at that moment a factor to be reckoned with in support of France. Great Britain had not recovered from the disasters to her military organization of the South African campaign. Her domestic politics were in a chaotic state. The Conservative Ministry was losing ground daily in bye elections; the Irish question was coming to the front again.

German intervention in Morocco was sudden and theatrical. On March 31, 1905, a date of far-reaching importance in history, Emperor William entered the harbour of Tangier upon his yacht, the *Hohenzollern*. When he disembarked, he gave the cue to German policy by saluting the representative of the Sultan, with peculiar emphasis, as the representative of an independent sovereign. Then, turning to the German residents in Morocco who had gathered to meet him, he said: "I am happy to greet in you the devoted pioneers of German industry and commerce, who are aiding in the task of keeping always in a high position, in a *free land*, the interests of the mother country."

The repercussion of this visit to Tangier in France and in Great Britain was electrical. It seemed to be, and was, a direct challenge on the part of Germany for a share in shaping the destinies of Morocco. It was an answer to the Anglo-French accord, in which Germany had been ignored. Great Britain was in no position to go beyond mere words in the standing behind France. France knew this. So did Germany. After several months of fruitless negotiations between Berlin and Paris, on June 6th, it was made plain to France that there must be a conference on the Moroccan question.

M. Delcassé, at that time directing with consummate skill and courage the Ministry of Foreign Affairs, urged upon the Cabinet the necessity for accepting Germany's challenge. But the Cabinet, after hearing the sorrowful confessions of the Ministers of War and Navy, and learning that France was not ready to fight, refused to accept the advice of the Minister of Foreign Affairs. M. Delcassé resigned. A blow had been struck at French prestige.

For six months the crisis continued in an acute stage. The chauvinistic— or shall we say, patriotic?—elements were determined to withstand what they called the Kaiser's interference in the *domestic* affairs of France. But France seemed isolated at that moment, and prudence was the part of wisdom. M. Rouvier declared to the Chamber of Deputies on December 16th: "France cannot be without a Moroccan policy, for the form and direction which the evolution of Morocco will take in the future will influence in a decisive manner the destinies of our North African possessions." France agreed to a conference, but won from Germany the concession that France's special interests and rights in Morocco would be admitted as the basis of the work of the conference.

On January 17, 1906, a conference of European States, to which the United States of America was admitted, met to decide the international status of Morocco. For some time the attitude of the German delegates was uncompromising. They maintained the Kaiser's thesis as set forth at Algiers: the *complete* independence of Morocco, and sovereignty of her Sultan. But they finally yielded, and acknowledged the right of France and Spain to organize in Morocco an international police.

The Convention was signed on April 7th. It provided for: (1) police under the sovereign authority of the Sultan, recruited from Moorish Moslems, and distributed in the eight open ports; (2) Spanish and French officers, placed at his disposal by their governments, to assist the Sultan; (3) limitation of the total effective of this police force from two thousand to two thousand five hundred, of French and Spanish officers, commissioned sixteen to twenty, and non-commissioned thirty to forty, appointed for five years; (4) an Inspector General, a high officer of the Swiss army, chosen subject to the approval of the Sultan, with residence at Tangier; (5) a State Bank of Morocco, in which each of the signatory Powers had the right to subscribe capital; (6) the right of foreigners to acquire property, and to build upon it, in any part of Morocco; (7) France's exclusive right to enforce regulations in the frontier region of Algeria and a similar right to Spain in the frontier region of Spain; (8) the preservation of the public services of the Empire from alienation for private interests.

Chancellor von Bülow's speech in the *Reichstag* on April 5, 1906, was a justification of Germany's attitude. It showed that the policy of Wilhelmstrasse had been far from bellicose, and that Germany's demands were altogether reasonable. The time had come, declared the Chancellor, when German interests in the remaining independent portions of Africa and Asia must be considered by Europe. In going to Tangier and in forcing the conference of Algeciras, Germany had laid down the principle that there must be equal opportunities for Germans in independent countries, and had demonstrated that she was prepared to enforce this principle.

When one considers the remarkable growth in population, and the industrial and maritime evolution of Germany, this attitude cannot be wondered at, much less condemned. Germany, deprived by her late entrance among nations of fruitful colonies, was finding it necessary to adopt and uphold the policy of trying to prevent the pre-emption, for the benefit of her rivals, of those portions of the world which were still free.

Neither France nor Spain had any feeling of loyalty toward the Convention of Algeciras. However much may have been written to prove this loyalty, the facts of the few years following Algeciras are convincing. After 1908, Spain provoked and led on by the tremendous expenditures entailed upon her by the Riff campaigns began to consider the region of Morocco in which she was installed as exclusively Spanish territory. French writers have expended much energy and ingenuity in proving the disinterestedness of French efforts to enforce loyally the decisions of Algeciras. But they have explained, they have protested, too much. There has never been a moment that France has not dreamt of the completion of the vast colonial empire in North Africa by the inclusion of Morocco. It has been the goal for which all her military and civil administrations in Algeria and the Sahara have been working. To bring about the downfall of the Sultan's authority, not only press campaigns were undertaken, but anarchy on the Algerian frontier was allowed to go on unchecked, until military measures seemed justifiable.

In a similar way, the German colonists of Morocco did their best to bring about another intervention by Germany. Their methods were so despicable and outrageous that they had frequently to be disavowed officially. In 1910, the German Foreign Office found the claims of Mannesmann Brothers to certain mining privileges invalid, because they did not fulfil the requirements of the Act of Algeciras. But the Mannesmann mining group, as well as other German enterprises in Morocco, were secretly encouraged to make all the trouble they could for the French, while defending the authority of the Sultan. The Casablanca incident is only one of numerous affronts which the French were asked to swallow.

Great Britain had her part, though not through official agents, in the intrigues. There is much food for thought in the motives that may, not without reason, be imputed to the publication in the *Times* of a series of stories of Moroccan anarchy, and of Muley Hafid's cruelties.

In the spring of 1911, it was realized everywhere in Europe that the Sultan's authority was even less than it had been in 1905. The Berber tribes were in arms on all sides. In March, accounts began to appear of danger at Fez, not only to European residents, but also to the Sultan. The reports of the French Consul, and the telegrams of correspondents of two Paris newspapers, were most alarming. On April 2d, it was announced that the Berber tribes had actually attacked the city and were besieging it. Everything was prepared for the final act of the drama.

A relief column of native troops under Major Bremond arrived in Fez on April 26th. The very next day, an urgent message for relief having been received from Colonel Mangin in Fez, Colonel Brulard started for the capital with another column. Without waiting for further word, a French army which had been carefully prepared for the purpose, entered Morocco under General Moinier. On May 21st, Fez was occupied by the French. They found that all was well there with the Europeans and with the natives. But, fortunately for the French plans, Muley Hafid's brother had set himself up at Mequinez as pretender to the throne. The Sultan could now retain his sovereignty only by putting himself under the protection of the French army. Morocco had lost her independence!

Germany made no objection to the French expeditionary corps in April. She certainly did not expect the quick succession of events in May which brought her face to face with the *fait accompli* of a strong French army in Fez. As soon as it was realized at Berlin that the fiction of Moroccan independence had been so skilfully terminated, France was asked "what compensation she would give to Germany in return for a free hand in Morocco." The *pourparlers* dragged on through several weeks in June. France refused to acknowledge any ground for compensation to Germany. She maintained that the recent action in Morocco had been at the request of the Sultan, and that it was a matter entirely between him and France.

Germany saw that a bold stroke was necessary. On July 1st, the gunboat *Panther* went to Agadir, a port on the Atlantic coast of Morocco. To Great Britain and to France, the dispatch of the *Panther* was represented as due to the necessity of protecting German interests, seeing that there was anarchy in that part of Morocco. But the German newspapers, even those which were supposed to have official relations with Wilhelmstrasse, spoke as if a demand for the cession of Mogador or some other portion of Morocco was contemplated. The Chancellor explained to the Reichstag that the sending of the *Panther* was "to show the world that Germany was firmly resolved not to be pushed to one side."

But in the negotiations through the German Ambassador in Paris, it was clear that Germany was playing a game of political blackmail. The German Foreign Office shifted its claims from Morocco to concessions in Central Africa. On July 15th, Germany asked for the whole of the French Congo from the sea to the River Sanga, and a renunciation in her favour of France's contingent claims to the succession of the Belgian Congo. The reason given to this demand was, that if Morocco were to pass under a French protectorate, it was only just that compensation should be given to Germany elsewhere. France, for the moment, hesitated. She definitely refused to entertain the idea of compensation as soon as she had received the assurance of the aid of Great Britain in supporting her against the German claims.

On July 1st, the German Ambassador had notified Sir Edward Grey of the dispatch of the *Panther* to Agadir "in response to the demand for protection from German firms there," and explained that Germany considered the question of Morocco reopened by the French occupation of Fez, and thought that it would be possible to make an agreement with Spain and France for the partition of Morocco. On July 4th, Sir Edward Grey, after a consultation with the Cabinet, answered that Great Britain could recognize no change in Morocco without consulting France, to whom she was bound by treaty. The Ambassador then explained that his Government would not consider the reopening of the question in a European conference, that it was a matter directly between Germany and France, and that his overture to Sir Edward Grey had been merely in the nature of a friendly explanation.

Germany believed that the constitutional crisis in Great Britain was so serious that the hands of the Liberal Cabinet would be tied, and that they would not be so foolhardy as to back up France at the moment when they themselves were being so bitterly assailed by the most influential elements of the British electorate on the question of limiting the veto power of the House of Lords. It was in this belief that Germany on July 15th asked for territorial cessions from France in Central Africa. Wilhelmstrasse thought the moment well chosen, and that there was every hope of success.

But the German mentality has never seemed to appreciate the frequent lesson of history, that the British people are able to distinguish clearly between matters of internal and external policy. Bitterly assailed as a traitor to his country because he advocates certain changes of laws, a British Cabinet Minister can still be conscious of the fact that his bitterest opponents will rally around him when he takes a stand on a matter of foreign policy. This knowledge of admirable national solidarity enabled Mr. Lloyd George on July 21st, the very day on which the King gave his consent to the creation of new peers to bring the House of Lords to reason, at a Mansion House banquet, to warn Germany against the danger of pressing her demands upon France. The effect, both in London and Paris, was to unify and strengthen resistance. It seemed as if the *Panther's* visit to Agadir had put Germany in the unenviable position of having made a threat which she could not enforce.

But the ways of diplomacy are tortuous. Throughout August and September, Germany blustered and threatened. In September, several events happened which seemed to embarrass Russia and tie her hands, as in the first Moroccan imbroglio of 1905. For Premier Stolypin was assassinated at Kiev on September 14th; the United States denounced its commercial treaty with Russia on account of the question of Jewish passports; and the Shuster affair in Persia occupied the serious attention of Russian diplomacy. Had it not been for the splendidly loyal and scrupulous attitude of the British Foreign Office towards Russia in the Persian question, Germany might have been tempted to force the issue with France.

German demands grew more moderate, but were not abandoned. For members of the House of Commons, of the extreme Radical wing in the Liberal party, began to put the British Government in an uncomfortable position. Militarism, entangling alliances with a continental Power, the necessity for agreement with Germany,—these were the subjects which found their way from the floor of the House of Commons to the public press. A portion of the Liberal party which had to be reckoned with believed that Germany ought not to have been left out of the Anglo-French agreement. So serious was the dissatisfaction, that the Government deemed it necessary to make an explanation to the House. Sir Edward Grey explained and defended the action of the Cabinet in supporting the resistance of France to Germany's claims. The whole history of the negotiation was revealed. The Anglo-French agreement of 1904 was published for the first time, and it was seen that this agreement did not commit Great Britain to backing France by force of arms.

Uncertainty of British support had the influence of bringing France to consent to treat with Germany on the Moroccan question. Two agreements were signed. By the first, Germany recognized the French protectorate in Morocco, subject to the adhesion of the signers of the Convention of Algeciras, and waived her right to take part in the negotiations concerning Moroccan spheres of influence between Spain and France. On her side, France agreed to maintain the open door in Morocco, and to refrain from any measures which would hinder the legitimate extension of German commercial and mining interests. By the second agreement, France ceded to Germany, in return for German cessions, certain territories in southern and eastern Kamerun.

There was a stormy Parliamentary and newspaper discussion, both in France and Germany, over these two treaties. No one was satisfied. The treaties were finally ratified, but under protest.

In France, the Ministry was subject to severe criticism. There was also some feeling of bitterness—perhaps a reaction from the satisfaction over Mr. Lloyd George's Mansion House speech—in the uncertainty of Great Britain's support, as revealed by the November discussions in the House of Commons. This uncertainty remained, as far as French public opinion went, until Great Britain actually declared war upon Germany in August, 1914.

In Germany, the *Reichstag* debates revealed the belief that the Agadir expedition had, on final analysis, resulted in a *fiasco*. An astonishing amount of enmity against Great Britain was displayed. It was when Herr Heydebrand made a bitter speech against Great Britain, and denounced the pacific attitude of the German Government, in the Reichstag session of November 10th, that the Crown Prince made public his position in German foreign policy by applauding loudly.

The aftermath of Agadir, as far as it affected Morocco, resulted in the establishment of the French Protectorate, on March 30, 1912. The Sultan signed away his independence by the Treaty of Fez. Foreign legations at Fez ceased to exist, although diplomatic officials were retained at Tangier. France voted the maintenance of forty thousand troops in Morocco "for the purposes of pacification." The last complications disappeared when, on November 27th, a Franco-Spanish Treaty was signed at Madrid, in which the Spanish zones in Morocco were defined, and both states promised not to erect fortifications or strategic works on the Moroccan coast.

But the aftermath of Agadir in France and Germany has been an increase in naval and military armaments, and the creation of a spirit of tension which needed only the three years of war in the Ottoman Empire to bring about the inevitable clash between Teuton and Gaul. Taken in connection with the recent events in Alsace and Lorraine, and the voting of the law increasing military service in France to three years, the logical sequence of events is clear.

CHAPTER V
THE PASSING OF PERSIA

The weakness of the Ottoman Empire and of Morocco served to bring the colonial and commercial aspiration of Germany into conflict with other nations of Europe. The recent fortunes of Persia, the third—and only other—independent Mohammedan state, have also helped to make possible the general European war.

The first decade of the twentieth century brought about in Persia, as in Turkey, the rise of a constitutional party, which was able to force a despotic sovereign to grant a constitution. The Young Persians had in many respects a history similar to that of the Young Turks. They were for the most part members of influential families, who had been educated in Europe, or had been sent into exile. They had imbibed deeply the spirit of the French Revolution from their reading, and had at the same time developed a narrow and intense nationalism. But to support their revolutionary propaganda, they had allied themselves during the period of darkness with the Armenians and other non-Moslems. As Salonika, a city by no means Turkish, was the *foyer* of the young Turk movement, so Tabriz, capital of the Azerbaidjan, a city by no means Persian, was the centre of the opposition to Persian despotism.

Young Turks, Young Persians, Young Egyptians, Young Indians, and Young Chinese have shown to Europe and America the peril—and the pity—of our western and Christian education, when it is given to eastern and non-Christian students. They are born into the intellectual life with our ideas and are inspired by our ideals, but have none of the background, none of the inheritance of our national atmosphere and our family training to enable them to live up to the standards we have put before them. Their disillusionment is bitter. They resent our attitude of superiority. They hate us, even though they feign to admire us. Their jealousy of our institutions leads them to console themselves by singling out and forcing themselves to see only the weak and vulnerable points in our civilization. Educated in our universities, they return to their countries to conspire against us. The illiterate and simple Oriental, who has never travelled, is frequently the model of fidelity and loyalty and affection to his Occidental master or friend. But no educated non-Christian Oriental, who has travelled and studied and lived on terms of equality with Europeans or Americans in Europe or America, can ever be a sincere friend. The common result of social contact and intellectual companionship is that he becomes a foe,— and conceals the fact. Familiarity has bred more than contempt.

The Young Persians would have no European aid. They waited, and suffered. Finally, after a particularly bad year from the standpoint of financial exactions, the Moslem clergy of the North were drawn into the Young Persia movement. A revolution, in which the Mohammedan *mullahs* took part, compelled the dying Shah, Muzaffereddin, to issue a decree ordering the convocation of a *medjliss* (committee of notables) on August 5, 1906. This improvised Parliament, composed only of delegates of the provinces nearest the capital, drafted a constitution which was promulgated on New Year's Day, 1907. The following week, Muzaffereddin died and was succeeded by his son, Mohammed Ali Mirza, a reactionary of the worst type.

Mohammed Ali had no intention of putting the Constitution into force. A serious revolution broke out in Tabriz a few weeks after his accession. He was compelled to acknowledge the Constitution granted by his father. In order to nullify its effect, however, the new Shah called to the Grand Vizierate the exiled Ali Asgar Khan, whom he believed to be strong enough to overrule the wishes of the Parliament. The Constitutionalists formed a society of *fedavis* to prevent the return to absolutism. At their instigation, Ali Asgar Khan was assassinated. The country fell into an anarchic state.

Constitutional Persia, as much because of the inexperience of the Constitutionalists as of the ill-will of the Shah, was worse off than under the despotism of Muzaffereddin. There was no money in the treasury. The peasants would not pay their taxes. One can hardly blame them, for not a cent of the money ever went for local improvements or local government. Throughout Persia, even in the cities, life was unsafe. The Persians, no more than the Turks, could call forth from the ranks of their enthusiasts a progressive and fearless statesman of the type of Stambuloff or Venizelos. In their Parliament they all talked at once. None was willing to listen to his neighbour. It may have been because there was no Mirabeau. But could a Mirabeau have overcome the fatal defects of the Mohammedan training and character that made the Young Persians incapable of realizing the constitutionalism of their dreams? Every man was suspicious and jealous of his neighbour. Every man wanted to lead, and none to be led. Every man wanted power without responsibility, prestige without work, success without sacrifice.

It was at this moment that one of the most significant events of contemporary times was helped to fruition by the state of affairs in Persia. Great Britain and Russia, rivals—even enemies—in western and central Asia, signed a convention. Their conflicting ambitions were amicably compromised. Along with the questions of Afghanistan and Thibet, this accord settled the rivalry that had done much to keep Persia a hotbed of diplomatic intrigue like Macedonia ever since the Crimean War.

In regard to Persia, the two Powers solemnly swore to respect its integrity and its independence, and then went on to sign its death warrant, by agreeing upon the question of "the spheres of influence." In spite of all sophisms, this convention marked the passing of Persia as an independent state. Persia is worse off than Morocco and Egypt. For one master is better than two!

Here enters Germany. For many years German merchants had looked upon Persia as they looked upon Morocco and Turkey. Here were the legitimate fields for commercial expansion. Probably there were also dreams of political advantages to be gained later. In their dealings with the three Moslem countries that were still "unprotected" when they inaugurated their *Weltpolitik*, the Germans had been attentive students of British policy in the days of her first entry into India and to Egypt. There were many Germans who honestly believed that their activities in these independent Moslem countries would only give them "their place under the sun," and a legitimate field for the overflow of their population and national energy, but that it would also be a distinct advantage to the peace of the world. Great Britain and Russia and France had already divided up between them the larger part of Asia and Africa. In the process, Great Britain had *recently* come almost to blows with both her rivals. If Germany stepped in between them, would this not prevent a future conflict? But the rivals "divided up." Germany was left out in the cold. It is not a very far cry from Teheran and Koweit and Fez to Liège and Brussels and Antwerp. Belgium is paying the bill.

The Anglo-Russian convention of August 31, 1907, was the first of three doors slammed in Germany's face. The Anglo-French convention of April 8, 1904, had been an attempt to do this. But by Emperor William's visit to Tangiers in 1905, Germany got in her foot before the door was closed! In Persia there was no way that she could intervene directly to demand that Great Britain and Russia bring their accord before an international congress.

Germany began to work in Persia through two agencies. She incited Turkey to cross the frontier of the Azerbaidjan, and to make the perfectly reasonable request that the third limitrophe state should be taken into the *pourparlers* which were deciding the future of Persia. Then she sent her agents among the Nationalists, and showed them how terrible a blow this convention was to their new constitutionalism. Just at the moment when they had entered upon a constitutional life, Great Britain and Russia had conspired against their independence, went the German thesis.

If only there had been a sincerity for the Constitution in the heart of the Shah, and an ability to establish a really constitutional *régime* in the leaders of Young Persia, the Anglo-Russian accord might have proved of no value. But—unfortunately for Persia and for Germany—the Shah, worked upon skilfully by Russian emissaries and by members of his *entourage*, who were paid by Russian gold, attempted a *coup d'état* against the Parliament in December, 1907. He failed to carry it through. With a smile on his lips and rage in his heart, he once more went through the farce of swearing to be a good constitutional ruler. But in June, 1908, he succeeded in dispersing the Parliament by bombarding the palace in which it sat.

It would be wearisome to go into the story of the revolts and anarchy in all parts of Persia in 1908 and 1909. After a year of fighting and Oriental promises, of solemn oaths and the breaking of them, the constitutionalists finally drove Mohammed Ali from Teheran in July, 1909. The Shah saved his life by taking refuge in the Russian legation. A few days later, he took the road to exile. He has since reappeared in Persia twice to stir up trouble in the north. On both occasions, it was when the Russians were finding it hard to justify their continued occupation of the northern provinces.

Mohammed Ali was succeeded by his son Ali Mirza, a boy of eleven years, who was still too young to be anything more than a mere plaything in the hands of successive regents.

The civil strife in Persia gave Great Britain and Russia the excuse for entering the country. In accord with Great Britain, Russia sent an expedition to occupy Tabriz on April 29, 1909. Later, Russian troops occupied Ardebil, Recht, Kazvin, and other cities in the Russian sphere of influence. Owing to the anarchy in the south during 1910, Great Britain prepared to send troops "to protect the safety of the roads for merchants." This was not actually done, for conditions of travel slightly ameliorated. But Persia has rested since under the menace of a British occupation.

Every effort made to bring order out of chaos in Persia has failed. Serious attempts at financial reform were undertaken by an American mission, under the direction of a former American official in the Philippine Islands.

The new American Treasurer-General would not admit that the Anglo-Russian accord of 1907 was operative in Persia. One day in the summer of 1911, I was walking along the Galata Quay in Constantinople. I heard my name called from the deck of a vessel just about to leave for Batum. Perched on top of two boxes containing typewriters, was a young American from Boston, who was going out to help reform the finances of Persia. I had talked to him the day before concerning the extreme delicacy and difficulty of the task of the mission whose secretary he was. But his refusal to admit the political limitations of Oriental peoples made it impossible for him to see that constitutional Persia was any different, or should be treated any differently, from constitutional Massachusetts.

From the sequel of the story, it would seem that Mr. Shuster had the same attitude of mind as his secretary. He refused to appoint fiscal agents in the Russian "sphere" on any other ground than personal fitness and ability. Russia protested. Mr. Shuster persisted. A march on Teheran to expel the Americans was threatened. Persia yielded and gave up the American mission—and her independence.

When Germany saw that the Russian troops had entered northern Persia with the consent of Great Britain, and had come to stay, there was nothing for her to do but to treat with Russia.

In November, 1910, when the Czar was visiting the Kaiser, Russian and German ministers exchanged views concerning the ground upon which Germany would agree to the *fait accompli* of Russia's exclusive political interests in Northern Persia, and the Russian military occupation. Satisfactory bases were found for an agreement between Russia and Germany concerning their respective interests in Persia and Asiatic Turkey. The Accord of Potsdam, as it is called, was made in the form of a note presented by the Russian Government to Germany, and accepted by her. Russia declared that she would in no way oppose the realization of the project of the Bagdad railway up to the Persian Gulf, and that she would construct to the border of Persia a railway to join a spur of the Bagdad railway from Sadije to Khanikin. In return for this, Germany was to promise not to construct railway lines outside of the Bagdad railway zone, to declare that she had no political interest in Persia, and to recognize that "Russia has special interests in Northern Persia from the political, strategic, and economic points of view." The German Government was to abandon any intention of securing a concession for a trans-Persian railway. On the other hand, Russia promised to maintain in Northern Persia the "open door," so that German commercial interests should not be injured.

The accord between Russia and Germany was badly received everywhere. France feared that Germany was trying to weaken the Franco-Russian alliance. Great Britain did not look with favour upon a recognition by Russia of German interests in Asiatic Turkey. The Sublime Porte felt that Russia and Germany had shown a disregard for the elementary principles of courtesy in discussing and deciding questions that were of tremendous importance to the future of Turkey without inviting the Sublime Porte to take part in the negotiations. Turkey in the Potsdam accord was ignored as completely as Morocco had been in the Algeciras Convention and Persia in the Russo-British accord.

The Potsdam stipulations brought prominently before Europe the possible significance of Germany's free hand in Anatolian and Mesopotamian railway constructions. It also aroused interest in the possibility of an all-rail route from Calais to Calcutta, in which all the Great Powers except Italy would participate.

The trans-Persian and all other railway schemes in Persia came to nothing. Between 1872 and 1890 twelve district railway projects had received concessions from the Persian Government. One of these, the Reuter group, actually started the construction of a line from the Caspian Sea to the Persian Gulf. A French project for a railway from Trebizond to Tabriz had gained powerful financial support. All these schemes were frustrated by Russian diplomacy. In 1890, Russia secured from the Persian Government the exclusive right for twenty-one years to construct railways in Northern Persia. Needless to say, no lines were built. Russia had all she could do with her trans-Siberian and trans-Caucasian schemes. But she deliberately acted the dog in the manger. By preventing private groups from building railways in Persia which she would not build herself, Russia has retarded the economic progress, and is largely responsible for the financial, military, and administrative weakness, of contemporary Persia. By the accords of 1907 with Great Britain and 1911 with Germany, Russia secured their connivance in still longer continuing this shameful stagnation. To this day no railroad has been built in the Shah's dominions.

Just a month before the outbreak of the European war, the boy Shah of Persia was solemnly crowned at Teheran. It was an imposing and pathetic ceremony. The Russians and British saw to it that full honour should be given to the sovereign of Persia. The pathos of the event was in the fact that the Russian and British legations at Teheran paid the expenses of the coronation. The Shah received his crown from the hands of his despoilers. A similar farce was enacted a little while before in Morocco. Turkey alone of Moslem nations remains.

The last effort of Persia to shake off the Russian octopus was made on October 8, 1914, when Russia was requested once more to withdraw her troops from the Azerbaijan. The Russian Minister at Teheran, without going through the form of referring the request to Petrograd, answered that the interests of Russia and other foreign countries could be safeguarded only by the continued occupation. To this response his British colleague gave hearty assent.

The importance of the passing of Persia is two-fold. It shows how in one more direction Germany found herself shut out from a possible field of expansion. Through the weakness of Persia, Great Britain and Russia, after fifty years of bitter struggle, were able to come to a satisfactory compromise. It was in Persia that their animosity was buried, and that co-operation of British democracy and Russian autocracy in a war against Germany was first envisaged. The failure of the Persian constitutional Government was a tremendous blow to Germany. It strengthened the bases of the Triple Entente. For the events of 1908 and 1909 put the accord to severe test, and proved that it was built upon a solid foundation. The agony of one people is often the joy of another. Has Persia suffered vicariously that France may be saved?

CHAPTER VI
THE PARTITIONERS AND THEIR POLES

[*] This chapter has not been written without giving consideration to the Russian point of view. There is an excellent book on Russia since the Jajpanese War (from 1906 to 1912) by Peter Polejaïeff.

When Russia, Austria, and Prussia partitioned Poland at the end of the eighteenth century, there were at the most six million Poles in the vast territory stretching from the Baltic nearly to the Black Sea. Of these a large number, especially in Eastern Prussia and in Silesia, had already lost their sense of nationality. Poland was a country of feudal nobles, whose inability to group under a dynasty for the formation of a modern state, made the disappearance of the kingdom an inexorable necessity in the economic evolution of Europe, and of ignorant peasants, who were indifferent concerning the political status of the land in which they lived.

To-day there are twenty million Poles. Although they owe allegiance to three different sovereigns, they are more united than ever in their history. For their national feeling has developed in just the same way that the national feeling of Germans and Russians has developed, by education primarily, and by that remarkable tendency of industrialism, which has grouped people in cities, and brought them into closer association. This influence of city life upon the destinies of Poland comes to us with peculiar force when we realize that since the last map of Europe was made Warsaw has grown from forty thousand to eight hundred thousand, Lodz from one thousand to four hundred thousand, Posen from a few hundreds to one hundred and fifty thousand, Lemberg and Cracow from less than ten thousand to two hundred thousand and one hundred and fifty thousand respectively. These great cities (except Lodz, which Russia foolishly allowed to become an outpost of Pan-Germanism in the heart of a Slavic population) are the *foyers* of Polish nationalism.

The second and third dismemberments of Poland (1793 and 1795) were soon annulled by the Napoleonic upheaval. The larger portion of Poland was revived in the Grand Duchy of Warsaw. The Congress of Vienna, just one hundred years ago, made what the representatives of the partitioning Powers hoped would be a definite redistribution of the unwelcome ghost stirred up by Napoleon. Poznania was returned to Prussia, and in the western end of Galicia a Republic of Cracow was created. The greater portion of Poland reverted to Russia, *not as conquered territory, but as a separate state, of which the Czar assumed the kingship and swore to preserve the liberties.* The unhappiness, the unrest, the agitation, among the Poles of the Muscovite Empire, just as among the Finns, came from the breaking of the promises by Russia to Europe when these subjects of alien races were allotted to her.

The story of modern Poland is not different from that of any other nationalistic movement. A sense of nationality and a desire for racial political unity are not the phenomena which have been the underlying causes of the evolution of Europe since the Congress of Vienna. In Italy, in Germany, in Poland, in Alsace-Lorraine, in Finland, among the various races of the Austro-Hungarian Empire and the Balkan Peninsula, as well as in Turkey and Persia, the underlying cause of political agitation, of rebellions and of revolutions has been the desire to secure freedom from absolutism. Nationalism is simply the tangible outward manifestation of the growth of democracy. There are few national movements where separatism could not have been avoided by granting local self-government. Mixed populations can live together under the same government without friction, if the lesser races are granted social, economic, and political equality. But nations that have achieved their own unity and independence through devotion to a nationalistic movement have shown no mercy or wisdom with smaller and less fortunate races under their domination. The very methods that European statesmen have fondly believed were necessary for assimilation have proved fatal to it.

The Polish question, as we understand it to-day, has little connection with the Polish revolutions of 1830 and of 1863. These movements against the Russian Government were conducted by the same elements of protest against autocracy that were at work in the larger cities and universities throughout Europe during the middle of the nineteenth century. Nationalism was the reason given rather than the cause that prompted. The revolutions were unsuccessful because they were not supported by the nation. The mass of the people were indifferent to the cause, just as in other countries similar revolutions against despotism failed for lack of real support. The apathy of the masses has always been the bulwark of defence for autocracy and reactionary policies. Popular rights do not come to people until the masses demand them. Education alone brings self-government. This is the history of the evolution of modern Europe.

The Poles *as a nation* began to worry their partitioners in the decade following the last unsuccessful revolution against Russia. To understand the contemporary phases of the Polish question, it is necessary for us to follow first its three-fold development, as a question of internal policy in Russia,

Germany, and Austria. Only then is its significance as an international question clear.

THE POLES SINCE 1864 IN RUSSIA

The troubles of Russia in her relationship to the Poles have come largely from the fact that the distinction between Poland proper, inhabited by Poles, and the provinces which the Jagellons conquered but never assimilated, was not grasped by the statesmen who had to deal with the aftermath of the revolution. What was possible in one was thought to be possible in the other. What was vital in one was believed to be vital in the other. In the kingdom of Poland, as it was bestowed upon the Russian Czar by the Congress of Vienna, there were massed ten million Poles who could be neither exterminated nor exiled. Nor was there a sound motive for attempting to destroy their national life. The kingdom of Poland was not an essential portion of the Russian Empire, and was not vitally bound to the fortunes of the Empire. So unessential has the kingdom of Poland been to Russia, and so fraught with the possibilities of weakness to its owner, that patriotic and far-sighted Russian publicists have advocated its complete autonomy, its independence or its cession to Germany. Because it was limitrophe to the territories occupied by the Poles of the other partitioners, there was constantly danger of weakening the defences of the empire and of international complications. Through failing to treat these Poles in such a way that they would be a loyal bulwark against her enemies, Russia has done irreparable harm to herself as well as to them.

The Polish question in Lithuania, Podolia, and the Ukraine was a totally different matter. These provinces had been added to Russia in her logical development towards the west and the south-west. Their possession was absolutely essential to the existence of the Empire. Their population was not Polish, but Lithuanian, Ruthenian, and Russian. From the Baltic to the Black Sea, the acquisition of these territories made possible the entrance of Russia into the concert of European nations. They had been conquered by Poland during the period of her greatness, and had naturally been lost by her when she became weak. In these portions of Greater Poland, the Poles were limited to the landowning class, and to the more prosperous artisans in the cities and villages. They were the residue of an earlier conquering race that had never assimilated the country. They had abused their power, and were heartily disliked. These provinces were vital to Russia, and she was able to carry out the policy of uprooting the Poles. Their villages were burned, their fortunes and their lands confiscated, the landed proprietors deported to Siberia, and others so cruelly persecuted that, when their churches and schools were closed and they found themselves forbidden to speak their language outside of their own homes, they emigrated. In Lithuania, the Lithuanian language was also proscribed. The Russians had no intention of blotting out a Polish question in order to make place for a Lithuanian one.

Where the Poles were few in number, these measures, which were exactly the same as the Poles had employed themselves in the same territories several centuries before, were successful. The peasants were glad to see their traditional persecutors get a taste of their own medicine. It was not difficult to make these provinces Russian. They have gradually been assimilated into the Empire. In all fairness, one can hardly condemn the Russian point of view, as regards the Poles in Lithuania, Podolia, and the Ukraine. Only youthful Polish irredentists still dream of the restoration of the Empire of the Jagellons.

In the kingdom of Poland, the situation was entirely different. This huge territory had been given to Russia by the Congress of Vienna upon the solemn assurance that it was to be governed as a separate kingdom by the Romanoffs. There was no thought in the Congress of Vienna of the disappearance of the Poles as a separate nationality from the map of Europe. But the autonomy of Poland was suppressed after the rebellion of 1830.

After the rebellion of 1863, Russia tried to assimilate the kingdom of Poland as well as the Polish marches. The repression was so severe that Polish nationalism was considered dead. The peasants had been indifferent to the movement. Not only had they failed to support it, but they had frequently shown themselves actually hostile to it.

It was because the nobles and priests were believed to be leaders of nationalistic and separatist movements, not only in Poland but in other allogeneous portions of the composite Empire, that Czar Alexander II emancipated the serfs. The policy of every autocratic government, when it meets the first symptoms of unrest in a subject race, is to strike at their church and their aristocracy. The most efficient way to weaken the power of the nobles is to strengthen the peasants. Alexander himself may have been actuated by motives of pure humanity, but his ministers would never have allowed the *ukase* to be promulgated, had they not seen in it the means of conquering the approaching revolution in Poland. For the moment it was an excellent move, and accomplished its purpose. The Polish peasants were led to believe that the Czar was their father and friend and champion against the exactions of the church and landowner. Was not their emancipation proof of this?

But in the long run the emancipation of the serfs proved fatal to Russian domination in Poland. For the advisers of Alexander had not realized that freemen would demand and attend schools, and that schools, no matter how careful the surveillance and restrictions might be, created democrats.

Democrats would seize upon nationalism to express their aspiration for self-government. The emancipation of the serfs, launched as a measure to destroy Poland, has ended in making it. Emancipation created Polish patriots. It was a natural and inevitable result. The artificial aid of a governmental persecution helped and hastened this result. The Irishman expressed a great truth when he said that there are things that are not what they are.

A flock of hungry Russian functionaries descended upon Poland in 1864. They took possession of all departments of administration. The Polish language was used in courts only through an interpreter, and was forbidden as the medium of instruction in schools. No Polish signs were tolerated in the railways or post-offices. In the parts of the kingdom where there were bodies of the Lithuanians, their nationalism was encouraged, and they were shown many favours, in contradiction to the policy adopted towards the Lithuanians of Lithuania. Catholics who followed the Western Rite were forced to join the national church. There was a clear intention to assimilate as much as possible the populations of the border districts of Poland.

After thirty years of repression, Russia had made no progress in Poland. In 1897, Prince Imeretinsky wrote to the Czar that the policy of the Government had failed. Polish national spirit, instead of disappearing, had spread remarkably among the peasant classes. The secret publication and importation of unauthorized journals and pamphlets had multiplied. The number of cases brought before the courts for infraction of the "law of association," which forbade unlicensed public gatherings and clubs, had so increased that they could not be heard. Heavy fines and imprisonment seem to have had no deterring effect.

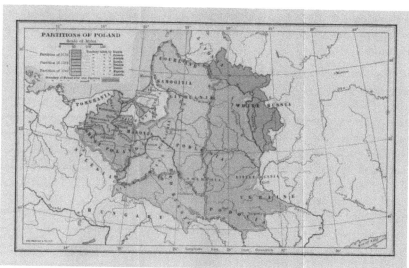

Map—Partitions of Poland

Could Russia hope to struggle against the tendencies of modern life? Free press and free speech are the complement of education. When men learn to read, they learn to think, and can be reached by propaganda. When men increase in prosperity, they begin to want a voice in the expenditure of the money they have to pay for taxes. When men come together in the industrial life of large cities, they form associations. No government, no system of spies or terrorism, no laws can prevent propaganda in cities. From 1864 to 1914, the kingdom of Poland has become more Polish than ever before in her history. Instead of a few students and dreamers, fascinated by the past glories of their race, instead of a group of landowners and priests, thinking of their private interests and of the Church, there is awakened a spirit of protest against Russian despotism in the soul of a race become intelligently nationalistic.

The issue between Russia and her Poles has become clearer, and for that reason decidedly worse, since the disastrous war with Japan. The Poles have demanded autonomy in the fullest sense of the word. The Russians have responded by showing that it is their intention to destroy Poland, just as they intend to destroy Finland. There is an analogy between the so-called constitutional *régimes* in Russia and Turkey. In each Empire, the granting of a constitution was hailed with joy by the various races. These races, who had been centres of agitation, disloyalty, and weakness, were ready to co-operate with their governments in building up a large, broad, comprehensive, national life upon the principles of liberty, equality, and fraternity. But in both Empires, the dominant race let it soon be understood that the Constitution was to be used for a destructive policy of assimilation. In the Ottoman Empire, the Constitution was a weapon for destroying the national aspirations of subject races. In Russia it has been the same.

After the Russo-Japanese War, Czar Nicholas and his ministers had their great opportunity to profit by the lessons of Manchuria. But the granting of a constitution was a pure farce. Blind to the fact that the enlightened Poles were interested primarily in political reforms, and in securing equity and justice for the kingdom of Poland, instead of for the advancement of a narrow and theoretical nationalistic ideal, the Russians repulsed the proffered loyalty of the Poles to a free and constitutional Russian Empire. In the second Duma, Dmowski and other Polish deputies unanimously voted the supplies for strengthening the Russian army. They stated that the Poles were willing to cast their lot loyally and indissolubly with constitutional Russia. Were they not brethren, and imbued with the same Pan-Slavic idea? Was it not logical to look to Russia as the defender of all the Slavs from Teutonic oppression?

But Poland, like Finland, was to continue to be the victim of Russian bureaucracy and of an intolerant nationalism which the Russians were beginning to feel as keenly and as arrogantly as the Prussians. Is the Kaiser, embodying the evils of militarism, more obnoxious and more dangerous to civilization than the Czar, standing for the horrors of bureaucratic despotism and absolutism? Have not the Armenian massacres, ordered from Constantinople, and the Jewish pogroms, ordered from Petrograd, associated Christian Czar with Mohammedan Sultan at the beginning of the twentieth century?

The first deliberate violation of the integrity of the kingdom of Poland was sanctioned by the Russian Duma in the same session in which it approved violation of Russian obligations to Finland. A law separating Kholm from the kingdom of Poland was voted on July 6, 1912. The test of the law declared that Kholm was still to be regarded as a portion of the kingdom of Poland, but to be directly attached to the Ministry of the Interior without passing by the intermediary of the Governor-General of Warsaw; and to preserve the Polish adaptation of the Code Napoléon for its legal administration, but to have its court of appeal at Kief.

The elections of 1913 from the kingdom of Poland to the Duma gave a decided setback to the party of Dmowski, who had so long and so ably pled for a policy of Pan-Slavism through accommodation with Russia. The law concerning Kholm had been the response of the Duma to Dmowski's olive branch. The moderates were discredited. But the failure of the radical nationalists to conciliate the Jewish element caused their candidates to lose both at Warsaw and Lodz.

The birth of an anti-Semitic movement has been disastrous to Polish solidarity during recent years. The Polish nationalists suspected the Jews of working either for German or Russian interests. They were expecially bitter against the *Litvak*, or Lithuanian and south Russian Jews, who had been forced by Russia to establish themselves in the cities of Poland. Poland is one of the most important pales in the Empire. The Jewish population is one-fifth of the total, and enjoys both wealth and education in the cities. Their educated youth had been courageous and forceful supporters of Polish nationalism. Before the Russian intrigues of the last decade and the introduction of these non-Polish Jews, there had never been a strong anti-Semitic feeling in Poland. The Polish protests against the encroachment of the Russians upon their national liberties have been greatly weakened by their antagonism to the Jews. The anti-Semitic movement, which has carried away both the moderate party of Dmowski and the radical nationalists, as was expected, has played into the hand of Russia.

The Muscovite statesmen, while endeavouring to use the Balkan Wars for the amalgamation of south Slavic races under the wing of Russia against Austria have treated the Poles as if they were not Slavs. During 1913 and the first part of 1914, the policy of attempting to russianize the Poles has proved disastrous to their feeling of loyalty to the Empire. The government announced definitely that the kingdom of Poland would be "compensated" for the loss of Kholm by a law granting self-government to Polish cities. This promise has not been kept. The municipal self-government project presented to the Duma was as farcical in practical results as all democratic and liberal legislation which that impotent body has been asked to pass upon.

THE POLES SINCE 1867 IN AUSTRIA-HUNGARY

The disappearance of Austria from Germany after the battle of Sadowa led to the organization of a new state, the Austro-Hungarian Empire. We must divorce in our mind the Austria before 1867 from the Austria-Hungary of the Dual Monarchy. The political situation changed entirely when Austrians and Hungarians agreed to live together and share the Slavic territories of the Hapsburg Crown. Austria no longer had need of her Galicians to keep the Hungarians in check. But there was equally important work for them to do.

The Austrians have always treated the Poles very well. Galicia, which had been Austria's share in the partition of Poland, was given local self-government, with its own Diet, and proper representation in the Austrian *Reichsrath*. Poles were admitted in generous numbers to the functions of the Empire.

The Polish nationalists of Russia and Prussia feel very bitter about the indifference of the Galicians to the nation at large—or rather in captivity. They claim that the lack of national feeling among the Austrian Poles is due to the fact that they have been bribed by the Austrians to desert not only their brethren of Russia and of Prussia, but also their fellow-Slavs of the Austro-Hungarian Empire. I have heard this criticism ably and feelingly presented, but I do not think it just. Since national aspirations are awakened and sustained by the effort to secure political equality and justice, the enjoyment of these takes away need or desire to plot against the Government. The Poles of Austria are like the French of Canada. Their nationalism is literary and religious in character. There is no reason for its being anti-governmental.

Of late years, however, there has been a national Polish agitation in Galicia. It is directed not against the Government, but against the Ruthenians, who, to the number of three millions—nearly forty per cent. of the total population—inhabit the eastern section of Galicia. This local racial conflict, which has strengthened rather than weakened the attachment of the Poles to the Vienna Government, arose after the introduction of universal suffrage, when eastern Galicia began to send in large numbers Ruthenian deputies to the Galician Diet and to the Austrian Parliament.

On April 12, 1908, Count Potocki was assassinated by a Ruthenian student, whose death sentence was commuted to twenty years' imprisonment. With the complicity of wardens, the assassin escaped from jail after three years. There has never been peace between the Poles and the Ruthenians since that time. After serious disorders at the University of Lemberg, where the Ruthenian students were treated disgracefully, Polish and Ruthenian leaders tried to find common ground for reconciliation in December, 1911. The Ruthenians demanded electoral reform with greater representation, and the creation of a Ruthenian university. The imperial government communicated to the representatives of the two nationalities the project of a decree of public instruction in Galicia in January, 1913. The project was a marvel of ingenuity. A Ruthenian university was to be established after four years, but if by October 1, 1916, the law voting credits for it was not yet passed, a special school for Ruthenians would be attached to the University of Lemberg, until their own university was a reality. The teaching of the Ruthenian language would cease in the University of Lemberg when this "special school" was inaugurated. The Ruthenians were suspicious of a trick in the project. They could not understand its vagueness. It looked as if they would be giving up their present rights in the University of Lemberg, limited as they were, for an uncertainty. Why was no definite date for opening specified, or indication given of the new university's location? Would it be maintained by Galicia with a budget appropriation in proportion to the taxes paid by Ruthenians?

The Ruthenian question in Galicia has been cited here to show how there are wheels within wheels in the complex questions of nationalities. European racial questions seem to follow the law of the animal world. The littlest animals are eaten by little animals, who in turn serve as food for larger animals. Nations which have suffered most cruelly from race persecution are generally themselves relentless and fanatical when the power to persecute is in their hands.

The Ruthenian question shows also how Poles and Austrians work together, and are content with the mutual advantages of their union. I have never met an Austrian Pole, who lived in Galicia and had a settled profession or business there, who was not a loyal—even ardent—supporter of the Hapsburg Monarchy. Austrian Poles are dismayed as they face the terrible dilemma of union with Russia or Germany.

THE POLES SINCE 1870 IN GERMANY

Germany, like Russia, has had a twofold Polish question: The acquisition of Polish territory on either side of the Vistula to the Baltic Sea was as essential to the creation of a strong Prussian kingdom as was the acquisition of Pomerania. The portion of Poland which, before the partition, cut off eastern from western Prussia was fully as much German as Polish,—in fact more so. It became German by logical and natural conquest in the course of Prussia's evolution.

The situation was different in Poznania. This territory of the later partition reverted to Prussia at the Congress of Vienna. In 1815, its population was only twenty per cent. German. For fifty years the process of Germanization went on naturally—in no way forced. When the German Empire was formed, nearly half of Poznania was German. Many of the leading Poles had lost their sense of Polish nationality. They had become German in language and in culture. How many families there are in Prussia whose Polish origin is betrayed only by their names!

But the Germanized Poles, for the most part, retained their religion. The notorious *Kulturkampf* of Bismarck aroused again the sense of nationality which had been lost, not only among the prosperous Poles of Poznania, but even of Silesia. Only the bureaucratic classes were unaffected by this renaissance of nationalism awakened by revolt against religious persecution.

Just after the formation of the Empire, when Prussia needed all her strength and force to preserve her hegemony in the new confederation and to lead modern Germany in the path of progress and civilization, on either side of her kingdom she had to cope with nationalist movements of Danes and of Poles. But she did not fear to undertake also the assimilation of Alsace and Lorraine!

Since the *Kulturkampf*, the Polish renaissance in Prussia has thrived in spite of persecution. As in Russia, the Polish language was banished, Polish teachers were transferred to schools in other parts of the Empire, and about forty thousand Poles of Russian and Austrian nationality were expelled from the country. The persecution has been carried on in the schools, in the army, and in the church. School children have been forbidden to pray in the Polish language. Two unconstitutional laws have been passed by the Prussian Diet. The first of these forbade the Poles to speak Polish in public gatherings. The second, sanctioned by the *Landtag* on March 8, 1908, authorized the Government to expropriate land owned by Poles *for the purpose of selling it to Germans.*

The Prussian scheme for getting rid of the Poles was to drive them from their lands and instal German colonists. Private enterprise was first tried. A "colonization society" was formed, with a large capital, and given every encouragement by Prussian officialdom. But economic laws are not controlled by politics. The colonists were boycotted. Enormous sums of money were lost in wasted crops. The farms of the colonists had to be resold by the sheriff, and were bought in by Poles. To discourage the buying back of the German farms, a law was passed forbidding Poles to build upon land acquired by them after the date of the colonization society's failure. The Poles got around this law most cleverly. If one goes into Poznania to-day, he will see farmhouses, barns, dairies, stables—even chicken-coops—on wheels. The people live in glorified wagons. They do not build. Will there be a law now against owning wagons?

When the failure of private enterprise was demonstrated, the Prussian Government announced its intention of applying the law of expropriation "for the use of the commission of colonization." This was in October, 1912. At the beginning of 1913, the Polish deputies to the *Reichstag* brought before their colleagues of all Germany the question of the expropriation of Polish lands in Prussia. They asked the representatives of a supposedly advanced and constitutional nation what they thought of this injustice. Chancellor von Bethmann-Hollweg tried to keep the question from being debated. He argued with perfect reason that it was a purely internal Prussian matter, which the Imperial Parliament was incompetent to discuss. But the Catholic centre and the Socialist left combined to vote an order of the day allowing the discussion of the Polish lands question.

In the history of the German confederation, it was the first time that an imperial chancellor had received a direct defiance. This vote is mentioned here to show how Prussian dealings with the Poles, just as with Alsace-

Lorraine, have tended to weaken the purely Prussian substructure of the German confederation, and to arouse a dangerous protest against Prussian hegemony. Contempt for the elementary principles of justice has been the key-note of Chancellor von Bethmann-Hollweg's career. His mentality is typical of that of German bureaucracy—no, more than that, of German statesmanship. It is possible to have sympathy with German national aspirations, but not with the methods by which those aspirations are being interpreted to the world. To show how little regard he had for parliamentary opinion in the German confederation, the Chancellor forced through the Prussian *Landtag*, on April 22, 1913, only three months after his rebuke from the *Reichstag*, an infamous law, voting one hundred and twenty-five million marks for German colonization in Prussian Poland. Shortly before the European war broke out, another unconstitutional law was passed, which makes possible the arbitrary division of large landed properties owned by Poles.

THE INTERNATIONAL ASPECT OF THE POLISH QUESTION

During the war with Japan, the Czar and the Kaiser understood each other perfectly on the Polish question. The neutrality of Germany was essential to Russia at that time. The Russians owe much to Germany for her benevolent attitude of those trying days. The Poles have since paid the bill.

As in Prussia, the Poles of Russia have seen their liberties menaced more than ever before during the past decade, and have had to struggle hopelessly against a policy of ruthless extermination. If on the one hand the Prussian persecution is more to be condemned because Germany asks the world to believe that she is an enlightened, constitutional nation, and "the torch-bearer of civilization," while Russia is admittedly reactionary and still half-barbarous, on the other hand there is less excuse for the Russian persecution of the Poles. For in Russia it is not Teuton against Slav, but Slav against Slav.

Germany and Russia have had the common interest of fellow-criminals in their relation to the Polish nation. Russia has not hesitated to co-operate with Germany through diplomatic and police channels in riveting more securely the fetters of the Poles. Her championship of the south Slavs against Teutonic aggression has been supposedly on the grounds of "burning love for our brothers in slavery, in whose veins runs the same blood as ours." The sham and hypocrisy of this attitude is revealed when we consider the fact that Russia has never protested to Germany against the treatment of the Poles of Poznania, nor shown any inclination to treat with equity her own Poles. Here are "brothers in slavery" nearer home. There is ground for suspicion that her interest in the south Slavs has been purely because they are on the way to Constantinople and the Mediterranean. One who reads the recent history of Russia stultifies himself if he allows himself to believe that Russia has entered into the present war to defend Servia from Austrian aggression *through any love for or humanitarian interest in the Servians.* If Russia gets the opportunity, will her treatment of Servian national aspirations be any different from that of Austria-Hungary? When we try to answer this question, let us think of Bulgaria after 1878 (the last "war of liberation") and of Poland *in 1914.*

On August 16, 1914, when I read the proclamation of Czar Nicholas to the partitioned Poles, promising to restore administrative autonomy to the kingdom of Poland, and posing as the liberator of Poles now under the yoke of Austria and of Prussia, it was hard to be enthusiastic. For the Jews of Odessa and Kief, and the Finns of Helsingfors, rise up to add their cry of warning to the bitter comments of Polish friends. Only two years ago I saw in those cities subjects of the Czar suffering cruelly from fanaticism and broken promises, and deprived of that which is now being held out as bait to the Poles, and as a sop to Russia's Allies.

Austria-Hungary has been able to use the Russian treatment of Poland as a means of strengthening her own hold on the border regions of the Empire. It was at the instigation of Ballplatz that the Galician deputies, on December 16, 1911, made a motion in the Reichsrath, inviting the Minister of Foreign Affairs "to undertake steps among the Powers who signed the conventions at Vienna in 1815 to assure the maintenance of the frontiers of the kingdom of Poland, of which Russia, in violation of her international obligations, was threatening the integrity. For the separation of Kholm from Poland is an attack upon Polish historic and national consciousness." It was tit for tat with the two Eastern Powers. Russia burned with indignation for the feelings of Servia when Austria-Hungary annexed Bosnia-Herzegovina. Austria-Hungary burned with indignation for the feelings of her own loyal Polish subjects, when Russia separated Kholm from Poland. Both had violated international treaties. Russia had no genuine interest in the Servians, and Austria none in the Poles. They merely seized upon weapons with which to attack each other.

It is a mystery how French and British public opinion, always so traditionally favourable to downtrodden races, and especially to the Poles, can hail the Russian entry into Lemberg as a "victory for civilization." To the Austrian Poles, the coming of the Cossacks is as the coming of the Uhlans to the Belgians. They look upon the Russian invasion of Galicia as a calamity to their national life. Fighting with the Austrians are thirty thousand young Poles who call themselves Sokols (falcons). Their organization is something like the German *Turnverein*, but more purely military. The Poles of Austria-Hungary are a unit against Russia.

One can make no such positive statement about the attitude of the Poles of the other two partitioners. They have little hope of any amelioration of their lot from a change of masters through the present war. As I write, the thunder of German cannon is heard at Warsaw, and the unhappy kingdom of Poland is the centre of conflict between Russia and Germany. The Poles are fighting on both sides, and Polish non-combatants are suffering from the brutality of both "liberating" armies. The situation is exactly expressed by a Polish proverb which is the fruit of centuries of bitter experience: *Gdzie dwóch panów sie, bije, ch[l-tilde]op w skur[e-cedille], dostaje*—"When two masters fight, the peasant receives the blows."

CHAPTER VII
ITALIA IRREDENTA

Irredentism grew inevitably out of the decisions of the Congress of Vienna, whose members were subjected to two influences in making a new map of Europe. The first consideration, so common and so necessary in all diplomatic arrangements, was that of expediency. The second consideration was to prevent the rise of liberalism and democracy. The decisions on the ground of the first consideration were made under the pressure and the play and the skill of give and take by the representatives of the nations who fondly believed that they were making a lasting peace for Europe. The decisions on the ground of the second consideration were guided by the idea that the checking of national aspirations was the best means of preventing the growth of democracy.

The decisions of Vienna, like the later modifications of Paris and Berlin, could not prevent the development of the national movements which have changed the map as it was rearranged after the collapse of the Napoleonic *régime*.

During the past hundred years, ten new states have appeared on the map of Europe: Greece, Belgium, Servia, Italy, the German Confederation, Rumania, Montenegro, Norway, Bulgaria, and—possibly—Albania. With the exception of Albania (and is this the reason why we have to qualify its viability by the word *possibly?*), *all of these states have appeared upon the map against the will of, and in defiance of, the concert of the European Powers.* They have all, again with the exception of Albania, been born through a rise of national consciousness preceded and inspired by a literary and educational revival. The goal has been democracy. None of them, in achieving independence, has succeeded in including within its frontiers all the territory occupied by people of the same race and the same language. *Irredentism is the movement to secure the union with a nation of contiguous territories inhabited by the same race and speaking the same language.* It is the call of the redeemed to the unredeemed, and of the unredeemed to the redeemed.

If we were to regard the present unrest in Europe and the antagonism of nations from the standpoint of nationalism, we could attribute the breaking out of contemporary wars to five causes: the desire of nations to get back what they have lost, illustrated by France in relationship to Alsace-Lorraine; the desire of nations to expand according to their legitimate racial aspirations, illustrated by the Balkan States in relationship to Turkey and Austria-Hungary, and Italy in relationship to Austria-Hungary; the desire of nations to expand commercially and politically because of possession of surplus population and energy, illustrated by Germany in her *Weltpolitik*; the desire of nations to prevent the commercial and political expansion of their rivals, illustrated by Great Britain and Russia; and the desire of nations to stamp out the rise of national movements which threaten their territorial integrity, illustrated by Austria-Hungary and Turkey.

The irredentism of the Balkan States led, first, to their war with Turkey; second, to their war with each other; and third, to Servia becoming the direct cause of the European war. The aspirations of none have been satisfied. Rumanian irredentism has stood between Rumania and the Triple Alliance. The irredentism of Italy has not yet led to anything, but it is so full of significance as a possible factor in bearing upon and changing the whole destinies of Europe during the winter of 1914-1915, that it cannot be overlooked in a study of contemporary national movements and wars.

The entrance of Italy into an alliance with the Teutonic Powers of Central Europe was believed by her statesmen to be an act of self-preservation.

The opposition of the French clerical party to the completion of the unification of Italy during the last decade of the Third Empire destroyed whatever gratitude the Italian people may have felt for the decisive aid rendered to the cause of Italian unity at Solferino. On the part of the moving spirits of Young Italy, indeed, this gratitude was not very great. For the first great step in the unification of Italy had been accompanied by a dismemberment of the territories from which the royal house of Piedmont took its name. Young Italy felt that the French had been paid for their help against Austria, and paid dearly. The cession of his birthplace, at the moment when the nation for which he had suffered so terribly and struggled so successfully came into being, hurt Garibaldi more than the French bullets lodged in his body eight years later at Mentana. When the French look to-day with joy upon Italian irredentism as the hopeless barrier between Italy and Austria-Hungary, they should not forget that, even though fifty years have passed, Italian irredentism includes also Savoy and Nice.

After the Franco-German War, there were two tendencies in the policy of the Third Republic to prevent an understanding between France and Italy. The first of these was the recurrence in France of the old bitter clericalism of the Empire. Italy feared that French soldiers might again come to Rome. The second was the antagonism of France to the budding colonial aspirations of Italy. When France occupied Tunis, Italy felt that she had been robbed of the realization of a dream, which was hers by right of history, geography, and necessity.

So Italy joined the Triple Alliance. It is argued with reason in France that the alliance of Teuton and Latin was unnatural. Since Italy had become wholly Guelph to realize its unity, why this sudden return to Ghibellinism? The alliance of Italy with Germany and Austria-Hungary, however, was not more paradoxical than the alliance of increasingly democratic and socialistic and anti-clerical France with mediæval Russia. The reasons dictating the alliance were practically the same.

But there was this difference. Italy entered into an alliance with a former enemy and oppressor, who was still holding certain unredeemed territories of the united Italy as it had existed in the minds of the enthusiasts of the middle of the nineteenth century.

Too many books have been written about the distribution of populations in the Austro-Hungarian Empire to make necessary going into the details here of the Italian populations of the Austrian Tyrol and of the Austrian provinces at the north of the Adriatic Sea. The Tyrolese Italians are undoubtedly Italian in sympathies and characteristics. But is their union with Italy demanded by either internal Italian or external European political and economic considerations more than would be the union with Italy of the Italian cantons of the Swiss confederation?

Italian irredentism in regard to the Adriatic littoral is a far more serious and complicated problem. One is struck everywhere in the Adriatic, even as far south as Corfu, by the Italian character of the cities. Cattaro, Ragusa, Spalato, Zara, Fiume, Pola, and Trieste, all have an indefinable Italian atmosphere. It has never left them since the Middle Ages. It is in the buildings, however, rather than in the people. One hesitates to attribute even to the people of Fiume and Trieste Italian characteristics in the narrower sense of the word. On the Dalmatian coast, the Slavic element has won all the cities. In Fiume and Trieste, it is strong enough to rob these two cities of their distinctive Italian character. One's misgivings concerning the claims of Italian irredentists grow when he leaves the cities. There are undoubtedly several hundred thousands of Italians in this region. Italian is the language of commerce, and on the Austrian-Lloyd and Hungaro-Croatian steamship lines, Italian is the language of the crews. But the people who speak Italian are not Italians, in every other case you meet, nor do they resemble Italians. Why is this?

Nationality, in the twentieth century, has a mental and civic, rather than a physical and hereditary basis. *We are the product of our education and of the political atmosphere in which we live.* This is why assimilation is so strikingly easy in America, where we place the immigrant in touch with the public school, the newspaper, and the ballot. Just as the Italians and Germans and French of Switzerland are Swiss, despite their differences of language, so the

Italians of the Adriatic littoral are the product of the dispensation under which they have lived. Unlike the Alsatians, they have never known political freedom and cultural advantages in common with their kin across a frontier forcibly raised to cut them off; unlike the Poles, they have not been compelled to revive the nationalism of an historic past as a means of getting rid of oppression; unlike the Slavs of the Balkans, their national spirit has not been called into being by the tyranny of a race alien in civilization and ideals, because alien in religion.

I have among my clippings from French newspapers during the past five years a legion of quotations from Vienna and Rome correspondents, concerning the friction between Austria-Hungary and Italy, and between the Italian-speaking population of Austria and the Viennese Government, over the question of distinct Italian nationality of Austro-Hungarian subjects. There have been frontier incidents; there have been demonstrations of Austrian societies visiting Italian cities and Italian societies visiting Trieste; there has been much discussion over the creation of an Italian Faculty of Law at the University of Vienna, and the establishment of an Italian University at Trieste or Vienna; and there have been occasional causes of friction between the Austrian Governor of Istria and the Italian residents of the province. But the general impression gained from a study of the incidents in question, and the effort to trace out their aftermath, leads to the conclusion that these irredentist incidents have been magnified in importance. A clever campaign of the French press has endeavoured to detach Italian public opinion from the Triple Alliance by publishing in detail, on every possible occasion, any incident that might show Austrian hostility to the Italian "nation."

In 1844, Cesare Balbo, in his *Speranze d'Italia*, a book that is as important to students of contemporary politics as to those of the Risorgimento, set forth clearly that the hope of Italy to the exclusion of Austria from Lombardy and Venetia was most reasonably based *upon the extension of the Austrian Empire eastward through the approaching fall of the Ottoman Empire*. Balbo was a man of great vision. He looked beyond the accidental factors in the making of a nation to the great and durable considerations of national existence. He grasped the fact that the insistence of the Teutonic race upon holding in subjection purely Italian territories, and its hostility to the unification of the Italian people, was based upon economic considerations. Lombardy and Venetia had been for a thousand years the pathway of German commerce to the Mediterranean. If Austria, Balbo argued, should fall heir to a portion of the European territories of the Ottoman Empire, she would have her outlet to the Mediterranean more advantageously than through the possession of Lombardy and Venetia. Once these Ottoman territories were secured, Austria would be ready to cede Lombardy and Venetia to a future united Italy.

After the unity of Italy had been achieved, and Austria had been driven out of Lombardy and Venetia, she did receive compensation in Bosnia and Herzegovina, and, just as Balbo predicted, there was born the Austrian ambition to the succession of Macedonia. *That this ambition has not been realized, and that Russia was determined to prevent the attempt to revive it, explains the Austro-Hungarian willingness to fight Russia in the summer of 1914.*

Austria and Hungary, from the very beginning of existence as a Dual Monarchy, have been caught in the vise between Italian irredentism and Servian irredentism. They have not been able to secure their outlet through Macedonia to the Ægean Sea. They have been constantly threatened by their neighbours on the south-east and south-west with exclusion altogether from the Adriatic, their only outlet to the Mediterranean.

From the economic point of view, one cannot but have sympathy with the determination of the Austrians and Hungarians to prevent the disaster which would certainly come to them, if the aspirations of Italian and Servian irredentism were realized. The severity of Hungary against Croatia and the oppression of the Servians in Bosnia-Herzegovina and Dalmatia by Austria have been dictated by the same reasons which led England and Scotland to attempt to destroy the national spirit of Ireland for so many centuries after they had robbed her of her independence. They could not afford to have their communications by sea threatened by the presence and growth of an independent nation, especially since this nation was believed to be susceptible to the influence of hereditary enemies.

It has been fortunate for Austria-Hungary that the claims of the irredentists at the head of the Adriatic have overlapped and come into conflict in almost the same way that the claims of Greece and Bulgaria have come into conflict in Macedonia. From time immemorial, the Italian and Greek peoples, owing to their position on peninsulas, have been seafaring. Consequently, it is they who have developed the commercial life of ports in the eastern Mediterranean. Everywhere along the littoral of the Ægean and the Adriatic, Greeks and Italians have founded and inhabited, up to the present day, the chief ports. But, by the same token, those engaged in commercial and maritime occupations have never been excellent farmers, shepherds, or woodsmen. So, while the Italians and Greeks have held the predominance in the cities of the littoral, the *hinterland* has been occupied by other races. Just as the *hinterland* of Macedonia is very largely Bulgarian, the *hinterland* of the upper end of the Adriatic is very largely Slavic. Just as the realization of the dreams of Hellenic irredentists would give Greece a narrow strip of coast line along European Turkey to Constantinople, with one or two of the larger inland commercial cities, while the Slavs would be cut off entirely from the sea, the realization of the dreams of Italian irredentists would give to Italy the ports and coast line of the northern end of the Adriatic, with no *hinterland*, and the Slavs, Hungarians, and Germans an enormous *hinterland* with no ports.

Italian irredentism, in so far as the Tyrol goes, is not unreasonable. But its realization in Istria and the Adriatic littoral is impracticable. Our modern idea of a state is of people living together in a political union that is to their economic advantage. Only the thoughtless enthusiasts could advocate a change in the map of Europe by which fifty million people would be cut off from the sea to satisfy the national aspirations of a few hundred thousand Italians.

The Italian Society *Dante Alighieri* has gotten into the hands of the irredentists, and, before the Tripolitan conquest, was successful in influencing members of Parliament to embarrass the Government by interpellations concerning the troubles of Italians who are Austrian subjects. This society has advocated for Italy the adoption of a law so modifying the legislation on naturalization that Italians who emigrate can preserve their nationality even if they acquire that of the countries to which they have gone. It was a curious anticipation of the famous Article XXV, of the German Citizenship Law of 1914. In 1911, a Lombard deputy tried to raise the old cry of alarm concerning German penetration into Italy, and emphasized the necessity of the return to the policy of the Ghibelline motto, "*Fuori i Tedeschi*"—"Expel the Germans."

Italian statesmen, however, have never given serious attention to the claims of the irredentists. The late Marquis di San Giuliano deplored their senseless and harmful manifestations. In trying for the impossible, and keeping up an agitation that tended to make friction between Italy and Austria-Hungary, he pointed out that they harmed what were the real and *attainable* Italian interests.

The antagonism between Italy and Austria-Hungary has had deeper and more logical and justifiable foundation than irredentism. The two nations have been apprehensive each about allowing the other to gain control of the Adriatic. Up to 1903, Spezzia was the naval base for the whole of Italy. Since that time, Tarento has become one of the first military ports, important fortifications have been placed at Brindisi, Bari, and Ancona, and an elaborate scheme has been drawn up for the defence of Venice. The Venetians have been demanding that Venice become a naval base.

Italian naval and maritime activity having increased in the Adriatic, there has naturally been more intense opposition and rivalry between the two Adriatic Powers over Albania. The spread of Austro-Hungarian influence has been bitterly fought by the Italian propaganda. This problem was becoming a serious one for the statesmen of the two nations while Albania was still under Turkish rule. Since, at the joint wish of Italy and Austria-Hungary, Albania has been brought into the family of European nations, the question of the equilibrium of the Adriatic has only become more unsettled. For free Albania turned out to be a fiasco.

If the relations between Austria-Hungary, fighting for life, and her passive ally of the Triple Alliance have become more strained since the European war began, let it be hoped for the future stability of Europe that it has not been because Italian irredentism has gained the upper hand at Rome. For if Italy were to intervene in the war for the purpose of taking away from Austria-Hungary the Adriatic littoral inhabited by Italians, she would be menacing her own future, and that of Switzerland as well. To entertain the hope of taking and keeping Trieste would be folly.

CHAPTER VIII
THE DANUBE AND THE DARDANELLES

The River Danube and the Straits leading from the Black Sea to the Ægean Sea have been the waterways of Europe whose fortunes have had the greatest influence upon the evolution of international relations during the last half century. The control of these two waterways, as long as the Ottoman Empire remained strong, was not a question of compelling interest to Europe. It was only when the decline of the Ottoman power began to foreshadow the eventual disappearance of the empire from Europe that nations began to think of the vital importance of the control of these waterways to the economic life of Europe.

There is an extensive and interesting literature on the history of the evolution of international law in its relationship to the various questions raised by the necessarily international control of the Danube and the Dardanelles. In a book like this, an adequate statement of the history and work of the Danube Commission, and of the various diplomatic negotiations affecting the Bosphorus and the Dardanelles, their freedom of passage, their fortifications, their lighthouses, and their life-saving stations, cannot be attempted. It is my intention, therefore, to treat these great waterways only in the broader aspect of the important part that the questions raised by them have played in leading up to the gigantic struggle which foreshadows a new political reconstruction of the world.

The Danube is navigable from Germany all the way to the Black Sea. On its banks are the capitals of Austria, Hungary, and Servia. It traverses the entire Austro-Hungarian Empire, forms a natural boundary between Austria and Servia, Rumania and Bulgaria, and then turns north across Rumania to separate for a short distance Rumania and Russia before finally reaching the Black Sea.

The volume of traffic on the Danube has increased steadily since the Crimean War. It has become the great path of export for Austrian and Hungarian merchandise to the Balkan States, Russia, Turkey, and Persia, and for Servian, Bulgarian, and Rumanian products to Russia and Turkey. The passenger service on the Danube has kept pace with the competition of the railways. Eastward, it is frequently quicker, cheaper, and more convenient than the railway service. You can leave Vienna or Buda-Pesth in the evening, and reach Buda-Pesth or Belgrade in the morning. From Belgrade to the Hungarian and Rumanian frontier towns, the Danube furnishes the shortest route. From Bulgaria to Russia, the Danube route, via Somovit and Galatz to Odessa, is in many ways preferable to the through train service. It is by spending days on the Danube that I have come to realize how vital the river is to freight and passenger communications between Austria-Hungary, the Balkan states, and Russia. Travel gives life and meaning to statistics. The Danube interprets itself.

The Congresses of Paris and Berlin considered carefully the entrance of the Danube question into international life through the enfranchisement of the Balkan States. International laws, administered by an international commission, govern the Danube. It is a neutral waterway. Problems, similar to those of the Scheldt, have arisen, however, in the present war between Austria-Hungary and Servia. If Rumania and Bulgaria should join in the European war, no matter on which side they should fight, the whole Danube question would become further complicated. When war actually breaks out, the rulings of international law concerning neutrality are invariably violated. States act according to their own interests.

In its larger European aspect, the Danube, as an international waterway, is dependent upon the Dardanelles. Were Rumania to close the navigation of the Danube, or were she to preserve its neutrality, she would only be preventing or assisting the commerce of the riverain states with the Black Sea. Unobstructed passage to the outside world for Danube commerce depends upon the control of the outlet from the Black Sea to the Ægean Sea. The Hungarian and Servian peasant looks beyond his own great river to the narrow passage from the Sea of Marmora. The question of the Danube is subordinated to the question of the Dardanelles.

That the passage from the Black Sea to the outside world remain open and secure from sudden stoppage or constant menace is of vital importance to the riverain Danube states, Austria-Hungary and Servia, to the states bordering the Black Sea, Russia, Rumania, and Turkey, and to Persia, whose nearest communications with Europe are by way of the Black Sea. Austria-Hungary, however, has another outlet through the Adriatic, Servia is pressing towards the Adriatic and the Ægean, Bulgaria has recently secured an Ægean littoral, Persia is dependent upon Russia, and Turkey holds the straits. There remain Russia and Rumania, to whom the question of the Dardanelles is a matter of life and death.

The international position of Rumania is most unfortunate. She must make common cause with Germanic Europe or with Turkey to prevent her only waterway to the outside world from falling into the hands of Russia, or she must ally herself with Russia, and, by adding Bukovina and Transylvania, increase her numbers to the point where she can hope to resist the tide of Slavs around her. In discussing the neutrality of Rumania, the French and British press have given too much emphasis to the loyalty of King Carol for the Hohenzollern family, of which he was a member, as the cause of the failure of Rumania to join the enemies of the Germanic Powers, and to the hope that the death of the sovereign who made Rumania may result in a favourable change in the policy of the Bukarest Cabinet. The new sovereign, King Ferdinand, is also a Hohenzollern. The hesitation of Rumania has not been, and is not, primarily because of the family ties of her rulers. The Rumanians in Hungary may call for union with their enfranchised brethren, just as the Italians in Austria may call for union with the Italians who were liberated in 1859 and 1866. But is irredentism the only factor in influencing the policy of Italy and Rumania? For Rumania, at least, the hope of acquiring Transylvania and Bukovina in the international settlement following the war is offset by the apprehension of seeing Russia at the Dardanelles.

The Dardanelles has been the scene of struggles for commercial supremacy since the days of the Peloponnesian wars. It was in the Dardanelles that the great battle was fought which brought about the downfall of Athenian hegemony. It was over the question of fortifying the island of Tenedos that Venice and Genoa in the latter half of the fourteenth century fought the war during which the Genoese occupation of Chioggia nearly caused the destruction of Venice. Then came the Ottoman occupation to put a stop to international jealousies until modern times.

The political development of Russia from Moscow has been a consistent forward march towards ocean waterways. There have been six possible outlets for Russia, the Baltic Sea, the Black Sea, the White Sea, the Yellow Sea, the Persian Gulf, and the Adriatic. At different periods of her history, Russia has expended her efforts continuously in these various directions. To reach the Baltic, Peter the Great built Petrograd. One has to stand on the Kremlin on a beautiful summer day and look out over the sacred city of the Russians to grasp the fulness of the sacrifice and the marvellous daring of the man who abandoned Moscow to build another capital on piles driven into dreary salt marshes. It was for the sea and contact with the outside world! To reach the Pacific Ocean, Russia patiently conquered the former empire of the Mongols, steppe by steppe, and when she thought the moment of realization had arrived, did not hesitate to throw a band of steel across the continent of Asia. To reach the Persian Gulf, she crossed the Caucasus and launched her ships upon the Caspian Sea. To reach the Black Sea, she broke the military power of the houses of Jagello and Osman, building laboriously upon the ruins of Poland and the Ottoman Empire. Is it to reach the Adriatic that her forces are now before Przemysl?

In spite of her struggles through three centuries, Russia is still landlocked. The ice is an insurmountable barrier to freedom of exit from the White Sea, her only undisputed outlet. Japan has arisen to shatter the dreams of the future of Port Dalny, and make useless the sacrifices to gain the Pacific. The control by Germany of the exit from the Baltic Sea has been strengthened in recent years by the construction and fortification of the Kiel Canal. The Persian Gulf has been given up by the accord of 1907 with Great Britain. There has remained what has always been the strongest hope, and the one for the realization of which Russia has made consistent and stupendous efforts.

Radetsky, in his memoirs, has summed up the attitude of Russia towards the Ottoman Empire in words that give the key to the whole Eastern Question during the past century:

"Owing to her geographical position, Russia is the national and eternal enemy of Turkey.... Russia must therefore do all she can to take possession of Constantinople, for its possession alone will grant to her the security and territorial completeness necessary for her future."

Three times during the nineteenth century Russia endeavoured to destroy the Ottoman Empire in Europe so that she might gain control of the exit to the Ægean Sea. In 1828, her armies reached Adrianople, and half a century later the suburbs of Constantinople. In both instances, especially the second, it was the opposition of Great Britain that forced Russia to make peace without having attained her end. In 1854, France and Italy joined Great Britain in the invasion of the Crimea to preserve "the integrity of the Ottoman Empire." In 1856, at the Congress of Paris, Russia saw the western Powers uphold the principle that the Czar had no right to sovereignty even on the Black Sea, a half of which his ancestors had wrested from the Turks. It was no use for Russia to plead that she had "special interests" in her own territorial waters. The Black Sea was neutralized. The expression "*selon nos convenances et intérêts*" was understood by Great Britain to refer only to British interests! It was by right of might that Russia was held in check. In 1870, Bismarck purchased the neutrality of Russia in his war against France by agreeing to Russia's denunciation of the Paris treaty clauses which held her impotent in the Black Sea. But again, in 1878, Great Britain interfered to bottle up Russia. Since then the Russian navy has been a prisoner in the Black Sea. Will it continue to be so after the war of 1914?

Just when Ottoman power was receding, the rapid development of steam power began to make southern Russia the bread basket of Europe. Steam machinery increased the yield of these vast and rich lands, steam railways enabled the farmers to send their harvests to Black Sea ports, and steamships made possible the distribution of the harvests throughout Europe. I used to live on the Bosphorus, and from my study window I could see every day the never-ceasing procession of grain ships of all nations going to and coming from the Black Sea. In May, 1912, when the Dardanelles was closed for a month during the Italian war, two hundred steamships lay at anchor in the harbour of Constantinople.

Another influence whose importance cannot be overestimated has constantly turned the eyes of Russians towards Constantinople. Slavs are idealists. For an ideal, one makes sacrifices that material considerations do not call forth. To the Russians, Constantinople is Tsarigrad, the city of the Emperor. It is from Constantinople that the Russians received their religion. Their civilization is imbued with the spirit of Byzantium. Just as one sees in the Polish language the influence of Latin in the construction of the sentence, one sees in the kindred Russian tongue the influence of Greek. I have frequently been struck with the close and vital relationship between Constantinople and Russia during the period of the development of the Russian nation. *Now that Russia seems to be entering upon a period of national awakening, the sentiment is bound to be irresistible among the Russians that they are the rightful inheritors of the Eastern Empire, eclipsed for so many centuries by the shadow of Islam and now about to be born again.*

On a July evening in 1908, when the constitutional revolution in Turkey was beginning to occupy the attention of Europe, I sat with my wife in the winter garden of the Grand Hotel in Paris. We were listening to a charming and intelligent Russian gentleman explain to us the aims of the political parties in the Duma of 1907. A waiter came to tell us that our baggage was ready. "Where are you going?" asked the Russian. "To Constantinople," we answered. An expression of wistful sadness or joy—you can never tell which it is meant to be with a Russian—came across his face. "Constantinople!" he murmured, more to himself than to us: "This revolution will fail. You will see. For we must come into our own."

The political aspect of the question of the Dardanelles has changed greatly since Great Britain and France fought one war with Russia, and Great Britain stood ready to fight a second, in order to prevent this passage from falling into Russian hands.

Almost immediately after the crisis of San Stefano and the resulting revision of the Russo-Turkish treaty at Berlin, the interests of Great Britain were diverted from the north-east to the south-east Mediterranean. She decided that her permanent route to India was through the Suez Canal, and made it secure by getting possession of the majority of the shares of the Canal and by seizing Egypt. The Bulgarians began to show themselves lacking in the expected docility towards their liberator. British diplomats realized that they had been fearing what did not happen. They began to lose interest in the Dardanelles. This loss of interest in the question of the straits as a vital factor in their world interests has grown so complete in recent years that Russia has no reason to anticipate another visit of the British fleet to Besika Bay if—I refrain from prophesying. It is safe to say, however, that London has forgotten Mohammed Ali, the Crimea, and the Princes' Islands, while the traditions of Unkiar Skelessi are still dominating the foreign policy of Petrograd.

For, while the future of the Dardanelles has come to mean less to Great Britain, it means more than ever before to Russia. Russia has been turned back from the Pacific. The loss of Manchuria in the war with Japan caused her once again to cast her eyes upon the outlet to the Mediterranean. To the increase in her wheat trade has been added also the development of the petroleum trade from the Caucasus wells. Since the agreement for the partition of Persia with Great Britain in 1907, and the mutual "hands off" accord with Germany at Potsdam in 1910, the expectations of a brilliant Russian future for northern Persia and the Armenian and Kurdish corner of Asiatic Turkey have been great.

Since the Congress of Berlin, Germany has come into the place of Great Britain as the enemy who would keep Russia from finding the Ægean Sea. The growth of German interests at Constantinople and in Asia Minor has become the India—in anticipation—of Germany. When Russia, after her ill-fated venture in the Far East, turned her efforts once more towards the Balkan peninsula, it began to dawn upon her that the *Drang nach Oesten* might prove a menace to her control of the Dardanelles, fully as great as was formerly the British fetish of the integrity of the Ottoman Empire to keep open the route to India. Diplomacy endeavoured to ward off the inevitable struggle. But the Balkan wars created a new situation that broke rudely the accords of Skierniewice and Potsdam. Austria-Hungary in the Balkans and Germany in Asia Minor became the nightmare of Russia.

CHAPTER IX
AUSTRIA-HUNGARY AND HER SOUTH SLAVS

It has often been predicted in recent years that the union between Austria and Hungary would be broken by internal troubles. Hungary has been credited with desiring to cut loose from Austria. The frequent and serious quarrels between the members of the Dual Monarchy have caused many a wiseacre to shake his head and say, "The union will not outlive Franz Josef!" But the Austro-Hungarian Empire has been founded upon sound political and economic principles, which far transcend a single life or a dynasty. Austrians and Hungarians may be unwilling yoke-fellows. But they know that if they do not pull together, they cannot pull at all. They have too many Slavs around them.

The principle upon which Austrians and Hungarians have founded a Dual Monarchy is the old Latin proverb, *divide et impera*. In the Empire, Austrians and Hungarians are in the minority. In each kingdom, by dividing the Slavs cleverly between them, they hold the upper hand. The German race is, therefore, the dominant race in Austria, and the Hungarian race is the dominant race in Hungary.

If one looks at the map, and studies the division of the Empire, he will readily see that it is much more durably constructed than he would have reason to believe from statistics of the population. *The Slavic question in the Dual Monarchy is not how many Slavs of kindred races are to be found in Austria-Hungary, but how they are placed in relationship to each other and to neighbouring states.* It is a question of geography rather than of census. The student needs a map instead of columns of figures.

In only one place is the Austro-Hungarian Monarchy very weak, and that is in the south. The sole port for the thirty millions of Austria is Trieste. To reach Trieste one passes through a belt of Slavic territory, and Trieste itself is more Italian than German. The sole port of Hungary is Fiume. To reach Fiume one passes through a belt of Slavic territory, and there are hardly any Hungarians in Fiume itself. The Slavs which cut off Fiume from Hungary and the Slavs of the Dalmatian coast and of all Bosnia and Herzegovina belong to the same family. They speak practically the same language as the Servians and Montenegrins.

The Hungarians, then, have exactly the same interest as the Austrians in every move that has been made since the proclamation of the constitution of Turkey to prevent the foundation of a strong independent Servian State on the confines of the Austro-Hungarian Empire, and to prevent the Slavs from reaching the Adriatic Sea.

Austria has not been necessarily influenced in her attitude towards the Balkan problem by Germany. Although her *Drang nach Osten* is frequently interpreted as a part of the Pan-Germanic movement, the Germans of Austria have needed no German sentiment and no German prompting to arrive at their point of view in regard to the Balkan nationalities. It must be clearly kept in mind that the Convention of Reichstadt in 1876, which was the beginning of Austria's consistent policy towards the Balkan peninsula, was signed before the alliance with Germany; that it was the conception of a *Hungarian* statesman, and that *the occupation of Bosnia and Herzegovina had nothing whatever to do with Pan-Germanism.* It was a measure of self-protection to prevent these remote provinces of Turkey from forming a political union with Servia, should the Russian arms, intervening on behalf of the south Slavs against Turkey, prove successful. The extension of sovereignty over Bosnia-Herzegovina in 1908 was to prevent the constitutional *régime* from trying to weaken the hold of Austria-Hungary upon these provinces. Austria-Hungary certainly would have preferred the more comfortable status of an occupation to the legal adoption of a *Reichsland.* But she could take no chances with the Young Turks. Her military occupation of the *Sandjak* of Novi Bazar was inspired as much by the necessity of preventing the union of Montenegro and Servia as by the desire to provide for a future railway extension to Salonika.

Hungary has had to grapple with two Balkan problems, the rise of Rumania and the rise of Servia. She has had within her kingdom several million Rumanian subjects and several million South Slavic subjects. Most of her Rumanians, however, have been separated from Rumania from the natural barrier of the Carpathian mountains, and have not found their union with Hungary to their disadvantage. For the Rumanians of Hungary enjoy through Buda-Pesth and Fiume a better outlet to the markets of the world, and a cheaper haul, than they would find through Rumania. They have benefited greatly by their economic union with Hungary. It is not the same with the Croatians. They are situated between Buda-Pesth and the Adriatic. They have a natural river outlet to the Danube. They are not separated by physical barriers from their brothers of race and language in Servia, Bosnia, and Dalmatia. Were they to separate from Hungary, they would not find their economic position in any way jeopardized.

Many South Slavs have advocated a trialism to replace the present dualism. They have claimed that the most critical problems of the Austro-Hungarian Empire could be solved in this way. Added to Hungary and Austria, there could be a Servian kingdom, perhaps enlarged by the inclusion of independent Servia and Montenegro, whose crown could be worn by the Hapsburg ruler.

But this solution has never found favour, simple and attractive though it sounds on first sight, with either Hungarians or Austrians. For it would mean the cutting off of both kingdoms from the sea. The Hungarians would be altogether land-locked, and surrounded on all sides by alien races. Austria would be forced into hopeless economic dependence upon Germany. The Germans of Austria and the Hungarians of Hungary have felt that their national existence depended upon keeping in political subjection the South Slavs, and upon repressing mercilessly any evidences of Italian irredentism upon the littoral of the Adriatic. Italian irredentism is treated in another place. The repression of national aspirations among the South Slavs, which interests us here, has been the corner-stone of Austro-Hungarian policy in the Balkans. For Hungary it has also been an internal question in her relationship with Croatia.

The Serbo-Croatian movement in southern Hungary has been repressed by Hungary with the same bitterness and lack of success that have attended the attempts to stifle national aspirations elsewhere in Europe. No weapon has been left unused in fighting nationalism in Croatia. Official corruption, bribery, manipulation of judges, imprisonment without trial, military despotism, gerrymandering, electoral intimidation,—this has been for years and is still, the daily record in Croatia. If there were a Slavic Silvio Pellico, the world would know that the ministers of the aged Franz Josef are not very different from the ministers of the young Franz Josef, who crushed the Milanese and tracked Garibaldi like a beast. Radetzkys and Gorzkowskis are still wearing Austrian livery. To Austria and Hungary, Salonika and Macedonia may have been the dream. But Trieste, Fiume, and Dalmatia have always been the realities. If Hungary took her heel off the neck of the Croatians, Buda-Pesth might become another Belgrade and Hungary another Servia, land-locked with no other outlet than the Danube. This does not excuse, but it explains. In this world the battle is to the strong. The survival of the fittest is a historical as well as a biological fact.

In spite of their juxtaposition, the Serbo-Croats have never been able to unite. There have been more reasons for this than their political separation. They are divided in religion. The Servians are Orthodox, and the Croatians and Dalmatians Catholic. In Bosnia and Macedonia, the race adhered to both confessions, though in majority Orthodox, and has also a strong Mohammedan element. The Orthodox Servians of Servia use the Cyrillic alphabet, and the Catholic Croatians and Dalmatians of Austria-Hungary the Latin alphabet.

Until the recent Balkan Wars, the Croatians and Dalmatians considered themselves a much superior branch of the race to the Servians. They have certainly enjoyed a superior education and demonstrated a superior civilization. The probable reason for this is that they did not have the misfortune to be for centuries under the Ottoman yoke. The Croatians have never been willing to play the understudy to the Servians. Agram has considered itself the centre of the Serbo-Croat movement rather than Belgrade. It is a far more beautiful and modern city than Belgrade. Few cities of all Europe of its size can equal Agram for architecture, for municipal works, and for keen, stimulating intellectual life. Its university is the *foyer* of Serbo-Croat nationalism and of *risorgimento* literature. It was here that the one Roman bishop of the world, who dared to speak openly in the Vatican Council of 1870 against the doctrine of papal infallibility and remain within the Church, gave to his people the prophetic message that nationality transcended creeds. Here also another Catholic priest taught the oneness of Servians and Croatians in language and history, and proved by scholarly research which is universally admired, that Croatia, Slavonia, and Dalmatia formed a triune kingdom, whose juridic union with the Austro-Hungarian Empire was wholly personal connection with the Hapsburg Crown, and had never been subjection to the Magyar. The Hungarians, during the past few years of bitterest persecution at Agram, have not been able to drive away the ghosts of Strossmayer and Racki. In Croatia, the pen has proved mightier than the sword.

Until recently, Austria-Hungary has not felt uneasy about the relationship between the Croatians and the Servians of the independent kingdom. But there has never been a minute since the annexation of 1908 that the statesmen of the Ballplatz have not been nervous about the Servian propaganda in Bosnia and Herzegovina. To keep Catholic Croatians and Orthodox Servians in antagonism with each other and with the Moslems, to prevent the education and economic emancipation of the Orthodox peasants, and to introduce German colonists and German industrial enterprises everywhere, has been the Austro-Hungarian program.

Vienna has used the Catholic Church and the propaganda of Catholic missions for dividing the Orthodox Servians in Bosnia from their Croatian brothers of the Catholic rite. Missionaries give every encouragement to Servians to desert the Orthodox Church. In the greater part of Bosnia, the Government has made it absolutely impossible for a child to receive an education elsewhere than in the Catholic schools. There are only two hundred and sixty-eight schools supported by the Government, of which one-tenth are placed in such a way that they serve exclusively other populations. The Bosnian budget provides four times as much money for the maintenance of the *gendarmerie* as for public schools.

Moslem law provides that all conquered land belongs to the Khalif. He farms it out in annual, life, or hereditary grants. In the Ottoman conquest of the Balkan Peninsula, the territories acquired were granted to successful soldiers on a basis which provided for a feudal army. The feudal proprietors, or *beys*, left the land to the peasants who occupied it, in consideration of an annual rental of a third of the yield of the land. The peasants had in addition to pay their tenth to the tax collectors of the Sultan. In territories that were on the borders of the Ottoman Empire, like Bosnia and Albania, the lands were largely retained by their former proprietors, who became Moslems. So the landed aristocracy remained indigenous.

The lot of the peasants in Bosnia, who were largely Orthodox Servians was not intolerable under Turkish rule, except when Moslem fanaticism was aroused by Christian separatist propaganda. Austria-Hungary claimed, however, that her occupation of the province was a measure dictated by humanity to ameliorate the lot of the enslaved Christians. But the Austrian administration has accomplished just the opposite. The new government from the beginning supported its authority upon the Moslem landowners, upon whose good-will they were dependent to prevent the awakening of national feeling among the peasants. Vienna was more complacent in overlooking abuses of the *beys* than had been Constantinople. For the Turks held their *beys* in check when exactions grew too bad. The Sublime Porte was afraid of giving an excuse for Christian intervention. But the Austrians encouraged the exactions of the *beys* in order to keep in abject subjection the Servian peasant population.

From the first moment of the Austro-Hungarian occupation, the peasants found that they would no longer enjoy undisturbed possession of their lands. The exodus of Mohammedan Bosnians, who, as we have seen elsewhere, were urged to follow the Ottoman flag, gave the Germans the opportunity of settling colonists on the vacated lands. This process of colonization was afterwards pursued to the detriment of the indigenous Christian population. Ernest Haeckel, the great philosopher, once said in a lecture at Jena that "the work of the German people to assure and develop civilization gives it the right to occupy the Balkans, Asia Minor, Syria, and Mesopotamia, and to exclude from these countries the races actually occupying them which are powerless and incapable." This statement, publicly made before a body of distinguished German thinkers, reveals the real ulterior ideal of the *Drang nach Osten*. Professor Wirth, dealing specifically with present possibilities, stated that the policy of Austria-Hungary in Bosnia must be to keep the peasantry in slavery and, as much as possible, to encourage them by oppression to emigrate. The reason given for this was: "*To render powerful the Bosnian peasant is to render powerful the Servian people, which would be the suicide of Germany."* Can we not see from this how public sentiment in Germany has stood behind the Austro-Hungarian ultimatum to Servia?

From 1890 to 1914, the theory of Haeckel and the advice of Wirth have been followed by the Austrian functionaries in Bosnia. No stone has been left unturned to drive the peasants from their lands. Right of inheritance has been suppressed, a tax collector has been introduced between the bey and his peasants, the taxes have been raised in many cases arbitrarily to the point where the peasants have been compelled to abandon their land. To German immigrants have been given communal lands which were necessary to the peasants for pasturage and the forests where their swine fed on acorns.

The population of Bosnia hardly surpasses thirty-five inhabitants to the kilometre. The total population is about two millions, of whom eight hundred thousand are Orthodox, six hundred thousand Moslem, and five hundred thousand Catholic. But practically all of this population—except one hundred thousand who are Jews, Protestants, and other German immigrants—is Servian or Servian-speaking. There are thirty-five thousand Germans, as opposed to one million eight hundred thousand Slavs. And yet German is the language of the administration, and the only language of the railways and posts and telegraphs, which in Bosnia have not ceased to be under the control of the military government. Many functionaries after thirty years of service in Bosnia do not know the language of the country. Two German newspapers are supported at the expense of the public budget to attack indigenous elements. In German schools, pupils are taught the history of Germany, but in Slavic schools the history of the south Slavs is excluded from the curriculum. There are fourteen schools for ten thousand Germans, and one school for every six thousand Slavs.

In the administration of Bosnia, only thirty-one out of three hundred and twenty-two functionaries are Servians, only twelve out of one hundred and twenty-five professors of lyceums, only thirty-one out of two hundred and thirty-seven judges and magistrates. And yet the Orthodox Servians form forty-four per cent. of the population. The young Bosnians who have graduated from the Austro-Hungarian universities find themselves excluded from public life. Turning to commercial life, they find eighty per cent. of the large industries controlled by German capital and managed exclusively by Germans. Turning to agriculture, they find economic misery and hopeless ignorance among the peasants of their race, and every effort made by the Government to prevent the bettering of their lot. Turning to journalism and public speaking to work for their race, they find an unreasoning censorship and a law against assemblies. As one of them expressed it to me, "We must either cease to be Slavs or become revolutionaries."

Did Austria-Hungary need to look to Servian propaganda, to influences *from the outside*, to find the cause of the assassination of Franz Ferdinand? Political assassinations were not new in the south Slavic provinces of the monarchy. A young Bosnian student attempted to assassinate the Governor of Bosnia at Sarajevo on June 6, 1910, at the time of the inauguration of the Bosnian *Sabor* (Diet). Two years later the royal commissioner in Croatia was the object of an attempt at assassination by a Bosnian at Agram. In September of the same year, a Croatian student shot at the Ban of Croatia. The same Ban, Skerletz, was attacked again at Agram by another young Croatian on August 18, 1913. These assassinations preceded those of the Archduke and his wife. They were all committed by students of Austro-Hungarian nationality. Only the last one had ever been in Servia.

In theory, Bosnia has had since February 20, 1910, a constitution with a deliberative assembly. But the *Sabor* can discuss no projects of law that have not been proposed by the two masters. Once voted, a law has to pass the double veto of Vienna and Buda-Pesth. As if this were not enough, the Viennese bureaucracy has so arranged the qualification of the electorate and the electoral laws that the suffrage does not represent the country. Then, too, the constitution decides arbitrarily that the membership of the *Sabor* must be divided according to religions, one Jew, sixteen Catholics, twenty-four Moslems, and thirty-one Orthodox. The Government has reserved for itself the right of naming twenty members! The constitution provides for individual liberty, the inviolability of one's home, liberty of the press and speech, and secrecy of letters and telegrams. This enlightened measure of the Emperor was heralded to the world. But of course there was the joker, Article 20. Vienna held the highest card! In case of menace to the public safety, all public and private rights may be suspended by a word from Vienna. Public safety always being menaced in Bosnia, the constitution is perpetually suspended. The Government even goes as far as to prosecute deputies for their speeches in Parliament. Newspapers are continually censored. Their telegraphic news from Vienna and Buda-Pesth is suppressed without reason. Particularly severe fines—sometimes jail sentences—are passed upon offending journalists.

Is it necessarily because of instigation and propaganda from Belgrade that of the three Servian political parties in Bosnia two (the *Narod* and the *Otachbina*) are closely allied to the Pan-Servian Society *Narodna Obrana*, and that these two parties openly support the separatist movement?

In Bosnia, Dalmatia, and Croatia in 1914 the bureaucracy of Vienna has been engaged in the same process of repression and police persecution as in Italy during the half century from 1815 to the liberation of Italy. The local constitutions have been suspended everywhere. Why have the Austrians, in spite of the lessons of the beginning of the present reign, dared to tempt providence in exactly the same way after the Golden Jubilee?

The victories of the Allies in the Balkans were a terrible blow to Austria-Hungary. Not only was her dream of reaching the Ægean Sea through the *sandjak* of Novi Bazar and Macedonia shattered by the Greek occupation of Salonika, but the aggrandizement of Servia, caused by a successful war, threatened to have a serious effect upon the fortunes of the Empire. The appearance of the Servians on the Adriatic would mean really the extension of Russian influence through Bulgaria and Servia to the Austrian and Italian private lake, and would cut off Austria for ever from her economic outlet to the Ægean. But there was more than this to cause alarm both in Austria and in Hungary. Bosnia-Herzegovina, Croatia, and Dalmatia—would they remain loyal to the Empire, if once they came under the spell of the idea of Greater Servia? Leaving Russia entirely out of the calculation, an independent, self-reliant, and enlarged Servia, extending towards the Adriatic and Ægean Seas, if not actually reaching it,—would it not be, as Professor Wirth declared, "the suicide of Germany"? The statesmen of the Hohenzollern and Hapsburg Empires determined that it should not occur.

From the very moment that the Servian armies drove the Turks before them, Austria-Hungary began to act the bully against Servia. The Austrian consuls at Prisrend and Mitrovitza were made the first cause of Austrian interference. It was pretended that Herr Prochaska had been massacred and mutilated at Prisrend, and that the life of Herr Táhy had been threatened so that he was forced to flee for safety from Mitrovitza. A formal inquest showed that the first of these consuls was safe, and that the trouble had been merely a discussion between Servian officers and Herr Prochaska over some fleeing Albanians who had taken refuge in the consulate, in the other case, there seemed to be no ground at all for complaint. But on January 15, 1913, the Servians acceded to the demand of Austria that the reparation be granted for the Prisrend incident. A company of Servian soldiers saluted the Austro-Hungarian flag as Consul Prochaska solemnly raised it. This incident seems too petty to mention, but in that part of the world and at that moment we thought it very serious. For it showed how anxious Austria-Hungary was to pick a quarrel with Servia in the midst of the Balkan War.

Two other incidents of an even more serious character immediately followed. Servia refused the Austrian demand that Durazzo be evacuated, supporting herself upon the hope that Russia would intervene. During December and January, deluded by unofficial representatives of Russian public sentiment and by demonstrations against Austria-Hungary in Moscow and Petrograd, Servia held out. It was only when she saw that Russian support was not forthcoming that she withdrew from Durazzo. The international situation during January, 1913, was similar to that during July, 1914, and the cause of the crisis was practically the same. In both cases Servia backed down, but the second time Austria-Hungary and Germany determined to provoke the war which they believed would be the end of Servia and the destruction of Russia's power to influence the political evolution of Balkan Peninsula.

After Durazzo, it was Scutari. Servia for the third time bowed before the will of Austria.

The next move against Servia was the annexation on May 12, 1913, of the little island of Ada-Kaleh on the Danube, which had curiously enough remained Turkish property after the Treaty of Berlin. It had actually been forgotten at that time. This island, situated in front of Orsova, would have given Servia a splendid strategic position at the mouth of the river. Austria-Hungary anticipated the Treaty of London.

It was to reduce Servia that secret encouragement was given to Bulgaria to provoke the second Balkan war. There is no doubt now as to the rôle of the Austro-Hungarian Minister at Sofia in allowing this crisis to be precipitated.

Had Germany been willing to stand behind her at Bukarest, Austria-Hungary would have prevented the signing of the treaty between the Balkan States by presenting an ultimatum to Servia. But Germany did not seem to be ready. The reason commonly given that Emperor William did not want to embarrass King Carol of Rumania, a prince of his own house, and his brother-in-law, the King of Greece, does not seem credible. In view of the events that have happened since, the signing of the Treaty of Bukarest is a mystery not yet cleared up.

The second Balkan war acted as a boomerang to Austria-Hungary. It increased tremendously the prestige of Servia abroad, and the confidence of the Servians in themselves. The weakness of the Turkish armies in the first Balkan war had been so great that Servia herself hardly considered it a fair test of her military strength. To have measured arms successfully with Bulgaria was worth as much to Servia as the territory that she gained.

We have seen how strained were the relationships of Austria-Hungary as separate kingdoms and together as an empire in their relationship with their south Slavic subjects. The Croatians, the Dalmatians, and a major portion of the inhabitants of Bosnia-Herzegovina were Servian in language and sympathies. They had never thought of political union with Servia, the petty kingdom which had allowed its rulers to be assassinated, and which seemed to be insignificant in comparison with the powerful and brilliant country of which they would not have been unwilling, if allowed real self-government, to remain a part. But a large and glorified Servia, with an increased territory and a well-earned and brilliant military reputation— would this prove an attraction to win away the dissatisfied subjects of the Dual Monarchy?

Austria-Hungary by the annexation of Bosnia-Herzegovina had taken to herself more Servians in a compact mass than she could well assimilate. They were not scattered and separated geographically like her other Slavic subjects. It was a danger from the beginning. After the Balkan wars, it became an imminent peril.

The death sentence of Servia was decided by the statesmen of Austria-Hungary and Germany the moment their newspapers brought to them the story of the battle of Kumonova.

I shall never forget my presentiment when I heard on June 29, 1914, down in a little Breton village, that a Bosnian student had celebrated the anniversary of the battle of Kossova by assassinating the Archduke Franz Ferdinand. The incident for which Austria was waiting had happened. There came back to me the words of Hakki Pasha, "If Italy declares war on Turkey, the cannon will not cease to speak until all Europe is in conflagration."

NOTE.—As a commentary on Austrian rule in Bosnia, particularly in connection with the statistics on pages 152-153 of this chapter, consider von Kállay who, as Governor of Bosnia-Herzegovina, fought so bitterly the rise of national feeling among the Servians through the teaching in their schools. This same von Kállay, in his earlier days, wrote a scholarly history of Servia, which I have had occasion to use. It is admirably written and accurate in detail. As a research scholar, von Kállay believed that Bosnians, Serbs, and Croats were *the same race*, and supported this thesis; but, as an Austrian official, he disclaimed such dangerous teaching by placing the ban upon his own book, which he forbade to be introduced into the provinces of which he was governor!

CHAPTER X
RACIAL RIVALRIES IN MACEDONIA

In the latter half of the nineteenth century, the peace of Europe was twice disturbed, and terrible wars occurred, over the question of the integrity of the Ottoman Empire. Since it is still the same question which has had most to do—directly at least—with bringing on the general European war of 1914, it is important to consider what has been, since the Treaty of Berlin, the very heart of the Eastern question in relation to Europe, the rivalry of races in Macedonia.

When the European Powers, following the lead of Great Britain, intervened after the Russo-Turkish War of 1877-78 to annul the Treaty of San Stefano, they frustrated the emancipation from Moslem rule of the Christian populations in Macedonia. A Balkan territorial and political *status quo* was decided upon by a Congress of the Powers at Berlin in 1878. In receiving back Macedonia, Turkey solemnly promised to give equal rights to her Christian subjects. In taking upon themselves the terrible responsibility of restoring Christians to Turkish rule, the Powers assumed at the same time the obligation to watch Turkey and *compel her to keep her promises.*

The delegates of the Powers brought to the Congress of Berlin a determination to solve the problems of South-eastern Europe, according to what they believed to be the personal selfish interests of the nations they represented. From the beginning of the Congress to the end, there was never a single thought of serving the interests of the people whose destinies they were presuming to decide. They compromised with each other "to preserve the peace of Europe." This formula has always been interpreted in diplomacy as the getting of all you can for your country without having to fight for it!

Practically every provision of the Treaty of Berlin has been disregarded by the contracting parties and by the Balkan States. The policy of Turkey in this respect has not been different from that of the Christian Powers. Great Britain and France, as their colonial empires increased, ignored the obligations of the treaty which they had signed, because they feared the effect upon their commercial and colonial interests overseas, were they to press the Khalif. The only effective pressure would have been force of arms. When popular sympathy was stirred to the depths by the cruelty of Abdul Hamid's oppression and massacres, successive British and French Cabinets washed their hands of any responsibility towards the Christians in

Turkey. Pan-Islamism was their nightmare. They had an overwhelming fear of arousing Mohammedan sentiment against them in their colonies. Germany refused to hold Abdul Hamid to his promises, because she wanted to curry favour with him to get a foothold in Asiatic Turkey. Russia and Austria, the Powers most vitally interested in the Ottoman Empire, because they were its neighbours, were agreed upon preserving the Sultan's domination in the Balkan Peninsula, no matter how great the oppression of Christians became. Neither Power wanted to see the other increase in influence among the Balkan nationalities.

The centres of intrigue were Bulgaria, Albania, Thrace, Bosnia and Herzegovina, and Macedonia, the portions of the Peninsula which had been refused emancipation by the Congress of Berlin. Bulgaria worked out her own emancipation. She refused the tutelage of Russia, annexed Eastern Rumelia in defiance of the Powers in 1885, and proclaimed her independence in 1908. The fortunes of Albania have been followed in another chapter. Thrace was too near Constantinople, the forbidden city, too unimportant economically, and too largely Moslem in population to be coveted by the Balkan States. Bosnia and Herzegovina, administered by Austria-Hungary since 1878, were annexed in defiance of treaty obligations in 1908. The principal victim of the mischief done by the Congress of Berlin was Macedonia.

The future of Macedonia has been the great source of conflict between Austria-Hungary and Russia, and between the Balkan States. At Athens, Sofia, Belgrade, Bukarest, and Cettinje, the diplomats of Russia, Austria-Hungary, and Turkey, from the morrow of the Berlin Congress to the eve of the recent Balkan Wars, played a game against each other, endeavouring always to use the Balkan States as pawns in their sordid strife. Turkey was backed by France and England, whenever it suited opportune diplomacy to do so. Austria-Hungary was backed by Germany, who at the same time did not hesitate to play a hand with the Turks. Russia has always stood more or less alone in the Balkan question, even after the conclusion of the alliance with France. Except at Cettinje, Italian activity in this diplomatic game has never been particularly marked.

What has been the object of the game? This is difficult to state categorically. Aims have changed with changing conditions. For example, during the five years immediately following the Congress of Berlin, British diplomacy was directed strenuously towards keeping down emancipated Bulgaria, and towards preventing the encroachment of Servia in the direction of the Adriatic and the Ægean. But when she saw that Bulgaria had refused to be the tool of Russia, and when her problem of the trade route of India had been solved by the buying up of the majority of shares in the Suez Canal and the occupation of Egypt, Great Britain championed

Bulgaria and sustained her in the annexation of Eastern Rumelia. British policy remained anti-Servian for thirty years. There was more in the withdrawal of the British Legation from Belgrade than disapproval of a dastardly regicide. But the moment British commerce began to fear German competition, and an accord had been made with Russia to remove causes of conflict, the British press began to change its tone towards Servia. What a miracle has been wrought in the decade since "an immoral race of blackguards, with no sense of national honour" has become "that brave and noble little race, spirited defenders of the liberties of Europe!" I quote these two sentiments from the same newspapers. If Premier Asquith is sincere in his belief that this present war is to defend the principle of the sanctity of treaties, will he insist, when peace is concluded, that Servia make good her oath to Bulgaria, and Russia her international treaty obligations in regard to the kingdom of Poland? Great Britain is the least of the offenders when it comes to diplomatic cant and hypocrisy. For the British electorate has a keen sense of justice, and an intelligent determination that British influence shall be exerted for the betterment of humanity. Cabinets must reckon with this electorate when they decide questions of foreign policy.

But we do not want to lose ourselves in a maze of diplomatic intrigue, which it is fruitless to follow, even if we could. We must limit ourselves to an exposition of the ambitions of Austria-Hungary and of the Balkan States to the possession of this coveted province.

Since the creation of modern Italy, the great German trade route to the Mediterranean has been changed. The influence in Teutonic commercial evolution of the passing of Lombardy and Venetia from the political tutelage of a thousand years has been of tremendous importance, for the connection between Germany and Italy had always been vital. It was the first Napoleon who broke this connection. It was the third Napoleon who nullified the effort of the Congress of Vienna to re-establish it. United Italy gave a new direction to Teutonic expansion. United Germany gave to it a new impulsion. The *Drang nach Osten* was born.

By the Convention of Reichstadt in 1876, Austria-Hungary secured from Russia the promise of the Turkish provinces of Bosnia and Herzegovina in return for her neutrality in the "approaching war of liberation" of Russia against Turkey. In order to liberate some Slavs, Russia changed the subjection of others. The Convention of Reichstadt is really the starting-point of the quarrel which has grown so bitterly during the last generation between Austria and Russia over the Slavs of the Balkan Peninsula. Russia paid dearly for a "free hand" with Turkey in 1877. She is paying still.

In her attitude towards the Balkans, Austria has had three distinct aims: the prevention of a Slavic outlet to the Adriatic, the realization of a German outlet to the Ægean, and the effectual hindrance of the growth in the Balkans of a strong independent south Slavic state, which might prove a fatal attraction to her own provinces of Croatia and Dalmatia. It was this triple consideration that led her to the occupation and annexation of Bosnia and Herzegovina, and to the policy of hostility to Servia, which is developed in another chapter. Desiring to possess for herself the wonderful port of Salonika on the Ægean bea, to reach which her railroads would have to cross Macedonia, the policy of Austria-Hungary towards Macedonia has been consistently to endeavour to uphold the semblance of Turkish authority, and at the same time to make that authority difficult to uphold through the exciting of racial rivalry among Greece, Servia, Bulgaria, Rumania, and Albania, in this turbulent country. Turkey and Austria met on the common ground of "keeping the pot boiling," although with a different aim. By keeping the pot boiling, Turkey thought that her sovereignty was safe, while Austria hoped that when Turkey and the Balkan States had worn themselves out, each opposing the other, she could step in and capture the prize.

Turkey and Austria-Hungary, then, conspired together to create as many points of conflict as possible among the Macedonians of different races. The most devilish ingenuity was constantly exercised in stirring up and keeping alive the hatred of each race over the other. While frequently aroused to the point of making perfunctory protests, the other nations of Europe, with the exception of Russia, let Austria and Turkey do as they pleased, just as Turkey was allowed a free hand in massacring the Armenians. The *laissez faire* policy of the Powers was a denial of their treaty obligations.

It was only when the Balkan States awoke to the realization of the fact that they were regarded as mere pawns upon the chessboard of world politics, to be sacrificed without compunction by the European Powers whenever it was to their interest, that they buried differences for a moment, and worked out their own salvation. If the Balkan Wars have brought the present terrible disaster upon Europe, it is no more than the contemptible diplomacy of self interest and mutual jealousy could expect.

Why was the Austro-Turkish policy possible, and why did it succeed for a whole generation?

The Ottoman Empire was founded in the Balkan peninsula by rulers whose military genius was coupled with their ability to use one Christian population against the other. The Osmanlis never fought a battle in which the Balkan Christians did not give valuable assistance in forging the chains of their slavery. The Osmanlis conquered the Balkan peoples by means of the Balkan peoples. They kept possession of the country just as long as they could pit one chief against another, and then, when national feeling arose, one race against another.

Gradually, in the portion of the Balkans where one race was predominant, nationalities began to form states, which secured independence as soon as they demonstrated the possibility of harmony. Greece was the first, and was followed by Servia. Moldavia and Wallachia united into the principality of Rumania. Last of all came Bulgaria. After having gained autonomy, independence was only a matter of form. But in the central portion of the Balkan Peninsula, from the Black Sea to the Ægean, through Thrace, Macedonia, and Albania, the sovereignty of Turkey, restored by the Treaty of Berlin, was able to endure. For the people were mixed up, race living with race, and in no place could the Christians of any one race claim that the country was wholly theirs.

As emancipated Greeks, Servians and Bulgarians formed independent states, they looked towards Macedonia as the legitimate territory for expansion. But here their claims, both historically and racially, overlapped. Greece regarded Macedonia as entirely Hellenic. Had it not always been Greek before the Osmanlis came, from the days of Philip of Macedon to the Paleologi of the Byzantine Empire? The Servians, on the other hand, invoked the memory of the Servian Empire of Stephen Dushan, who in the fourteenth century, on the eve of the Ottoman conquest, was crowned "King of Romania" at Serres. It was from the Servians and not from the Greeks, that the Osmanlis conquered Macedonia in the three battles of the Maritza, Tchernomen, and Kossova. The Bulgarians invoked the memory of their mediæval domination of Macedonia and Thrace. It was by the Bulgarians that northern Thrace was defended against the Ottoman invasion; a Bulgarian prince was the last independent ruler of central Macedonia; and long before the ephemeral Servian Empire of Stephen Dushan, the Bulgarian Czars were recognized from Tirnova to Okrida. This latter city, in fact, was the seat of the autonomous Bulgarian patriarchate in the Middle Ages.

These historical claims, to us of western Europe, would have only a sentimental value. They had been forgotten by the subject populations of European Turkey for many centuries. The first revival of political ambitions was that of Hellenism. Modern Greece, divorcing itself from the impossible and pagan dream of a restoration of classic Greece, with Athens as its capital, which had been woven for it by western European admirers during the first half century of its liberation, began to take stock of its Byzantine and Christian heritage during the latter part of the reign of Abdul Aziz. The new Hellenism, as the prestige of the Ottoman Empire decreased, took the definite form of a determination to succeed the Ottoman Empire, as it had preceded it, with Constantinople as capital.

The Greeks believed themselves to be the unifying Christian race of the Balkan Peninsula. They had a tremendous advantage over the Slavs, because the ecclesiastical organization, to which all the Christians of the Balkan Peninsula owed allegiance, was in their hands. When Mohammed the Conqueror entered Constantinople, he gave to the Patriarch of the Eastern Church the headship of the Balkan Christians. The spirit of Moslem institutions provides for no other form of government than a theocracy. Religion has always been to the Osmanli the test of nationality. The Christians formed one *millet*, or nation. This *millet* was Greek. During all the centuries of Ottoman subjection, the Balkan Christians owed allegiance to the Greek Patriarchate. Whatever their native tongue, the language of the Church and *of the schools* was Greek.

Unfortunately for Hellenism, the new Greek aspirations came into immediate conflict with the renaissance of the Bulgarian nation. Russia had long been encouraging, for the purposes of Pan-Slavism, the awakening of a sense of nationality in the south Slavs. Her agents had been long and patiently working among the Bulgarians. But they overshot their mark. When Bulgarian priests and the few educated men of the peasant nation turned their attention to their past and their language, it was not the idea of their kinship with the great Slavic Power of eastern Europe that was aroused, *but the consciousness of their own particular race.* Bulgaria had been great when Russia was practically unknown. Bulgaria could be great once more, when, by the disappearance of Ottoman rule, the Bulgarian Empire of the Middle Ages would be born again in the Balkans.

One can readily appreciate that *the first necessity of Bulgarian renaissance was liberation from the Greek Church.* Russia strenuously opposed this separatist agitation. What she wanted was a Slavic movement within the bosom of the Greek Orthodox Church, which, if bitterly persecuted by the Patriarchate, would throw the south Slavs upon the Russian Synod for protection, or, if tolerated, would give Russia a powerful voice in the councils of the Orthodox Church in the Ottoman Empire. But the Bulgarians had progressed too far on the road of religious separation from the Greeks to be arrested by their Russian godfather. It was a prophecy of the future independent spirit of the Bulgarian people, which Beaconsfield and Salisbury unfortunately failed to note, that the Bulgarians determined to go the length of uniting with Rome in order to get free from Phanar. Another Uniate sect would have been born had Russia not yielded. With bad grace, her Ambassador obtained from Sultan Abdul Aziz the *firman* of March 11, 1870, creating the Bulgarian Exarchate.

The cleverness of the Bulgarians outwitted the manoeuvre made to have the seat of the Exarchate at Sofia. The Greeks realized that a formidable competitor had entered into the struggle for Macedonia. From that moment there has been hatred between Greek and Bulgarian. In spite of the treaty of Bukarest, the end of the struggle is not yet. The policy and ambition of the modern state are dictated by strong economic reasons, of which sentimental aspirations are only the outward expression. If wars and the treaties that follow them were guided by honest confession of the real issues at stake, how much easier the solution of problems, and how much greater the chances of finding durable bases for treaties! The whole effort of Bulgaria in Macedonia may be explained by the simple statement that the Bulgarian race has been seeking its natural, logical, and inevitable outlet to the Ægean Sea.

During the middle of the nineteenth century, Servian national aspirations were directed toward Croatia, Dalmatia, and Bosnia-Herzegovina. The Servians thought only in terms of the west. It was the foundation of the Austro-Hungarian dual monarchy in 1867, followed by the Austrian occupation of Bosnia-Herzegovina and of the *sandjak* of Novi Bazar, that let Servia to enter into the struggle for Macedonia.

As soon as Russia saw that she could not control Bulgaria, she began to favour a Servian propaganda in the valley of the Vardar. Russian intrigues at Constantinople led to the suppression of the Bulgarian bishoprics of Okrida, Uskub, Küprülü (Veles) and Nevrokop. Bulgaria secured the restoration of these bishoprics through the efforts of Austria-Hungary and Great Britain. The story of Macedonia is full of instances like this of intrigue and counter intrigue by European Powers at the Sublime Porte. Combinations of interests changed sometimes over night. Is it any wonder that the Turks grew to despise the European alliances, and to laugh at every "joint note" of the Powers in relation to Macedonia?

Austria-Hungary opposed the Russian aid given to Servia by introducing a new racial propaganda. Ever since the Roman occupation there had been a small, but widely diffused, element in the population of Macedonia, which retained the Roman language, just as the Wallachians and Moldavians north of the Danube had done. Diplomatic suggestion at Bukarest succeeded in interesting Rumania in these Kutzo-Wallachians, as they came to be called. Rumania did not have a common boundary with European Turkey. But her statesmen were quick to see the advantage of having "a finger in the pie" when the Ottoman Empire disappeared from Europe. So Rumania became protector of the Kutzo-Wallachian. The Sublime Porte gladly agreed to recognize this protectorate. The development of a strong Rumanian element in Macedonia would help greatly to preserve Turkish sovereignty. For Rumania could have no territorial aspirations there, and would look with disfavour upon Rumania being swallowed up by Greece, Servia, or Bulgaria. Another propaganda, well financed, and encouraged by the Austro-Hungarian and Turkish Governments was added to the rivalry of races in Macedonia.

We cannot do more than suggest these intrigues. After 1885, the Macedonian question became gradually the peculiar care of the two "most interested" Powers. There was little to attract again international attention until the question of Turkey's existence as a state was brought forward in a most startling way by the repercussion throughout the Empire of the Armenian massacres of 1893-96. *By refusing to intervene at that time, the Powers, who fondly thought that they were acting in the interest of the integrity of the Empire, were really contributing to its further decline.*

Elsewhere we have spoken of the Cretan insurrection of 1896 and the train of events that followed it, ending in the formation of the Balkan alliance to drive Turkey out of Europe. Here we take up the other thread which leads us to the Balkan Wars. Bulgaria, remembering the happy result of her own sufferings from the massacres of twenty years before, was keen enough to see in the Asiatic holocausts of the "Red Sultan" a sign of weakness instead of a show of strength. The statesmen of the European Powers had not acted to stop the massacres of the Armenians. But their indecision and impolitic irresolution was not an expression of the sentiments of the civilized races whom they represented. The time was ripe for an insurrection in Macedonia. Public opinion in Europe would sustain it. The movement was launched from Sofia.

From that moment, Turkish sovereignty was doomed. Turkey did not realize this, however. Instead of adopting the policy of treating with Bulgaria, and giving her an economic outlet to the Ægean Sea, the Sublime Porte was delighted with the anticipation of a new era of racial rivalry in Macedonia. For it knew that Bulgaria's efforts to secure Macedonian autonomy would be opposed by Servia and Greece. In fact, the Greeks were so alarmed by the Bulgarian activity that immediately after their unhappy war with Turkey they gave active support to the Turks in putting down the Bulgarian rebels. The services of the Greek Patriarchate were particularly valuable to Turkey at this time.

Nor did Austria-Hungary and Russia appreciate the significance of the Bulgarian movement. In 1897, they signed an accord, solemnly agreeing that the *status quo* be preserved in the Balkan peninsula. Russia was anxious for this convention with Austria. For the moment all her energies were devoted to developing the policy in the Far East that was to end so abruptly eight years later on the battlefield of Mukden. Austria-Hungary was delighted to have the solution of the Macedonian problem delayed. *She*

felt that every year of anarchy in European Turkey would bring her nearer to Salonika.
The *Drang nach Osten* was to be made possible through the strife of Servian, Bulgarian, and Greek.

The moment was favourable for the Bulgarian propaganda. Russia was too much involved in Manchuria to help the Servians. The Greeks had lost prestige with the Macedonians by their easy and humiliating defeat at the hands of Turkey. Gathering force with successive years, and supported by the admirably laid foundation of the Bulgarian ecclesiastic and scholastic organizations throughout Macedonia, the Bulgarian bands gradually brought the *vilayets* of Monastir, Uskub, and Salonika into a state of civil war. In 1901 and 1902, conditions in Macedonia were beyond description. But the Powers waited for some new initiative on the part of Austria-Hungary and Russia.

Emperor Franz Josef and Czar Nicholas met at Mürszteg in the autumn of 1903. Russia, more and more involved in Manchuria, and on the eve of her conflict with Japan, found no difficulty in falling in with the suggestion of the Austrian Foreign Secretary that the two Powers present to the signers of the Treaty of Berlin a program of "reforms" for Macedonia. Europe received with delight this new manifestation of harmony between Austria-Hungary and Russia.

In 1904 the "Program of Mürszteg" was imposed upon Turkey by a comic-opera show of force on the part of the Powers. An international *gendarmerie* was their solution of the Macedonian problem. Different spheres were mapped out, and allotted to officers of the different Powers. Germany refused to participate in this farce, just as she had refused to participate in "protecting" Crete.

The international "pacification" failed in Macedonia for the same reasons that it had failed in Crete, and was to fail a third time ten years later in Albania. *It was a compromise between the Powers, dictated by considerations which had nothing whatever to do with the problem of which it was supposed to be the solution.* This is the story of European diplomacy in the Near East.

From the very moment that Turkey found herself compelled to accept the policing of Macedonia by European officers, she set to work to make their task impossible. Hussein Hilmi pasha was sent to Salonika as Governor. An accord was quickly established between him and the Austro-Hungarian agents in Macedonia. Where the Bulgarians were weak, the Turks and the Austrian emissaries encouraged the Bulgarian propaganda. Where the Greeks were weak, Hellenic bands were allowed immunity. Where the Servians were weak, the connivance of the Government. The European *gendarmerie* was powerless to struggle against Turkish, Austro-Hungarian, and Balkan intrigues. The correspondence of the European officers and consuls, and of journalists who visited Macedonia during this period, makes interesting reading. Their point of view is almost invariably that of their surroundings. It depended upon just what part of Macedonia one happened to be in, or the company in which one travelled, whether a certain nationality were "noble heroes suffering for an ideal" or "blood-thirsty ruffians." Why are so many writers who pretend to be impartial observers like chameleons?

Greece, Servia, and Bulgaria were alike guilty of subsidizing bands of armed men, who imagined that they were fulfilling a patriotic duty in brutally forcing their particular nationality upon ignorant peasants, most of whom did not know—or care—to what nation they belonged. There was little to choose between the methods and the actions of the different bands. Everywhere pillage, incendiarism, and assassination were the order of the day. When Christian propagandists let them alone, the poor villagers had to endure the same treatment from Moslem Albanians and from the Turkish soldiery.

In order to give the "reforms" of the Program of Mürszteg a chance, Athens, Sofia, and Belgrade ostensibly withdrew their active support of the bands. But the efforts of the Powers had still not only the secret bad faith of Austria-Hungary and Turkey to contend with, but also the determination of the Macedonians themselves not to be "reformed" *à l'européenne*, that is to say, *à la turque*. The powerful Bulgarian "interior organization" in Macedonia kept up the struggle in the hope that the continuation of anarchy would bring the Powers to see that there was no other solution possible of the Macedonian question *than the autonomy of Macedonia under a Christian governor.* Greeks and Servians opposed the project of autonomy, however, because they knew that it would result eventually in the reversion of Macedonia to Bulgaria. The history of Eastern Rumelia would be repeated. In considering the Macedonian problem, it must never be forgotten that the great bulk of the population of Macedonia is Bulgarian, in spite of all the learned dissertations and imposing statistics of Greek and Servian writers. But the difficulty is that this Bulgarian population is agricultural. In the cities *near the sea* and all along the seacoast from Salonika to Dedeagatch the Greek element is predominant. No geographical division of Macedonia can be made, viable from the economic point of view, which satisfies racial claims by following the principle of preponderant nationality.

After her disasters in the Far East, Russia began to turn her attention once more to the Near East. A reopening of the Macedonian question between Austria-Hungary and Russia was imminent when the Young Turk revolution of July, 1908, upset all calculations, and brought a new factor into the problem of the future of European Turkey. Austria-Hungary boldly challenged—more than that, defied—Russia by annexing Bosnia-

Herzegovina. In this action she was backed by Germany. Russia and France were not ready for war. Great Britain and Italy, each involved in an internal social revolution of tremendous importance, could not afford to risk the programs of their respective cabinets by embarking upon uncertain foreign adventures.

The Balkan States were left to solve the Macedonian problem by themselves. Their solution was the Treaty of Bukarest. The success of Servia in planting herself in the valley of the Vardar, and in occupying Monastir, is the result of the struggle of races in Macedonia. It is the direct, immediate cause of the European War of 1914.

CHAPTER XI
THE YOUNG TURK RÉGIME IN THE OTTOMAN EMPIRE

No event during the first decade of the twentieth century was heralded throughout Europe with so great and so sincere interest and sympathy as the bloodless revolution of July 24, 1908, by which the *régime* of Abdul Hamid was overthrown and the constitution of 1876 resuscitated.

Although the world was unprepared for this event, it was not due to any sudden cause. For twenty years the leaven of liberalism had been working in the minds of the educated classes in the Ottoman Empire. Moslems, as well as Christians, had been in attendance in large numbers at the American, French, Italian, and German schools in Turkey, and had gone abroad to complete their education. Just as in Italy and in Germany, Young Turkey had come into existence through contact with those free institutions in the outside world which other races enjoyed, had been emancipated from superstition and from the stultifying influences of religious formalism, and had grown, in the army, to numbers sufficient to dictate the policy of the Government.

From the beginning of his reign, Abdul Hamid had done all in his power to prevent the growth of the liberal spirit. The result of thirty years, in so far as civil officials of the Government were concerned, had been the stamping out of every man who combined ability with patriotism and devotion to an ideal. The best elements had taken the road to death, to imprisonment, or to exile, so that from the palace down to the humblest village, the Turkish civil service was composed of a set of men absolutely lacking in independence and in honour, and devoted to the master who ruled from Yildiz. But in the army, this same policy, though attempted, had not wholly succeeded. A portion at least of the officers received an education; many of them, indeed, had been sent abroad to Germany and to France in order to keep abreast with the development of military science, so essential to the very existence of Turkey. In the army, then, hundreds of officers of high character and high ideals were able to avoid the fate which had come to other educated Moslems in Turkey. They learned to love their country, and with that love came a sense of shame for the results of the despotism under which they existed. To have lived in Paris or in Berlin was enough to make them dissatisfied; to have visited Cairo or Alexandria, Sofia or Bukarest or Athens, and to have contrasted the conditions of life in these cities, recently their own, with Constantinople, Salonika, and Smyrna, was sufficient.

It is impossible in the limits of this book to tell how this bloodless revolution was planned by exiles abroad and officers at home. It was successful, as well as bloodless, because the army refused to obey the orders of the Sultan. To save his life and his throne, Abdul Hamid was compelled to resuscitate the constitution which he had granted, and then suppressed, at the beginning of his reign.

We who lived through those dream days of the beginning of the new *régime* will never forget the sense of joy of an emancipated people. The spy system was abolished, newspapers were allowed to tell the truth and express their own opinions, passports and *teskeres* (permissions to travel from one point to another within the Empire) were declared unnecessary, *bakshish* was refused at the custom house and police station. Moslem *ulema* and Christian clergy embraced each other in public, rode through the streets in triumph in the same carriages, and harangued the multitudes from the same platform in mosque and church. A new era of Liberty, Fraternity, and Equality, they said, had dawned for all the races in Turkey. The Sultan was the father, Turkey the fatherland, barriers and disabilities of creed and race had ceased to exist. It seemed incredible, but these scenes were really happening from the Adriatic to the Persian Gulf.

Optimism, hope for the future, was so strong that one had not the heart to express very loudly his belief that no real revolution was ever bloodless, that no real change in political and social life of the people could come in a single day or as a result of an official document. No one could think of anything else but the constitution, which had broken the chains for Moslem and Christian alike, the constitution which was going to restore Turkey to its lawful place among the nations of Europe, the constitution which was to heal the sick man and solve the question of the Orient. In Smyrna, in Constantinople, in Beirut, and in Asia Minor, I heard the same story over and over again. But there was always the misgiving, the apprehension for the future, from which the foreigner in Turkey is never free. It seemed too good to be true; it *was* too good to be true. It was against the logic of history. The most wonderful constitution that the world has ever known is that of England. It does not exist on paper; there is no need for a document. It is good, and it has endured, because it has been written in blood, in suffering, and in the agony of generations, on the pages of eight centuries of history. Could Turkey hope to be free in a day?

The first test of the constitution came, of course, with the election and composition of the Parliament. The election was held quietly, in some parts of the Empire secretly even, and when the Parliament assembled at

Constantinople, one began to see already the handwriting on the wall. For its composition was in no way in accordance with the distribution of population in the Empire. The Turk—and by the Turk I mean the composite Moslem race which has grown up through centuries of inter-marriage and forcible conversion—had always been the ruling race. With the establishment of a constitutional *régime*, the Young Turks did not mean to abdicate in favour of Moslem Arabs or Christian Greeks and Armenians. They had "arranged" the elections in such a way that they would have in the Parliament a substantial majority over any possible combination of other racial elements.

One cannot but have sympathy with the natural feeling of racial pride which is inborn in the Turks. A race of masters,—who could expect that they would be willing to surrender the privileges of centuries? But they forgot that a constitutional *régime* and the principles of Liberty, Equality, and Fraternity must necessarily imply the yielding of their unique position in the Empire. The Turk, as a race, is composed of two elements, a ruling class of land-owners and military and civil officials, arrogant though courteous, corrupt though honest in private life, parasitical though self-respecting, and a peasant class, hopelessly ignorant, lacking in energy, initiative, ambition, aspirations, and ideals. The great bulk of the Turkish element in the Empire looked with the indifference of ignorance and the hostility of jealous regard for their unique position in the community upon the granting of a constitution. I doubt if five per cent. of the Turkish population of the Empire has ever known what a constitutional *régime* means, or cared whether it exists or not.

There remains the five per cent. Of these the great bulk belong either to the corrupt official class, whose subjection to the tyranny of Yildiz Kiosk had totally unfitted them for service under the new *régime* on which they were entering, and the land-owners, whose wealth was dependent upon the unequal privileges that the law allowed to them as Moslems, and whose interests were totally at variance with the spirit of the constitution. There are left small groups of younger army officers and of professional men, who had been educated in foreign schools or by foreign teachers in Turkey and abroad. They were, for the most part, either without the knowledge of any other *métier* than the army, or, if civilian, unfitted by training and experience for governmental executive and administrative work. Consequently from the very beginning, the genuine Young Turks who were honest in their idealism had to make a compact with the higher army officers and with corrupt civil officials of Abdul Hamid. When the real Young Turks controlled the Cabinet, their disasters were those of theorists and visionaries. When they yielded the control of affairs to men more experienced than they, it was simply the renewal of the tyranny of Abdul

Hamid. It was because these two elements were united in the firm resolution to keep the control in the hands of Moslem Turks, that the constitutional *régime* in Turkey has gone from Scylla to Charybdis without ever entering port.

From the very beginning, thoughtful men pointed out that there was only one way of salvation and of liberal evolution for the Ottoman Empire. That was an honest and sincere co-operation with the Christian elements of the Empire, and with the Arabic and Albanian Moslem elements. Fanaticism and racial pride prevented the Young Turks from adopting the sole possible way of establishing the constitutional *régime*. From the very beginning, then, they failed, and it is their failure which has plunged Europe into the series of wars that has ended in the devastation of unhappy Belgium, so far remote from the cause and so innocent of any part in the events which brought upon her such terrible misfortunes. One could write a whole book upon the events of the first five years of constitutional government in Turkey and could show, beyond a shadow of a doubt, how from the very beginning there was no honest and loyal effort made to apply even the most rudimentary principles of constitutional government. Despotism means the subjection of a country to the will of its rulers. Constitutionalism means the subjection of the rulers to the will of the country. The Young Turks, embodied in the "Committee of Union and Progress," merely continued the despotism of Abdul Hamid. They were far worse than Abdul Hamid, however, for they were irresponsible and unskilled. One handling the helm, knowing how to steer, might have kept the ship of state afloat, all the more easily, perhaps, because the waters were so troubled. Many hands, none knowing where or how to go, steered the Ottoman Empire to inevitable shipwreck.

Although the vicissitudes of various Cabinets and Parliaments can have place in our work only so far as they have a direct bearing on foreign relations, there are six matters of internal policy which must be mentioned in order to explain how rapidly and surely the Ottoman Empire went to its destruction; the treatment of Armenians before and after the Adana massacres; the attempt to suppress the liberties of the Orthodox Church; the Cretan question, ending in the Greek boycott; the Macedonian policy; the Albanian uprisings; and the lack of co-operation and sympathy with the Arabs.

THE ARMENIANS AND THE ADANA MASSACRES

Among the various races of the Ottoman Empire, none was more overcome with joy at the proclamation of the constitutional *régime* than the Armenian. Scattered everywhere throughout the Empire, and in no region an element of preponderance, the Armenians had always made themselves felt in the commercial and intellectual life of Turkey far out of proportion to their numerical strength. They appreciated and understood, best of all the Christian populations, the significance of constitutional government. Honestly applied, it meant more to them than to any other element of the Empire.

In the first place, the burden of Turkish and Moslem oppression had fallen most heavily on them. It was not only the massacres of 1894 to 1896, horrible as they were, which had put the Armenians in continual fear for their lives; it was the centuries-old petty persecution, from which they believed they were now to be freed. Turkish officialdom had grown rich in extorting the last farthing from the Armenians. Only those who had seen this persecution and extortion can realize how large a part it played in the daily life of the Armenians, and how continuous and rich a source of revenue it was to the official Turk. For every little service the official expected his fat fee, always charging up to the limit his victim was able to pay. You could not carry on your business, you could not build a house, you could not enlarge or alter or repair your shop, you could not get a tax on your harvest estimated, you could not travel even from one village to another for the purpose of business or pleasure or study, without paying the officials. Very frequently between the local Turkish official and the Armenian stood a middle man who must also be paid for the purpose of carrying the fee or bribe to the official in charge. How people could have lived under such a *régime* and have prospered, is beyond the comprehension of the Occidental. Nothing speaks so eloquently for the business acumen of the Armenian race, as well as for devotion to the religion of its fathers.

Naturally, the Armenians expected that the constitution would bring to them a complete relief from economic repression, as well as from the terrors of massacre. They were led to believe this by the Young Turks who had so long plotted the overthrow of Abdul Hamid's despotism. During the campaign from 1890-1908, the Young Turks needed the money and the brains of Armenians in the larger centres of population where they had their *foyers*, and in the cities abroad where they lived in exile. It cannot be doubted that there were among the Young Turks during the period when they had to keep alive their ideals in the fire of hope, an honest intention to give the Armenians a share in the regeneration of the Ottoman Empire. But, as soon as they realized their ambitions, racial and religious fanaticism came to them with such force that they forgot the brilliant promises as well as the affectionate intercourse of the days of suffering and struggle.

In the second place, Armenians, unlike the Greeks, the Macedonians, and the Arabs, had, as a race, no separatist tendencies. They were not looking towards another state to come and redeem them. They feared Russia. They were too scattered to hope to form, by the break-up of the Ottoman Empire, a state of their own. They loved the land in which they lived with all the passion of their nature. In many regions, Turkish was their native tongue. They were industrious tillers of the soil, as well as merchants. The Sultan could have had no more loyal subjects than these, had he so desired.

Although the composition of the new Parliament chosen in October, 1908, and of the first constitutional Cabinet, was a prophecy of how they were to be left out in the cold, the Armenians were throughout that winter, when the constitution was new, firm and loyal, as well as intelligent, supporters of regenerated Turkey. The wish was father to the thought. For them there was no longer the barrier of race and creed. All were Osmanlis, and willing to lose their identity in the politically amalgamated race. The reign of Abdul Hamid was a nightmare, quickly forgotten. The future was full of hope. If only the Young Turks had realized what a tremendous influence the Armenians could have played in the creation of New Turkey, if only they had been willing to use these allies, we might have been able to write a different history of the past few years in Europe.

But the awakening was to be cruel. It came in a region of the Empire that never before experienced the horrors of a general massacre, where Christians felt not only at ease, but on friendly terms with their Moslem neighbours.

On April 14, 1909, on a morning when the sun had risen upon the peaceful and happy city of Adana, out of a clear sky came the tragedy which was the beginning of the end of the Ottoman Empire. Without provocation, the Moslem population began to attack and kill the Christians. The Governor of the province and his military officials not only did nothing whatever to stop the bloodshed, but they actually handed out arms and munitions to the blood-frenzied mob of peasants, who were pouring into the city. For three days, killing, looting, and burning of houses were aided by the authorities. The massacres spread west through the great Cilician plain to Tarsus, and east over the Amanus Range into northern Syria, as far as Antioch, where the followers of Jesus were first called Christians. The world, horrified by the stories which soon made their way to the newspapers, realized that the "bloodless revolution" had not regenerated Turkey. The blood had come at last, and without the regeneration! The Great Powers sent their warships to Mersina, the port of

Tarsus and Adana. Even from the distant United States came two cruisers, under pressure, over six thousand miles.

In the meantime, events of great importance, but not of equal significance in the future of Turkey, were taking place at Constantinople. On the eve of the first Adana massacre, Abdul Hamid, having corrupted the soldiers of the Constantinople garrison, set in motion a demonstration against the constitution. The soldiers shot down their officers in cold blood, marched to Yildiz Kiosk, and demanded of the Sultan the abolition of the constitution, which they declared was at variance with the *Sheriat*, the sacred law of Islam. Abdul Hamid gladly consented. Popular sympathy in Constantinople and throughout the Empire was with the Sultan, as far as the object of the revolution went. But the way in which it was brought about made it impossible for the Sultan to remain within the pale of civilization. Of all nations, none relied on its army more than Turkey. Were the assassination of the officers to go unpunished, the disintegration of the Empire necessarily followed. So the military hierarchy, "Old" Turks as well as "Young," rose against the Sultan. The army corps in Salonika under the command of Mahmud Shevket pasha, marched against the capital and with very little resistance mastered the mutiny of the Constantinople garrison. Abdul Hamid was deposed, and sent into exile at the Villa Alatini at Salonika. His brother, Reshid Mohammed, came to the throne, under the title of Mohammed V.

As soon as the Young Turks found themselves again in control of the situation, even before the proclamation of the new Sultan, they sent from Beirut to Adana a division of infantry to "re-establish order." These regiments disembarked at Mersina on the day Mohammed V ascended the throne, April 25th. Immediately upon their arrival in Adana they began a second massacre which was more horrible than the first. Thousands were shot and burned, and more than half the city was in ruins. This second massacre occurred in spite of the fact that a dozen foreign warships were by this time anchored in the harbour of Mersina.

It is impossible to estimate the losses of life and property in the *vilayets* of Cilicia and northern Syria during the last two weeks of April, 1908. Not less than thirty thousand Armenians were massacred. The losses of property in Adana alone were serious enough to cause the foremost fire insurance company in France to fight in the courts for two years the payments of its claims. But it is not in the realm of our work to follow out the local aftermath of this terrible story. We are interested here only in its bearing on the fortunes of the Empire and of Europe.

From the very beginning, the Young Turks, now re-established in Constantinople with a Sultan of their own creation, and having nothing more to fear from the genius and bad will of Abdul Hamid, protested before Europe that the massacres were due to the old *régime* and that they had been arranged by Abdul Hamid, whose deposition cleared them of responsibility. But the revelations of the *New York Herald*, the *Tribuna* of Rome, and the *Berliner Tageblatt*, translated and reprinted in the British, French, and Russian press, were so moving that it was necessary for the Young Turks to send special commissions to the capitals of Europe to counteract the impression of these articles.

Europe was willing to accept the explanation of the Constantinople Cabinet, and to continue its faith, though shaken, in the intentions of the Young Turks to grant to the Christians of Turkey the *régime* of equality and security of life and property which the constitution guaranteed. Even the Armenians, terrible as this blow had been, were also willing to forgive and forget. But the condition of forgiveness, and the proof of sincerity of the declarations of the Young Turks, both to the outside world and to the Armenians, would be the punishment of those who had been guilty of this most horrible blot upon the civilization of the twentieth century. This was to be the test.

The Court-Martial, sent to Adana from Constantinople after the new Sultan was established upon the throne and the Young Turks were certain of their position, had every guarantee to enable it to do its work thoroughly and justly. It was not influenced or threatened. There was, however, no honest intention to give decisions impartially and in accordance with the facts that the investigation would bring forth. The methods and findings of the Court-Martial were a travesty of justice. Its members refused absolutely to go to the bottom of the massacre, and to punish those who had been guilty. I happen to be the only foreign witness whose deposition they took. They refused to allow me to testify against the Vali and his fellow-conspirators. The line of conduct had been decided before their arrival. The idea was to condemn to death a few Moslems of the dregs of the population, who would probably have found their way to the gallows sooner or later any way. With them were to be hanged a number of Armenians, whose only crime was that they had defended the lives and honour of their women and children. The Vali of Adana, who had planned the massacre and had carried it out, and two or three Moslem leaders of the city who had co-operated with him and with the military authorities in the effort to exterminate the Armenians, were not even sent to prison. No testimony against them was allowed to be brought before the Court-Martial. They went into exile "until the affair blew over."

When a future generation has the prospective to make researches into the downfall of the Young Turk constitutional *régime* in Turkey, they will probably find the beginning of the end in the failure to punish the perpetrators of the Adana massacres. For this was a formal notification to the Christians of Turkey that the constitutional *régime* brought to them no guarantees of security, or justice, but, on the other hand, made their position in the Empire even more precarious than it had been under the despotism of Abdul Hamid. After Adana, the Armenian population became definitely alienated from the constitutional movement, and was convinced that its only hope lay in the absolute disappearance of Turkish rule.

THE ATTEMPT TO SUPPRESS THE LIBERTIES OF THE ORTHODOX CHURCH

When Mohammed the Conqueror entered Constantinople in 1453, he showed a wise determination to continue the policy of his predecessors by preserving the independence of the Orthodox Church. For he knew well that the success of the Osmanlis had been due to religious toleration, and that no durable empire could be built in Asia Minor and the Balkan Peninsula by a Moslem government, unless the liberties of the Christian inhabitants were assured through the recognition of the Greek patriarchate. The first thing that Mohammed did was to seek out the Greek patriarch, and confirm him in his position as the political, as well as the religious, head of Christian Ottoman subjects.

Islam is a theocracy. The spirit of its government is inspired by the sacred law, the *Sheriat*, based upon the Koran and the writings of the earliest fathers of Islam. Down to the smallest details, the organization of the state, of the courts of justice, and of the social life of Mohammedan peoples, is influenced by ecclesiastical law, and by the power of the Church. As this law does not provide for the inclusion of non-Moslem elements either in the political or social life of the nation, it has always been evident that people of another religion, within the limits of a Moslem state, can exist only if they have an ecclesiastical organization of their own, with well-defined liberties, privileges, and safeguards.

This principle was recognized by the Osmanlis for over five hundred years; even the most despotic of sultans never dreamed of abandoning it. There might be persecutions, there might be massacres, there might be even assassination of patriarchs, but, until the Young Turk *régime*, no Ottoman ministry ever dreamed of destroying the organism which had made possible the life of Moslem and Christian under the same rule.

The thesis of the Young Turks was, from a theoretical standpoint, perfectly sound and just. They said that ecclesiastical autonomy was necessary under a despotism, but that it had ceased to have a *raison d'être* under a constitutional government. The constitution guaranteed equal rights, irrespective of religion, to all the races of the Empire. Therefore the

Greek Church must resign its prerogatives of a political nature, for they were wholly incompatible with the idea of constitutional government.

Many foreigners, carried away by the reasonableness of this argument, severely condemned the Orthodox Church for continuing to resist the encroachments of the new Government upon its secular privileges— secular in both senses of the word. They attributed the attitude of the Greek ecclesiastics to hostility to the constitution, to the reactionary tendency of every ecclesiastic organization, and to selfish desire to hold firmly the privileges which enabled them to keep in their clutches the Greek population of Turkey, and continue to enjoy the prestige and wealth accruing to them from these privileges. Such criticism only revealed ignorance of history and a lack of appreciation of the real issue at stake.

No ecclesiastical organization can, under a constitutional government, continue indefinitely to be a state within a state, and to enjoy peculiar privileges and immunities. But the application of the constitution must come first. It must enter into the life of the people. It must become the vital expression of their national existence, evolved through generations of testing and experimenting. The constitution is finally accepted and supported by a nation when, and because, it has been found good and has come to reflect the needs and wishes of the people. Then, without any great trouble, the ecclesiastical organization will find itself gradually deprived of every special privilege. For the privileges will have become an anachronism.

But, just as in the establishment of the constitution, in their attitude toward the Greek Church the Young Turks acted as if the work of generations in other countries could be for them, in spite of their peculiarly delicate problems and the differences in creed involved, the act of a single moment. This mentality of the half-educated, immature visionary has been shown in every one of the numerous senseless and disastrous decisions which have brought the Ottoman Empire so speedily to its ruin.

The Greek Church resisted bitterly every move of the Young Turks to bring about the immediate millennium. The patriarch was a man of wide experience, of sound common sense, and of undaunted courage. Backed by the Lay Assembly, which has always been an admirable democratic institution of the Orthodox Church, he refused to give up realities for chimeras. With all its privileges and all its power, it had been hard enough for the Orthodox Church to protect the Greek subjects of Turkey. The patriarch did not intend to surrender the safeguards by which he was enabled to make tolerable the life of his flock for illusory and untested guarantees. Let the constitution become really the expression of the will of the people of Turkey, let it demonstrate the uselessness of any safeguards for protecting the Christians from Moslem oppression, let the era of liberty and equality and fraternity actually be realized in the Ottoman Empire, and then the Church would resign its privileges. For they would be antiquated, and fall naturally into desuetude. But in constitutions, as in other things, the proof of the pudding is in the eating.

What the Young Turks attempted to do was to destroy the privileges of the Orthodox Church, on the ground that these privileges were a barrier to the assimilation of the races in the Empire. Americans, above all nations, have deep sympathies for, and well justified reasons for having faith in, the policy of assimilation. Have not the various races of Europe, different in religion and in political and social customs, passed wonderfully through the crucible of assimilation on American soil? But by assimilation the Young Turks meant, not the amalgamation of races, each co-operating and sharing in the building up of the fatherland, as in America, but the complete subjection and ultimate disappearance of all other elements in the Empire than their own. They intended, from the very first days of the constitutional *régime*, to make Turkey a nation of Turks. Theirs was the strong, virile race, into which the other races would be fused. Turkey was weak, they declared, because it was the home of a conglomeration of peoples. If Turkey was to become like the nations of Europe, these different nationalities must be destroyed. To destroy them, the Government had first to aim at the *foyer* of national life, the ecclesiastical hierarchies.

I have talked with many a zealous Young Turk. What I have written here is not only the logical interpretation of the facts; it is also the faithful expression of the ideas of the most earnest and intelligent Turkish partisans of the new *régime*. They pointed out, with perfect logic, that this process had gone on in every European country, and that it was the only way in which a strong nation could be built. So far they were right. But, aside from the fact that in Europe this political and social evolution had taken centuries, there was also the working of the law of the survival of the fittest. In European nations it had been the element, always composite, which deserved to live, that formed the nucleus of a nationality. The whole root of the question in Turkey was, were the Young Turks justified in believing that the Turk was this element?

There is not space to discuss the reasons for the supremacy of the Osmanli in the Ottoman Empire. Up to the eighteenth century, the Osmanli was undoubtedly the "fittest" element. For the past two hundred years, the continued domination of Turk and the continued subjection of Christian populations, in Turkey, has been due to causes outside of the Empire. The Turk has remained the ruling race. But is he still the fittest? One may examine the different elements of the Ottoman Empire, and measure them by the tests of civilization. From the intellectual standpoint, from the business standpoint, from the administrative standpoint, the Turk is hardly able to sustain his claim to continue to be, in a twentieth-century empire, the element which can hope to assimilate Greek, Armenian, Albanian, Slav, and Arab. He is less fit than any of the others, especially than the Greek and Armenian in intellectual and business faculties, and than the Albanian in administrative faculties. There remains, then, as his sole claim to dominate the other races, his physical superiority. By history and by legend, he is the fighting man and rules by right of conquest and force.

It was always the sane—and only safe—policy of the Turks to keep Christians out of the army. They saw to it that the *métier* of arms remained wholly to the Moslems. In spite of the increasing wealth and education of the Christian elements of the Empire, the ascendancy was preserved to the Turk through the army. But at what a sacrifice! By reason of military service, the Turkish peasant has been kept in economic and intellectual serfdom, while his Christian neighbour progressed. The Turkish population has actually decreased, and the ravages of garrison life, due to dyspepsia and syphilis, have diminished fearfully the physical vigour of the race. By the same token, the upper classes, knowing only the life of army officers, have been removed from the necessity of competing in the world for position and success. Can manhood be formed in any other mould than that of competition, where the goal is achievement, and is reached only by continued effort of will and brain? The upper class Turk is a parasite, and, like all parasites, helpless when that upon which he feeds is taken from him.

Map—Europe in 1911

The attack of the Young Turk party upon the Greek Church failed. The patriarch refused to surrender his privileges. The Greek clergy and the Lay Council held out under persecution and threats. In October, 1910, when the Lay Council met in Constantinople, its members were arrested, and thrown into jail. In Macedonia and Thrace, in the Ægean Islands, along the coast of Asia Minor, the bishops and clergy suffered untold persecutions. Some were even assassinated. I shall never forget a memorable interview I had with Joachim III, during that crisis. His Holiness untied with trembling fingers the *dossier* of persecutions, which contained letters and sworn statements from a dozen dioceses. "They treat us like dogs!" he cried. "Never under Abdul Hamid or any Sultan have my people suffered as they are suffering now. But we are too strong for them. We refuse to be exterminated. I see all Europe stained with blood because of these crimes." How prophetic these words as I record them now!

The Turk could not hope to assimilate the Greek by peaceful methods, because he was his intellectual inferior. When he planned to use force, the Balkan Alliance was formed. The battle of Lulé Burgas took away from the Turk his last claim to fitness as dominant race. He could no longer fight better than Christians. The first Balkan War gave the *coup de grâce* to the final—and has it not been all along the only?—argument for Turkish racial supremacy.

THE CRETAN QUESTION AND THE GREEK BOYCOTT

The island of Crete had long been to Turkey, in relation to Greece, what Cuba had been to Spain, in relation to the United States. In both cases, and about the same time, wars of liberation broke out. But Greece was not as fortunate in her efforts for the emancipation of an enslaved and continually rebellious population as was the United States. Powerless and humiliated, after the war of 1897, Greece could no longer hope to have a voice, by reason of her own force, in the direction of Cretan affairs. Crete became the foundling of European diplomacy.

Together with the declaration of Bulgarian independence, and the annexation of Bosnia and Herzegovina by Austria-Hungary, the Young Turks had to face a decree of the Cretan assembly to the effect that Crete was indissolubly united to the kingdom of Greece. The Young Turks could do nothing against Bulgaria. For the ceremony of Tirnovo had been no more than the *de jure* sanction of a *de facto* condition. The only cause for conflict, the question of the railroads in eastern Rumelia, was solved by Russian diplomacy. Against Austria-Hungary a boycott was declared. It resulted in a few successful attempts to prevent the landing of mails and freights from Austrian steamers, and in the tearing up of several million fezes which were of Austrian manufacture. These, by the way, were soon replaced by new fezes from the same factories. The Sublime Porte settled the Bosnia-Herzegovina question by accepting a money payment from Austria-Hungary.

All the rancour resulting from these losses and humiliation, all the vials of wrath, were poured upon the head of Greece. The Cretan question became the foremost problem in European diplomacy. The Cretans stubbornly refused to listen to the Powers, and decided to maintain their decision to belong to Greece. But Greece was threatened with war by Turkey, if she did not refuse to accept the annexation decree voted by the Cretans themselves. In order to prevent Turkey from attacking Greece, the Powers decided to use force against the Cretans. Turkey, not satisfied with the efforts of the Powers to preserve the Ottoman sovereignty and Ottoman pride in Crete, demanded still more of Greece. She asked that the Greek Parliament should not only declare its disinterestedness in Crete, but should take upon itself the obligation to maintain that disinterestedness in the future.

To go into all the tortuous phases of the Cretan question up to the time of the Balkan War would make this chapter out of proportion; and yet Crete, like Alsace-Lorraine, has had a most vital influence upon the present European war. The one point to be emphasized here is, that to bring pressure to bear upon Greece in defining her attitude toward Crete, the Young Turks decided to revive the commercial boycott which they had used against Austria. I have seen from close range the notorious Greek boycott of 1910 to 1912. It was far more disastrous to the Turks than to the Greeks of Turkey. It threatened so completely, however, the economic prosperity of Greece, which is a commercial rather than an agricultural country, that it forced Greece into the Balkan Alliance much against her will, for the sake of self-preservation.

If this boycott had been carried on against the Greeks of Greece alone, it would not have affected vitally the prosperity of the Greeks in the Ottoman Empire. Their imports come from every country, and for their exports the freight steamers of all the European nations competed. But it was directed also against the Greeks who were Ottoman subjects. In Salonika, Constantinople, Trebizond, Smyrna, and other ports, commerce was entirely in the hands of Greeks. They owned almost every steamer bearing the Ottoman flag. They owned the cargoes. They bought and sold the merchandise. The Young Turks, working through the *hamals* or longshoremen and the boatmen who manned the lighters,—all Turks and Kurds,—succeeded in tying up absolutely the commerce of Ottoman Greeks. The Greek merchants and shippers were ruined. It was urged cleverly that this was the chance for Moslems to get the trade of the great ports of Turkey into their own hands. The Government encouraged them by buying and maintaining steamship lines. But the Turks had no knowledge of commerce, no money to buy goods, and no inclination to do the work and accept the responsibilities necessary for successful commercial undertakings. The result was that imports were stopped, prices went up, and the Moslems were hurt as much as, if not more than, the Christians. After several voyages, the new government passenger vessels were practically *hors de combat*. There was no longer first, second, and third class. Peasants squatted on the decks and in the saloons. Filth reigned supreme, and hopeless confusion. No European could endure a voyage on one of these steamers, and no merchant cared to entrust his shipments to them.

The boycott died because it was a hopeless undertaking. For many months, the Government lost heavily through the falling off in the custom house receipts. The labouring class (almost wholly Moslems) of the seaports suffered terribly, as our labouring class suffers during a prolonged strike. The boycott was removed, Greeks were allowed to resume their business, so essential for the prosperity of the community, and, as is always the case in Turkey, everything worked again in the same old way.

But, just as the failure to punish the perpetrators of the Adana massacre alienated definitely and irrevocably the sympathy and loyal support of the Armenian element from the constitutional *régime*, so the boycott, iniquitous and futile, lost to the Young Turks the allegiance of the Greeks of the Empire. Already alarmed by the attack upon the liberties of the patriarchate, the Greeks began to look to Greece for help; and, in the islands of the Ægean and in Macedonia, the hope was strong that a successful war might put an end to what they were suffering.

The Greeks of Turkey are not free from the universal characteristic of human nature. You can persecute and browbeat a man, you can bully him and do him physical injury, you can refuse him a share in the government and put him in an inferior social position, and he will continue to endure it. But, rob him of the chance of making a livelihood, and he will commence to conspire against the government. A man's vital point is his pocket-book. That vital point the Young Turks threatened by their boycott.

THE YOUNG TURKS AND THE MACEDONIAN PROBLEM

It was at Salonika that the Young Turk movement first gained its footing in the Ottoman Empire, and until the loss of European Turkey, after the disastrous war with the Balkan States, Salonika continued to be the centre of the "Committee of Union and Progress." Its congresses were always held there. From Salonika the third army corps went forth to suppress, in April, 1909, the counter-revolution in Constantinople. To the Young Turks, Salonika seemed the safest place in all the Ottoman dominions for the imprisonment of Abdul Hamid. Many of the leading members of the party were natives of Macedonia. In fact, it was because the Young Turks saw clearly that European Turkey would soon be lost to the Empire, unless there was a regeneration, that they precipitated in 1908 the revolution which had so long been brewing.

It is natural, then, that the Macedonian problem should be the first and uppermost of all the many problems that had to be solved in the regeneration of Turkey. The "Committee of Union and Progress" saw that immediate action must be taken to strengthen Ottoman authority, so severely shaken since the war with Russia, in the European *vilayets*.

We have already shown in a previous chapter how the struggle of races in European Turkey had made Macedonia the bloody centre of Balkan rivalry, and had reduced the *vilayets* of Uskub and Salonika to anarchy.

Up to the coming of the constitutional *régime*, there had been a very strong element in Macedonia, principally Bulgarian, which saw—oh, how prophetically!—that the liberation of Macedonia from Turkish rule would endanger, rather than aid, the propaganda for eventual Bulgarian hegemony in the Balkan Peninsula. These Bulgarians, wise in their day and generation beyond their emancipated brethren, advocated the intervention of Bulgarian arms, not to secure independence, but autonomy. They felt that by the creation, for a period of years, of an autonomous province of Macedonia under the suzerainty of the Sultan, the felicitous history of Eastern Rumelia would repeat itself.

The Young Turks decided to solve the Macedonian problem by strengthening the Moslem element in every corner of the *vilayets* of Salonika and Uskub. The means of doing this were at hand. After the annexation of Bosnia and Herzegovina, Turkish agents began to work among the Moslem population in these countries to induce them to emigrate and come under the dominion of the "Padishah," as the Sultan is called by his faithful subjects. They were brought in and settled, with the help of the Government, in those districts of Macedonia where the Moslem element was weak. This was a repetition of the policy of Abdul Hamid after the Congress of Berlin, when, in Eastern Rumelia and Thrace, to oppose the Bulgarians Circassians from the lost Caucasus were settled, and to oppose the Servians Albanian emigration into old Servia and the Sandjak of Novi Bazar was encouraged.

In addition to this, the Young Turks decided to secure the loyalty of their Christian subjects in European Turkey by abolishing the *karadj* (head tax) which exempted Christians from military service. Bulgarians, Greeks, and Servians were summoned to serve in the Ottoman army.

The first of these measures should never have been adopted. The bitter experience of former years should have taught the Young Turks the lesson that emigration of this nature not only tended to arouse religious fanaticism, but also introduced an element, ignorant and unruly, and wholly worthless from the economic point of view. It has often been recorded that Moslems, prompted to the sacrifice of abandoning everything for their love of remaining Turkish subjects, have made these "treks" after the unsuccessful wars of Turkey *of their own initiative*. Nothing is farther from the truth. There has never been an exodus of this sort which has not been due to the instigation of political agents. From the very fact that large industrious and influential Moslem elements have remained and prospered under Russian, Bulgarian, and Austrian rule, it can be inferred that those who yielded to the solicitation of Turkish agents were the undesirable Moslem element, who, never having acquired anything where they were, had nothing to lose by making a change. If one excepts a certain portion of the Circassians, the statement may well be made that these emigrants— *muhadjirs* they are called in Turkish—are an element forming the lowest dregs of the population, as worthless and shiftless as the great majority of the Jews whom the Zionist movement has attracted to Palestine. More than this, the *muhadjirs* have been fanatical and lawless, and it is they whose massacres of Christians have invariably ended in irretrievable disaster for Turkey.

In Macedonia, the muhadjirs, in conjunction with the Albanian Moslem immigrants, were responsible for the succession of massacres in 1912, such as those of Ishtip and Kotchana, which helped to bring about the Balkan alliance. The same thing is happening to-day in the coast towns of Asia Minor and Thrace, where the brutality and blood lust of the *muhadjirs* since 1913 will eventually cause another attack of Greece upon Turkey.

The second policy—that of enrolling Christians in the army—was recorded, back in the days of the first attempt at the emancipation of Christians, the *Tanzimat* of 1839, as a measure which would ameliorate their lot and bring about equality. The idea was splendid, but its application was impracticable. Ottoman Christians are so wholly incompatible, from their social and educational background, with Ottoman Moslems, that they cannot be placed in the army, in mixed regiments, without incurring humiliation, degradation, and persecution of the most cruel sort.

The only way in which Christians could be called to serve in the Ottoman army would have been the formation, at first, of separate regiments, where the soldiers would enjoy immunity from persecution. When this reform was made, there should have been also a provision from the very first, that the ranks of officers be recruited from the Christian elements in the Empire, in proportion to their numerical strength. But with both Christians and Jews, obligatory army service was used from the beginning—it is still used today—as a means of extorting money from those who could pay, and terrorizing and reducing to slavery those who could not raise the forty pounds required for exemption. Even if there were no religious fanaticism, even if it were not necessary for Christians of intelligence to serve in an army wholly officered by Moslems, the terrible and criminal conditions of service which they were called upon to suffer would have justified the Christians in adopting every possible measure to avoid military service.

Throughout the Empire, intelligent Christians who could not purchase their freedom from this obligation preferred exile to military service. From 1909 to 1914, Turkey has lost hundreds of thousands of its best young blood.

The result in Macedonia of the coming of the *muhadjirs* and the taking of Christians for the army, was that the Macedonians abandoned their advocacy of autonomy, under the suzerainty of the Sultan, and looked to the Balkan States for freedom from Turkish rule.

THE ALBANIAN UPRISINGS

Albania was never fully conquered by the Osmanlis. Like the Montenegrins, the Albanians were always able to resist the extension of Turkish authority in their mountains. Not only did the nature of the country favour them, but their proximity to the Adriatic, and their ability to call at will for Italian and Austrian help, made it advisable for the Supreme Porte to compromise with them. Many Albanians, including principally, as in Bosnia, the landowning families, were converted to Mohammedanism, and attached themselves to the fortunes of Turkey. Without ever giving up their local independence, these renegade Albanians became the most loyal and efficient supporters of Ottoman authority *outside of Albania.*

Turkey has gained much from the Albanians. Her higher classes, endowed with extreme intelligence and physical activity, have been the most valuable civil and military officials that the Government has ever enjoyed. Because they were Moslems, they were able to take high positions in the army and government service. It is one of the most remarkable facts of Ottoman history that the great majority of the really great statesmen and soldiers of the Empire, if not of Christian ancestry, have been, and still are, Albanians. In strengthening the Turkish domination in the European provinces, after the period of decline set in, the Albanians have been indispensable. Their emigration from their mountains into Epirus, Old Servia, the valley of the Vardar, and the coast towns of Macedonia checked for a long time the conspiracies and rebellions of the Christian elements.

The Sultans of Turkey and their counsellors have always recognized the value of the Albanians. In return for their great services to the Empire, they were allowed to retain their local privileges. This meant independence, in reality, rather than autonomy. They gave what taxes they pleased, or none. Military service was rendered upon their own terms. Christian Albanians, as well as Moslem, have preferred Ottoman sovereignty to any other. They have never thought of independence, because this would have brought them responsibilities and dangers from which, under the fetish of "the integrity of the Ottoman Empire," they were free. So they resisted every effort of Italian, Austrian, Slav, and Greek to weaken their allegiance to the Sultan. Turkey also allowed them to remain under the mediæval conditions in which they lived back in the fourteenth century. They wanted neither railways, roads, nor ports. Among all the subjects of the Sultan, the Albanians were best satisfied with the absolute lack of progress under Moslem rule. These are the reasons why the majority of Albanians want to return once more to the fold of Turkey.

The Young Turks were no more felicitous in their treatment of the Albanians than of the Greeks and Armenians. Without any consideration of the peculiar problems involved, they decided immediately, tackling every problem at once, that Albania must be civilized and that Ottoman sovereignty must work there in exactly the same way as in any other part of the Empire. Albanians must render military service, and submit to being sent wherever the authorities at Constantinople decided. Local independence must cease. Taxes must be paid regularly. When the Albanians resisted, as they did immediately, an army was sent to pacify the country.

One cannot but sympathize with the principle laid down by the Minister of the Interior at Constantinople, that the central authority must be recognized and that the only way to stamp out the Albanian anarchy was to disarm the population. But the Young Turks knew no other way of doing this than by force. They did not realize that anarchy and lawlessness disappear only with education and economic progress. Instead of starting to "civilize" the Albanians by establishing schools and opening up the country with railways, they sent rapid-firing guns. In the summer of 1909, the rebellion was stamped out with ruthless cruelty by the burning of villages, the destruction of crops, and the seizing of cattle. Such measures were a very poor argument for the Albanian to induce him to comply with the disarmament decree. Under ordinary circumstances an Albanian would rather lose his leg than his gun. Under these circumstances, he preferred risking his life to giving up what he considered his only means of defence.

Every year the Albanian rebellion broke out afresh. Every year the Young Turks exhausted the strength and spent the resources of their armies in

European Turkey against the invulnerable mountains of Albania. After every "pacification," Albania in arms was just as certain each May as the coming again of summer.

In 1912, when affairs were in a critical state as regards the Christian neighbours, the Cabinet in Constantinople was once more engaged in the hopeless task of subduing Albanian opposition. The Albanians, however, seemed to gain strength rather than lose it. In September, 1912, I was in Uskub just four weeks before the Balkan War broke out. The Albanian chieftains were there, having made a truce for Ramazan (the sacred month of the Moslem fasting). They said to me that the next year, if the Turks did not stop persecuting them, they would take their army to Constantinople. Others were to get ahead of them, and they were to win their independence without having to fight the Turks again. The poor showing of the Turkish arms against the Greeks and Servians is very largely due to the exhaustion which had come to them through continuous and unsuccessful attempts to get the better of the Albanian uprisings. The Balkan States knew how severely the western Macedonian army had suffered in July and August, 1912. It was one of the considerations which decided them to strike at that moment.

THE TREATMENT OF THE ARABIC ELEMENT

In Asiatic Turkey there are supposed to be about eight million Arabic-speaking inhabitants. These figures may be an exaggeration, for no census has ever been taken. But the *vilayets* are occupied almost exclusively by Arabs and races speaking Arabic. They form a half of the Empire's dominions in Asia, starting with the Taurus and Amanus ranges, south through Syria to Arabia and east and south-east through Mesopotamia to the Persian Gulf.

These large stretches of territory were never thoroughly conquered by the Turks. They did not settle there in the way they had done in the Balkan Peninsula, outside of Albania and Montenegro, and in Asia Minor. The race from whom they had taken their religion and from whom they soon absorbed whatever culture and art they can be said to possess, was never assimilated by the Turks. Their simple warrior and herdsman language was enriched by Arabic substantives, as Anglo-Saxon was enriched by the Latin gotten through the Normans and through the Church. But there was no racial fusion.

Only in appearance did Turkish officialdom and the authority of the Sultan ever get a real hold over the Arabs. By habit they came to respect the Sultan as Khalif. The allegiance which they gave him as ruler was altogether without value—a pure matter of form. An aggressive pasha found it easy to detach Egypt from Turkish rule. It was conglomerate populations and a lack of natural boundaries for forming states that prevented the other Arabic portions of the Ottoman Empire from following Egypt. In Arabia proper, and in the larger portion of Mesopotamia, up to the present day, the Arabs have been as independent of the Sublime Porte as have been the Albanians.

In the reign of Abdul Hamid, when the idea of the Pan-Islamic movement was conceived, the importance of joining the sacred cities of Medina and Mecca more closely with the Turkish Empire was recognized. French interests were building a railway across the Lebanon Mountains to Aleppo and Damascus. The Germans had launched their project for the *Bagdadbahn*. Abdul Hamid decided to create a railway directly under government control, from Damascus to Medina and Mecca. For the first time since they were joined to the Ottoman Empire, the Arabic provinces saw themselves in prospective connection with the capital. It had been for a long time easier and quicker to go from Constantinople to the United States or to China than to Bagdad or to Mecca. The railways would have one of two results: either the Arabs would be brought more closely into connection with the Empire, or they would be definitely alienated from it.

The Arabic question stood thus when the constitution was re-established in 1908. There are many Arabs among the Young Turks, but these, like the Slavs in the military and official service of Austria-Hungary, have been definitely alienated from their own nationality. Here was the opportunity to bring into sympathy with the constitutional movement the millions of Arabic-speaking subjects of the Sultan, who formed the most numerous Moslem element in the Empire. But the Young Turks were no more tactful in the treatment of the Arabs, who were mostly of their own religion, than of the Greeks and Armenians. In the first Parliament, they were almost as unfair to Moslem Arabs as to Christians. In the apportionment of places in the Cabinet, the Arabs were ignored. It is true that some Cabinet members, some high officials both in the military and civil administration, and some members of the inner council of the Committee of Union and Progress were of Arabic origin. But they must be counted practically as Turks, for they had lived so long away from their own country and their people that they had lost all Arabic sympathies. Some who were called Arabs were in reality members of the old Turkish families, who in Mesopotamia, as in Syria and Egypt, had received large tracts of land at the time of the conquest, and had always been Turks by interests and by atmosphere. The younger nationalistic Arabic element, educated, and living by professional or business interests in cities of the Arabic portion of the Empire, were from the very beginning ignored.

Two things soon became evident. In the first place, the Young Turks tried to impose their language in local administration as the sole official language of the Empire. In many places in Syria and Mesopotamia, civil officials, even in the courts of justice, were appointed without a knowledge of the language of the people among whom they had to serve. In the Balkans and in Asia Minor, where there were so many races and so many tongues, the Turks were acting reasonably and sensibly in imposing their own language as a medium for the transaction of government business, but in *vilayets* which were *wholly* Arabic speaking, the foisting of the Turkish language upon the people could be likened to a bastard child endeavouring to rule the branch of his family from which he had received his best and purest blood. Before a year had passed, the educated, intellectual Arabs were wholly out of sympathy with the new *régime*. Many of them began to dream of the revival of the Arabian khalifate, and looked to the nationalistic movement in Egypt as the seed from which their Pan-Arabic tree would some day grow. Others, older and less sentimental, did not hesitate to express a desire to see British or French sovereignty extended over Syria and Mesopotamia.

In the second place, among the quasi-independent tribes of the Syrian *hinterland*, and of the Arabian peninsula, the attempt of the Turks to destroy their privileges ended in the same way as it had done in Albania. From 1908 up to the outbreak of the Balkan War, millions of treasure and thousands of the best soldiers of the Empire were lost in fruitless efforts to realize the aspirations of the Young Turks. We cannot even enumerate these rebellions. They were as perennial as the Albanian uprisings, and as disastrous to the Turkish army. In Arabia, rebellious Arabs treated with the Italians. In Syria, beyond the Jordan, they made a practice of tearing up the tracks and burning the stations of the Hedjaz railway. In Mesopotamia, they refused to respond to the obligation of military service.

This incomplete summary of the Young Turk *régime* in the Ottoman Empire has been given to throw light upon the collapse of the constitutional *régime* and of the military reputation of Turkey. I have refrained from going into a discussion of party politics, of intrigues, and of the bickerings of Parliament. Enough has been told to show that the constitutional *régime* was marked for failure from the beginning for three reasons: There was no honest attempt to bring together the various races of the Empire in a common effort for regeneration. The Young Turks, having no statesmen among their leaders, depended upon untrained men and upon those Abdul Hamid had trained in sycophancy and despotism. In spite of the heroic and able efforts of the German military mission and the British naval mission, no progress was made in reforming the only force by which the Young Turks could have held in respect and obedience the Sultan's own subjects, as well as those foreign nations who were looking for the opportunity to dismember the Empire.

If the hopes of the true friends of Turkey had been realized, if only the constitution had been applied, if only there had been the *will* to regenerate Turkey, all the wars of the past few years, including the one which is now shaking Europe to its foundations, would have been avoided.

CHAPTER XII
CRETE AND EUROPEAN
DIPLOMACY

On November 19, 1910, the Cretan General Assembly made a stirring appeal "to the four Great Powers who are protectors of the island, to the two great Powers of Central Europe, to the great Republic of the New World, to the liberal and enlightened press of two Continents, and in general to all Christians, in favour of the rights of the Cretan people which it represents,—rights acquired and made legal by so many sacrifices and sufferings." The Cretans definitely included the United States and the American press in this manifesto. They wanted the American people to become acquainted with what was known to the chancelleries of Europe as "the Cretan question." For one fifth of the Cretans have members of their families in America. There are few hamlets in the island into which the spirit and influence of "the great Republic of the New World" has not penetrated.

A review of the relationship between Crete and the European Powers is as necessary in trying to throw light upon the events which led up to the war of 1914 as is the exposition of the later phases of the Albanian question. It helps us to grasp the attitude of the Powers towards Turkey in the years immediately after the proclamation of the constitution, the tremendous power of Hellenism under the wise and skilful guidance of a statesman such as M. Venizelos has proved himself to be, the importance of the Cretan question in precipitating the Balkan Wars, and the impotence of European diplomacy to preserve the *status quo*, and decide *ex cathedra* the destinies of countries like Crete and Macedonia, whose emancipated kinsfolk had acquired the spirit of the soldiers who sang:

"As Christ died to make men holy, let us die to make men free."

A century ago, Crete was cut off from the outside world. It had been for two hundred and fifty years under the Turks, who took a peculiar pride in the island from the fact that it was their last great conquest. Its Christian inhabitants, although forming the majority of the population, lived, or rather existed, under the same hopeless conditions as prevailed throughout Turkey. In the sea-coast towns the Christians prospered better than the Moslems, owing to their aptitude for commerce; but the bulk of the Christian population was in abject slavery to the Turkish *beys*, who were the great landowners.

The Greek war of liberation was shared in by the Cretans, who lent valuable aid to their brethren of the mainland. They endured all the sufferings of the war, but reaped none of its rewards. It is quite possible that they might have thrown off the Turkish yoke at that favourable moment had it not been for the astute policy of the Turks, who, seeing the danger of losing Crete, handed it over to Mehemet Ali in 1830 as a reward for Egyptian aid in the Greek war and compensation for the ships destroyed at Navarino. With the downfall of Mehemet Ali's schemes of conquest in 1840, the island reverted to Turkey. At this time the Powers could easily have united Crete with Greece, but deliberately sacrificed the Cretans to their commercial rivalries.

Turkey never succeeded in gaining her former ascendancy in Crete. Insurrection after insurrection was drowned in blood. During two generations the Turks sent into the unhappy island successive armies, whose orgies of cruelty and lust are better left undescribed. But the tortures of hell could not extinguish the flames of liberty. Every few years the Cretans would rise again and repay blood with blood until they were overwhelmed by Anatolian soldiers, of whom Turkey possesses an unlimited supply.

At the Congress of Berlin in 1878 the Greeks pled, with much force, for the privilege of annexing Crete. As we read them to-day, the arguments of M. Delyannis are a prophecy. The Powers put Crete back under Ottoman control, subject to a reformed constitution called the Pact of Holepa, which provided a fairly good administration, if a capable and sincere governor were chosen. Everything went well until Sultan Abdul Hamid in 1889 practically annulled the solemn agreement he had made by appointing a Moslem Governor-General, and reducing the representation in the General Assembly in such a way that the Moslem minority in the island came into power again. It would be fruitless to go into the complex history of the next seven years during which the lawlessness of former times was revived.

Christian refugees fled to Greece and carried the tale of their sufferings. A massacre in Canea in February, 1897, engineered by Turkish officers fresh from similar work in Armenia, had such a repercussion in Greece that King George would have lost his throne had he remained deaf to the popular demand that aid be sent to the Cretans. Greek soldiers crossed to the stricken island. This meant war with Turkey. In a few weeks Greece was overwhelmed in Thessaly, and the Powers were compelled to intervene. Much ridicule has been cast upon Greece for her impotence in the war of 1897. Her defeat was a foregone conclusion, and she was severely blamed for having jeopardized the peace of Europe just as the Balkan States are being blamed to-day.

But there are times when a nation simply has to fight. So it was with Greece in 1897. In exactly similar circumstances, but with conditions less serious and an issue not so long outstanding or so vital to national well-being, the United States a year later declared war on Spain. There was great similarity between the Cretan situation in 1897 and that of 1912 in Crete and Macedonia. Refugees, crossing the borders and telling unspeakable tales to their brothers of blood and religion, were continually before the eyes of the Bulgarians and Servians and Montenegrins and Greeks since the proclamation of the constitution in 1908. Each nationality suffered by massacres in Macedonia which were followed by no serious punishment.

Even though defeated in 1897, Greece forced the hand of the Powers and of Turkey. Crete was given autonomy, and placed under the protection of Italy, Great Britain, France, and Russia, who occupied the principal ports of the island. For a year and a half they searched for a "neutral" governor for the Cretans. The Turkish troops, however, remained at Candia, leaving the rest of the island to the revolutionaries. It was not until the British were attacked in the harbour of Candia, and their Vice-Consul murdered, that the Powers moved. But, as at Alexandria in 1882, it was a bluff admiral and not the diplomats who settled the status of the island. The Turkish troops were compelled to withdraw, and the Powers were told that they would either have to appease the Cretans by some encouragement of their aspirations or conquer the island by force. A way out of the dilemma was found in the appointment of Prince George of Greece as High Commissioner of the protecting Powers in Crete.

Here is where the Powers, if they had at that time any intention of "preserving the rights of Turkey" in Crete, made the first of their blunders. To call the son of the King of Greece to the chief magistracy of an island which had so long aspired to political union with Greece was, in the eyes of the people, a direct encouragement to their aspirations. How could they think otherwise? The Turkish Cretans, too, regarded this step as the end of Ottoman sovereignty, for they emigrated in so great a number that soon the Moslem population was reduced to ten per cent. Prince George's appointment, made in December, 1898, was for three years, but really lasted eight. In 1906 he withdrew because he had become hopelessly involved in party politics, and had "backed the wrong horses."

Now comes the second blunder, *unless the Powers were preparing Crete for union with Greece.* They sent a letter to the King of Greece, asking him to appoint a successor to his son! Let me quote from the exact wording of this letter:

"The protecting Powers, in order to manifest their desire to take into account as far as possible the aspirations of the Cretan people, and to recognize in a practical manner the interest which His Hellenic Majesty must always take in the prosperity of Crete, are in accord to propose to His Majesty that hereafter, whenever the post of High Commissioner of Crete shall become vacant, His Majesty, after confidential consultations with the representatives of the Powers at Athens, will designate a candidate capable of exercising the mandate of the Powers in this island...."

Turkey naturally protested against the change in the *status quo* which such a step implied, and pointed out that it was a virtual destruction even of the *suzerainty* of the Sultan. The Powers, however, did not object to the publication of their note to the King of Greece in the newspapers of Crete. M. Zaimis, a former prime minister of Greece, was appointed High Commissioner. The island had its own flag and postage stamps, and laws identical with those of Greece. Cretan officers in Greek uniform commanded the militia and constabulary of the island. Turkey treated Crete as a foreign country. For this statement there is no more conclusive proof than the records of the custom-houses at Smyrna and Salonika which show that Cretan products were subjected to the same duties as were applied to all foreign imports.

It would seem, then, that Crete was in practically the same position as Eastern Roumelia in 1885, or, in fact, as Bulgaria herself. Nothing was more natural than that the establishment of a constitutional *régime* in Turkey should lead to a proclamation of union with Greece. The motives which led to this action were identical with those which Austria-Hungary put forth as an explanation of her annexation of Bosnia and Herzegovina. The Cretans quite justly feared that the Young Turks would repudiate the obligations assumed by Abdul Hamid, and endeavour to bring Crete back into the Turkish fold. At the moment Turkey was so engrossed in the question of the Austrian annexation and the Bulgarian declaration of independence and seizure of the railways in Eastern Roumelia that she contented herself with a formal protest against the action of the Cretan Assembly.

What did the Powers do? Turkey, at the moment, could have done nothing had they recognized the union with Greece. But they did not want to go that far. On the other hand, they did not want to offend Greece and the Cretans. They made no threats, and took no action, although their troops were in the island. Inaction and indecision were made worse by the following note, which was sent by the four Consuls at Candia to the self-appointed provisional government:

"The undersigned, agents of France, Great Britain, Italy, and Russia, by order of their respective governments, have the honour of bringing to the knowledge of the Cretan government (*sic*) that the protecting Powers consider the union of Crete to Greece as depending upon the assent of the Powers who have contracted obligations with Turkey. Nevertheless they would not refuse to envisage with kindly and sympathetic interest the discussion of this question with Turkey, if order is maintained in the island and if the safety of the Moslem population is secured."

That diplomatic sanction would sooner or later be given to the action of the Cretans, if they showed their ability to preserve order in the island and treat the Moslems well, is an altogether justifiable interpretation of this note of the Powers. Otherwise would they not have protested against the illegality of the provisional government, and have forbidden the Cretan authorities to promulgate their decrees in the name of King George? Although the High Commissioner had disappeared, and the Cretans were running the island just as if the annexation were an assured fact, the Powers, far from protesting, announced their intention of withdrawing their troops of occupation!

What were their intentions concerning Crete, and what was their understanding of the *status quo* at the moment of withdrawal? This question they did not answer then, nor did they answer it afterwards. They simply withdrew from the island without stating what legal power was to succeed them. This was in the summer of 1909. M. Venizelos, then Prime Minister of Crete, asked the Powers to state definitely their intentions. He said that he did not wish to run counter to the orders of the Powers, but that he would have to raise the flag of Greece over the island when their troops left, unless they *formally* forbade him to do so. With admirable clearness and irrefutable logic he pointed out to the Powers that the only other alternative would be anarchy. But the Powers, pressed by their ambassadors at Constantinople, were afraid to assent to annexation. They were equally averse to taking the opposite course. So they contented themselves with giving M. Venizelos "friendly counsels" not to hoist the Greek flag. The result was the ludicrous spectacle of the cutting down of the Greek flag by marines landed from eight warships. It was like a scene from a comic opera, and M. Venizelos must have formed then the opinion which every succeeding action of the Powers strengthened and to which he gave expression after the Balkan War was declared—that the Powers were "venerable old women."

Crete now began to be menaced by the insensate chauvinism of the Young Turks, who thought they could avenge the loss of Bosnia-Herzegovina and the Bulgarian declaration of independence by destroying the autonomy of Crete and re-establishing the authority of the Sultan in this island which had been repudiating the Ottoman government for eighty years. In the spring of 1910, the *Tanine*, at that time official organ of the Committee of Union and Progress, laid down five points as the *minimum* which the Porte would accept in the definite and permanent solution of the status of Crete:

"1. Formal recognition of the rights of the Sultan.

"2. The right of the Sultan to name the Governor-General of the island among three Cretan candidates elected by the General Assembly.

"3. The right of the *sheik-ul-islam* to name the religious chiefs of the Cretan Moslems.

"4. Establishment in the Bay of Suda of a coaling-station for the Ottoman fleet, and the maintenance there of a permanent *stationnaire* like the *stationnaires* of the embassies at Constantinople.

"5. Restriction of the rights of the Cretan government in the matter of conclusion of treaties of commerce and agreements with foreign powers."

What the "rights of the Sultan" might be were not specified then, nor have they been since: but articles four and five were enough to throw the whole of Crete into a state of wildest excitement. The Turks, after having lost the island, were trying to win it back.

Left to themselves (as they had every reason to believe) the Cretans convoked the National Assembly for April 26, 1910. The Assembly was opened in the name of George I., King of the Hellenes. The Moslem deputies immediately presented a protest in which they rejected the sovereignty of Greece over Crete. The deputies were then asked to take the oath of allegiance in the name of King George. A second petition was presented by the Moslem deputies, declaring that, as the Sultan of Turkey held "sovereign rights" in the island, they, in the name of their Moslem constituents, protested against such an action. They refused to take the oath. Should they be excluded from the Assembly, or be allowed to sit without taking the oath?

Instead of insisting on the admission of the Moslem deputies, the Powers again gave "friendly counsels." Once more M. Venizelos pleaded that they speak out their mind in the matter of the legal status of the island. The diplomats "temporized" again, and the warships reappeared to assure to the Moslem deputies "their lawful rights." When M. Venizelos could get no statement from the Powers as to the grounds upon which these "lawful rights" rested, he saw that all hope of help from the Powers was over, and that he was only wasting his time. Like Cavour, when he turned with disgust from his efforts to interest the Powers and had the inspiration, *Italia fara da se*, the Cretan leader abandoned the antechamber of the chancelleries. While the Powers still sought a *modus vivendi* for Crete, M. Venizelos made one. From that moment the Balkan War was a certainty.

The Young Turk Cabinet, arrogant and drunk with the success of their boycott against Austria-Hungary, and at the same time knowing that they must turn public attention away from the loss of Bosnia and Herzegovina, began to press the Powers for the restoration in Crete of the *status quo* as it had existed before the diplomatic blunders I have outlined above, and, in addition, for the coaling station and for control over Crete's foreign relations. At the same time, they demanded of the Athens Cabinet that Greece renounce formally, not only for the present *but also for the future*, any intention of annexing Crete. The Young Turks represented that public opinion in Turkey was so wrought up over the Cretan question that war with Greece would certainly follow. To illustrate to the Powers and to Greece the force of this public opinion, a widespread boycott against everything Greek in Turkey was started. This economic warfare is described in another chapter. In some parts of Turkey the boycott has never ceased. There is no doubt that this boycott was one of the very most important factors in bringing on the Balkan War. For it taught the Greeks, who were continually being bullied and threatened with an invasion in Thessaly, the imperative necessity of reconciliation with Bulgaria by a compromise of rival claims in Macedonia.

Thinking that he could serve his country better in Greece than in Crete, M. Venizelos posed his candidacy to the Greek Chamber in the summer of 1910. Seemingly he was abandoning Crete to its fate, and he had to bear many unjust reproaches from his fellow-countrymen. His wonderful personality and extraordinary political genius soon brought him to the front in Greece. The Cretan revolutionary became Prime Minister of Greece. Steadfast in his purpose he began to negotiate with the other Balkan States and with Russia. He was able to accomplish the impossible. The war with Turkey is largely his personal success. No statesman since Bismarck has had so brilliant a triumph.

In 1910, M. Venizelos took the step which was the turning point in his career and in the history of Greece. Firmly persuaded that Crete could be annexed to Greece only by Greece proving herself stronger than Turkey, and not by diplomatic manoeuvres, he decided to desert Cretan politics, and enter the larger sphere open to him at Athens. It was easy to secure a seat in the Greek Parliament, but that was the only easy part about it. When one considered the fickle character of the Greek people in their politics, the selfish narrowness and bitter prejudices of their leaders, the inefficiency of the army and navy, whose officers had been ruined by political activity, the emptiness of the treasury, the unpopularity of the royal family, and the general disorder throughout the country, it seems incredible that M. Venizelos should have been willing to assume the responsibility of government, let alone succeed in his self-imposed task. Had you asked the leading statesmen of Europe five years ago what country presented the most formidable and at the same time most hopeless task tor a Premier, there would have been unanimity in selecting Greece.

But for Eleutherios Venizelos there was no difficulty which could not be overcome. It is the nature of the man to refuse to see failure ahead. "If one loves to work, and works for love," he has declared, "failure does not exist."

Called to be Prime Minister in August, 1910, M. Venezelos began to reform everything in sight. His first step was to endow Greece with a new constitution, whose most important changes were a Council of State, chosen for life and irremovable, to act as a Senate (Greece has single-chamber government), legalizing the state of siege, sanctioning the employment of foreigners in the service of the Government, fixing twenty-four hours as the maximum delay for bringing one who had been arrested before a magistrate, forbidding the publication of uncensored news relative to military and naval operations in time of war, establishing free, obligatory primary instruction, excluding from Parliament directors in corporations, and facilitating the expropriation of property for public purposes. I have given enough to show the practical character of the new constitution.

Although strongly urged to do so, both by the King and by the political leaders, M. Venizelos refused to turn his Constituent Assembly into an ordinary Parliament, and proceed to the legislation made possible by the new constitution. Seeing clearly that durable and effective ministerial power could be derived only from the people and supported only by their intelligent good-will, he balked the intrigues of the politicians, and overcame the dynastic fears of the King. The Constituent Assembly was dissolved. M. Venizelos went before the people, travelling everywhere and explaining his program for the reformation of the country. The result was a triumph such as no man has ever received in modern Greece. In November, 1910, followers of M. Venizelos were returned in so overwhelming a majority that he could afford to ignore the Athenian politicians who saw in him a menace to their personal rule, their sloth, and their "graft."

Since that day M. Venizelos has been the idol of Greece. Never has trust in public man been more amply justified. Every administration of the State was completely transformed within eighteen months. Even to outline what M. Venizelos has accomplished reads like a fairy tale. Only those who knew the Greece before his arrival and are able to contrast it with the Greece of today can appreciate the immensity of his labours and the radical character of the changes he has made. I cannot dwell on the talent shown by this Cretan in matters of financial reform. But his military and naval reforms, and his foreign policy, have been so important in making possible the Balkan alliance and its successes that they cannot be passed over.

M. Venizelos, when he first came to Athens, saw what was the matter with the Greek military and naval establishments. Like Peter the Great and the Japanese, he realized that the Greeks must learn from Europe by submitting to European teachers. To persuade his fellow-countrymen, who have a very exalted opinion of their own ability (the Greeks are always sure they were born to command, without first having learned to obey!), that they must not only call in foreign advisers, but must submit to their authority, has been the most Herculean of the tasks this great man set before him. Article three of the new constitution had authorized the appointment of foreigners as officers of the Government and given them temporarily Hellenic citizenship. From England was asked a naval mission, from France a military mission, and from Italy officers to reorganize the *gendarmerie*. In Greece the foreign officers were able to accomplish more in eighteen months than the foreign "advisers" of Turkey had accomplished in many long years. This is no assertion of personal opinion. The facts of the Balkan War speak for themselves. Why is this? In Turkey, the foreign teachers have never been given any real authority, and have seen every effort they put forth nullified by the insouciance, self-sufficiency, and cursed apathy of the Turk. The Greeks, on the contrary, "became as little children," and lo! a miracle was wrought!

When foreigners who visited Greece within recent years read about the successes of the Crown Prince at Salonika and Janina, the assassination of King George, the mourning of the Greek people, and the hearty acclamation of King Constantine, the national hero, they could think back to less than four years ago when the Crown Prince was practically banished from Greece, after having been dismissed from his command in the army by a popular uprising, and when the portrait of the King was removed from every coffee-house in Athens. What is the cause of the complete revulsion in public feeling towards the dynasty? It is due to the common sense of M. Venizelos. He saw that the present dynasty was necessary for Greece, and that the Crown Prince must come back and take command of the army. In defiance of public opinion, he insisted on this point. This attitude was a bitter disappointment to many who imagined that M. Venizelos would be anti-dynastic in his policy. As a result of his success in reconciling the Greeks with their sovereign and his family, the sympathies of Russia and Germany and Great Britain were not alienated from the Greek people, as was rapidly becoming the case. Emperor William especially, whose sister is wife of the new Greek King, was so delighted with the success of M. Venizelos in rehabilitating his brother-in-law that he asked the Greek Premier to visit him at Corfu.

This visit of the former Cretan revolutionary to the German Emperor in April, 1912, was hardly commented upon by the European press. But epoch-making words must have been spoken in the villa Achilleion, for immediately after that visit the semi-official German press began to prepare the public for the events which were to take place in the Balkans. The eloquence and remorseless logic which had carried the day among Cretan insurgents and Greek electors was not lost on the "war-lord of Europe." Emperor William carried back to Berlin the conviction that no diplomacy could outwit the Greek Premier's determination that Turkey should disappear from Crete and Macedonia.

I do not think I am exaggerating in saying that when the Young Turks, by their insensate chauvinism, caused M. Venizelos to despair of saving Crete through Crete itself, they signed their own death-warrant. If they had refrained from their boycott and let Crete alone, would M. Venizelos have gone to Greece? I think not. It is one of those strange coincidences of history that on the very day when Mahmud Shevket pasha, in the Ottoman Parliament, declared that if Greece did not make a public statement to the effect that she had no intention at any time to extend her sovereignty over Crete, a million Turkish bayonets would gleam upon the plains of Thessaly, Eleutherios Venizelos was quietly leaving Crete for Athens.

To bring together Greece, Bulgaria, Servia, and Montenegro into an alliance which would drive the Turk out of Europe was in the mind of M. Venizelos as far back as the summer of 1909, when he saw the international fleet at Canea land marines to cut down the Greek flag which he had raised. It became an obsession with him. It was possible, because he believed it was possible. But no one else regarded it as more than an idle dream. The rare friends to whom M. Venizelos vaguely hinted that such an alliance was the only way of solving the Balkan question called it the "acme of absurdity." I quote the words of an eminent diplomat to whom this solution was mentioned. At the opening of the Italian War, when I suggested to the Turkish Grand Vizier that such an alliance was possible, he looked at me pityingly, and said, "The questions you ask display your ignorance of conditions in this part of the world. My time is too valuable to discuss such an impossible hypothesis. Go to Hussein Hilmi pasha, and ask him if he thinks the Greeks and Bulgarians could ever unite." Hussein Hilmi pasha referred me to every single book that has ever been written about the Macedonian question. "I do not care which you read," said the ex-Governor-General of Macedonia, "they all tell the same story."

But M. Venizelos was not asking himself, "Can I do it?" but, "How shall I do it?" Once more he saw clearly. The pan-Hellenic national ideal must be given up. Greece must content herself with Epiros, the Ægean Islands, Crete, and a slice of Macedonia west of the Vardar—possibly including Salonika, if the army proved as victory-winning as those of Bulgaria and Servia. Everything else must be left to Bulgaria and Servia. When first proposed to the leaders of Greece, this proposition seemed so preposterous that M. Venizelos was accused of being a traitor to Hellenism. He is still denounced by the fanatics, after all that he has accomplished. But patiently he built up his argument, using all his magnetism and his eloquence to convince his colleagues. He showed how Greece was being constantly humiliated and menaced by the chauvinism of the Young Turks, how the boycott was ruining Greek shipping, how Crete itself would gradually get to like independence better than union with Greece, and how inevitable it was that the Slavs should in the course of time come to possess Thrace and Macedonia. Instead of sacrificing everything to Bulgaria, he maintained, "this is our only chance to get any part of European Turkey. We must give up our ideal, because it is impracticable. With Bulgaria, we can crush Turkey. Without Bulgaria, Turkey will crush us. And if Bulgaria helps, we must pay the price." It may be years—not until archives are open to historians and memoirs of present actors are published—before everything is clear concerning the formation of an alliance which was as great a surprise to Europe as it was to Turkey. But the famous telegram which M. Gueshoff, Prime Minister of Bulgaria, addressed to his colleagues at Athens after the first successes of the war were won, is sufficient testimony to the essential part played by M. Venizelos in forming the coalition.

After M. Venizelos left Crete, a last blunder made the protecting Powers the laughing-stock of Europe. The Cretans elected deputies to the Greek Chamber, and the warships of the Powers played hide-and-seek with small Cretan craft in a fruitless endeavour to prevent the chosen deputies from proceeding to Athens. This move was altogether unnecessary, for they had not yet learned the matchless worth of their opponent. M. Venizelos, knowing that Greece and her new allies were not yet ready for war with Turkey, "tipped off" both the Cretans and the leaders in the Greek Parliament that they would have to wait one or two years longer. But, to satisfy the *hoi polloi* on the one hand and the diplomats on the other, a little comedy was enacted before the Parliament House in Athens which threw wool over everybody's eyes.

As soon as he saw that war was inevitable and that his allies were ready, M. Venizelos admitted the Cretan deputies. Europe was face to face with a *fait accompli*. The Cretan and Macedonian questions were settled by war. The hand of Turkey and the diplomats was forced.

Now we see the importance of the Cretan question. The Balkan War could have been avoided by a courageous and straightforward policy of efficient protection of Christians who lived under the Ottoman flag. It is because the Powers did not fulfil the obligations of the Treaty of Berlin, and sacrificed Cretans and Bulgarians and Servians and Greeks to the furthering of their commercial interests at Constantinople, that all Europe is now stained with blood. By flattering the Turk and condoning his crimes, the Powers succeeded in destroying the "integrity of the Ottoman Empire," which they professed to uphold. In trying to be the friends of the Turk they proved his worst enemies.

The Cretan question is a commentary upon the utter futility of insincere and procrastinating diplomacy.

CHAPTER XIII
THE WAR BETWEEN ITALY AND TURKEY

Since the days when Mazzini, looking beyond the almost irrealizable dream of Italian unity, said in his Paris exile, "North Africa will belong to Italy," a new Punic conquest has been the steadfast hope of the Italians. France had already started her conquest of Algeria when Mazzini spoke, and was mistress of the richest portion of the southern Mediterranean littoral before the Italian unification was completed. Late though they were in the race, the Italians began to try to realize their dream by sending thousands of colonists to Egypt and to Tunis. But the events of the years 1881-1883 in these two countries, consummated by the Convention of London in 1885, gave Egypt to England and Tunis to France. Italy was too weak at the time to protest, and Germany had not yet begun to develop her *Weltpolitik*.

For some years Italian colonial aspirations were directed towards Somaliland and Abyssinia. The battle of Adowa in 1896 was a death-blow to the hopes of founding an Italian empire of Erythrea. Ten years ago Giolitti received a portfolio in the Zanardelli ministry, and ever since then there has been a new Cato at Rome, crying "Tripoli must be taken." By the Franco-Italian protocol of 1901, it was agreed that if France should ever extend her protectorate over Morocco, Italy should have the Tripolitaine and Barca, with the Fezzan as a *hinterland*. This "right" of Italy was recognized at the international conference of Algeciras in 1906, and has since been accepted in principle by the European cabinets.

During the past decade Italy quietly prepared to seize Tripoli,— peacefully, if possible, and if not, by force. Had Italy been ready, Turkey would have lost Tripoli in the autumn of 1908, when Bulgaria declared her independence and Austria annexed Bosnia and Herzegovina. Internal politics made a bold stroke impossible at that favourable moment.

To accomplish her purpose, Italy worked along two lines. She tried to make her economic position so strong in Tripoli that the country would virtually belong to her and be exploited by her without any necessity for a change in its political status, until Arabs and Berbers, choosing between prosperity under Italy and poverty under Turkey, would of their own accord expel the Turks. Foreseeing a possibility of failure in this plan, she at the same time prepared for a forcible occupation of the country.

Immediately after the Anglo-Boer War, the Italian Ministries of War and Marine began to make a study of the question of transporting troops and landing them under the cover of a fleet. Tourists who were in Italy during the summer of 1904 will remember the famous dress rehearsal of the Tenth Army Corps.

Some six thousand men, completely provided with horses, ammunition, artillery, and provisions, were embarked in eleven hours. The convoy put to sea, escorted by a squadron of battleships and torpedo-boats, in two columns of five transports each. Despite a heavy swell, these troops and all their stores were landed in the Bay of Naples in sixteen hours. I wonder if many who were watching and applauding on that memorable day understood why Italy was practising so assiduously landing from transports,—and under the protection of the fleet. For what war was she preparing in time of peace? In 1907, the Minister of Marine announced in the *Italia Militare* that Italy could send seventy thousand troops upon a distant expedition oversea and one hundred and fourteen thousand *for a short journey not exceeding two nights at sea*!

The peaceable conquest of Tripoli was cleverly conceived, and has been faithfully tried. Branches of the Banco di Roma were established at Tripoli and Benghazi, and, for the first time since the days of Imperial Rome, a serious attempt was made to develop the agricultural and commercial resources of the country. The natives were encouraged in every enterprise, and managed in such a way that they became—in the vicinity of the seaports and trading-posts, at least—dependent for their livelihood upon the Banco di Roma. Italian steamship lines, heavily subsidized, maintained regular and frequent services between Tunis and Tripoli and Benghazi and Derna and Alexandria. The more enterprising natives travelled for a few piastres to Alexandria, and the object-lesson of contrast was left without words to work its effect upon them. The admirable Italian parcel post system—one of the most successful in Europe—extended its operations into the *hinterland* and captured the ostrich feather trade. The Italians began to talk of making secure the routes to Ghadames and Ghat and Murzuk, and of establishing for the interior postal and banking facilities that these regions could never hope to have under Turkish administration. Railways were contemplated as soon as they could be financed entirely by Italian capital.

The Italian schemes were working beautifully when the birth of New Turkey in the revolution of July, 1908, changed the whole situation. The indolent and corrupt officials of the *vilayet* of Tripoli and *sandjak* of Benghazi, whose attention had been turned from Italian activities by Italian gold pieces, were replaced by members of the Union and Progress party. These new officials, owing to their utter inexperience and their sense of self-esteem, may have been no better than the old ones; probably they proved as inefficient, for executive power is not inherent in the Turkish character. But they were men who had passed through the fire of persecution and suffering for love of their fatherland, and the renaissance of Turkey was the supreme thing in their lives. Their patriotism and enthusiasm knew no bounds. Their ambitions for Turkey may have been far in advance of their ability to serve her. But criticism is silent before patriotism which has proved its willingness to sacrifice Life for country.

One can imagine the feelings of the Young Turks when they saw what Italy was doing. It is easy enough to say that they should have immediately reformed the administration of the country and given to the Tripolitans an efficient government. Reform does not come in a twelvemonth, and the Young Turks had to act quickly to prevent the loss of Tripoli. They took the only means they had. They began to thwart and obstruct every Italian enterprise, to extend the military frontiers of Tripoli into the Soudan, to bring all the Moslem tribes of Africa into touch with the Constantinople khalifate.

Italy saw her hopes being destroyed as other colonial hopes had been destroyed one after the other. Representations at Constantinople were without effect. The more her ambassador tried, the more he realized the hopelessness of his case. Surely it was a fruitless diplomatic task to persuade Young Turkey that her officials in Tripoli and Benghazi should be forbidden to hinder the onward march of Italian "peaceable conquest." The Italian economic fabric in Tripoli, so carefully and so patiently built, seemed to be for nothing. Austria-Hungary had begun the disintegration of the Ottoman Empire by the annexation of Bosnia and Herzegovina in 1908. No Power had successfully protested, much less the helpless Turks. So Italy began to prepare her coup.

The crisis could not be precipitated. Italian public opinion, wary of colonial enterprises since the terrible Abyssinian disaster, and opposed to the imposition of fresh taxes, had to be carefully prepared to sustain the Ministry in a hostile action against Turkey.

In January, 1911, the Italian press began to publish articles on Tripoli, dilating upon its economic value and its vital importance to Italy, if she were to hold her place among the great Powers of Europe. Every little Turkish persecution—and there were many of them—was made the subject of a first-page bit of telegraphic news. The Italian people were worked up to believe that not only in Tripoli, but elsewhere, the Young Turks were showing their contempt for Italian officials and for the Italian flag. An Italian sailing vessel was seized at Hodeidah in the Red Sea; the incident was magnified. An American archæological expedition was granted a concession in Tripoli; a similar concession had been refused to Italian applicants. The newspapers pretended that the Americans were really prospecting for sulphur mines, whose development would mean disaster to the great mines in Sicily! French troops reached the Oasis of Ghadames; the *hinterland* of Tripoli was threatened by the extension of French sovereignty into the Sahara. At this moment the reopening of the Morocco question by the Agadir incident gave Italy the incentive and the encouragement to show her hand.

In September, the press campaign against the Turkish treatment of Italians in Tripoli became daily and violent. Signor Giolitti succeeded in getting all parties, except the extreme Socialists, to promise their support.

It was not until the last moment that the Sublime Porte realized the danger. On September 26th, the *Derna*, a transport, arrived at Tripoli, with much-needed munitions of war. There had been a shameful neglect to keep up the garrisons in the African provinces, and when it was too late—as is so often the case at Constantinople—there dawned the realization that the provinces were practically without defence.

On September 27th, the first of the series of ultimatums which have brought all Europe into war was delivered to the Sublime Porte. Italy gave Turkey forty-eight hours to consent to the occupation of Tripoli, with the proviso of the Sultan's sovereignty under the Italian protectorate, and the payment of an annual subsidy into the Ottoman Treasury. In Italy, two classes were mobilized, General Caneva embarked his troops upon transports that had already been prepared, and the Italian fleet proceeded to Tripoli.

The Turks did not believe that there would be war. On the afternoon of September 29th, the Grand Vizier, as far-seeing in his understanding of international affairs as he was blind in grasping what was best for Turkey's interests, told me that he was sure Italy would hesitate before entering upon a war that would be the prelude to the greatest catastrophe that the world has ever known. "Italy will not draw the sword," he declared, "because she knows that if she does attack us, all Europe will be eventually drawn into the bloodiest struggle of history,—a struggle that has always been certain to follow the destruction of the integrity of the Ottoman Empire." Hakki pasha was right, except in one important particular. Perhaps Italy did know what an attack upon Turkey would eventually lead to. But two hours after my conversation with the Grand Vizier, he received a declaration of war.

Simultaneously with the news of the declaration of war, Constantinople learned that the first shots had already been fired. Without waiting for any formalities, the Italian fleet had attacked and sunk Turkish torpedo-boats off Preveza at the mouth of the Adriatic. The Turkish fleet had just left

Beirut to return to Constantinople, and for three days it was feared that the Italians would follow up their offensive by destroying the naval power of Turkey. They did not do so, although it would have been an easy victory. For it was the hope of the Giolitti Cabinet that there would be no real war.

The attack at Preveza had a double purpose of preventing the torpedo-boats from interfering with the Italian commerce, and of striking terror into the hearts of the Turks. The Italians did not want to widen the breach and draw upon themselves the hatred and enmity of Turkey by sinking her navy. Such an action would make difficult the negotiations which they still hoped to pursue. It was not war against the people of Turkey that they had declared; that was a mere form. What they wanted was a pretext for seizing Tripoli. So naval and military operations were directed not against Turkey, but against the coveted African provinces. Considerations of international diplomacy, also, dictated this policy.

The Italian warships opened fire upon Tripoli on September 30th. On October 2d and 3d, the forts were dismantled and the garrison driven out of the city by the bombardment. On October 5th, Tripoli surrendered. The expeditionary corps disembarked on the 11th. The next transports from Italy went farther east. Derna capitulated on the 8th, but a heavy sea prevented the troops from landing until the 18th. General Ameglio took Benghazi at the point of the bayonet on October 19th. Homs was occupied on the 21st.

The Turks and Arabs attempted to retake Tripoli on October 23d. While the Italian soldiers were in the trenches they were fired upon from behind by Arabs who were supposed to be non-combatants. Discovery of the assailants was practically impossible, because many clothed themselves like women and hid their faces by veils. The Italians had to repress this move from the rear with ruthless severity. They did what any other army would have done under the circumstances, for their safety depended upon putting down the enemy that had arisen in their rear. Failure to act quickly and severely would have encouraged a revolution in the city and its suburbs. Horror was excited throughout the world by the highly coloured stories of this repression. Details of Italian cruelty were emphasized. No effort was made to explain impartially the provocation which had led to this killing. There was an unconscious motive in these stories to embarrass Italy in her attempt to build a colonial empire, just exactly as there had been in the time of the Abyssinian War in 1896. The American Consul at Tripoli has assured me that the correspondents who were guests at the time of the Italian army did not give the facts as they were.

The French and English newspaper campaign against Italy was as violent as it had been against Austria in 1908, at the time of the first violation of

Ottoman territorial integrity. Attempts were made to denounce the high-handed act of piracy of which Italy had been guilty, and to poison the public mind against the Italian army. It is significant to note this attitude of the press of the two countries, which are now so persuasively extending the olive branch to Italy. Great Britain and France were alarmed over the menace to the "equilibrium" of the Mediterranean. This is why they did not hesitate to denounce unsparingly the successful effort of Italy to follow in their own footsteps! The tension between France and Italy was illustrated by the vehement newspaper protests against the Italian use of the right of search for contraband on French ships. Italy was taken to task for acting in exactly the same way that France has since acted in arresting Dutch ships in August and September, 1914.

The attempt of October 23d failed, in spite of the conspiracy behind the lines. A second attempt on the 26th was equally unsuccessful. On November 6th, the garrison of Tripoli started to take the offensive. But progress beyond the suburbs of the city was found to be impossible.

A decree annexing the African provinces of Turkey was approved by the Italian Parliament on November 5th. The Italian "adventure," as those who looked upon Italy's aggression with unfriendly eyes persisted in calling it, was now shown to be irrevocable. Turkey's opportunity to compromise had passed.

In Tripoli, as well as in the other cities, it took the whole winter to make the foothold on the coast secure. From November 27th to March 3d, Enver bey made three attempts to retake Derna. From November 28th to March 12th, six assaults of Turks and Arabs were made upon Benghazi. The Italian positions at Homs were not secure until February 27th. Italy was practically on the defensive everywhere.

Hakki pasha found himself compelled to resign when the war was declared. In fact, he considered himself fortunate not to be assassinated by army officers, who declared that he had been negligent to the point of treason in laying Turkey open to the possibility of being attacked where and when she was weakest. Saïd pasha became Grand Vizier—he had held the post six times under Abdul Hamid. Five members of the former Cabinet, including Mahmud Shevket pasha, remained in office.

The first appearance of Saïd pasha's Cabinet before Parliament is a scene that I shall never forget. No pains had been spared to make it a brilliant spectacle. The Sultan was present during the reading of his speech from the throne. Everyone expected an important pronouncement. The speech of Saïd pasha was typically Turkish. Instead of announcing how Turkey was to resist Italy, he gave it to be understood in vague language that diplomacy was going to save the day once more, and that Turkey was secure because the preservation of her territorial integrity was necessary for Europe.

The action of Italy, however, had upset the calculations of the Young Turks in the game they were trying to play in European diplomacy. It was their dream—more than that, their belief—that Turkey held the balance of power between the two great groups of European Powers. They thought that the destinies of Europe were in their hands. I heard Mahmud Shevket pasha say once that "the million bayonets of Turkey would decide the fortunes of Europe." Turkey was essentially mixed up in the European imbroglio. But it was the absence of those million bayonets, of which Mahmud Shevket pasha boasted, that changed the fortunes of Europe. The military weakness of the Ottoman Empire has brought us to the present catastrophe.

The embarrassment of the Young Turks was that Italy belonged to the Triple Alliance, and that Germany, while professing deep and loyal friendship, stood by and saw Turkey attacked by her ally, Italy, just as she had stood by in 1908, when the other partner of the Triple Alliance had annexed Bosnia and Herzegovina. Those who had based their hopes of Turkey's future upon the pan-Germanic movement had a bitter awakening. In what sense could Wilhelm II be called "the defender of Islam"?

I attended sessions of Parliament frequently during the five weeks between the outbreak of the war and the passing of the decree by which the African possessions of Turkey were annexed to the kingdom of Italy. Before this step had been taken by Italy, there was a possibility of saving the situation. But the Turks, instead of presenting a united front to the world, and finding ways and means of making a successful resistance against Italy, wasted not only the precious month of October, when there was still a way out, but also the whole winter that followed. In November, the opposition in the House and Senate formed a new party which they called the "Entente Liberale." The principal discussions in Parliament were about whether the Hakki pasha Cabinet should be tried for high treason, and whether the Chamber of Deputies could be prorogued by the Sultan without the consent of the Senate. The opposition grew so rapidly that the Committee of Union and Progress induced the Sultan to dissolve Parliament on January 18, 1913.

The new elections were held at the end of March. Throughout the Empire they were a pure farce. The functionaries of the Government saw to it that only members of the Committee of Union and Progress were returned. While the Young Turks were playing their game of parties, anarchy was rife in different parts of the Empire. The "Interior Organization" had been revived in Macedonia. The Albanians, who had been left entirely out of the fold in the new elections, were determined to get redress. In Arabia, the neutrality of Iman Yahia in the war with Italy was purchased only by the granting of complete autonomy. It was the surrender of the last vestige of Turkish authority in an important part of Arabia. Saïd Idris, the other powerful chief in the Yemen, refused to accept autonomy, and continued to harass the Turkish army.

The Committee of Union and Progress was not allowed to enjoy long its fraudulent victory. In the army an organization which called itself "The Military League for the Defence of the Country" was formed, and received so many adhesions that Mahmud Shevket pasha was compelled to leave the Ministry of War on July 10th, and Saïd pasha the Grand Vizirate eight days later. Ghazi Mukhtar pasha accepted the task of forming a new Cabinet. The Unionist Parliament refused to listen to his program. So he secured from the Sultan a second prorogation of Parliament on August 5th. The weapon the Unionists had used was turned against them.

While Turkey showed herself absolutely incapable of making any military move to recover the invaded provinces or to punish the invader, Italy had none the less a difficult problem to face. A few Turkish officers had succeeded in organizing among the Arabs of Tripoli and Benghazi a troublesome resistance. General Caneva went to Rome at the beginning of February, and told the Cabinet very plainly that it would take months to get a start in Africa, and years to complete the pacification of the new colonies, unless the Turks consented to withdraw the support of their military leadership and to cease their religious agitation.

The question was, how could Turkey be forced to recognize the annexation decree of November 5th? The Italian fleet could not be kept indefinitely, at tremendous expense and monthly depreciation of the value of the ships, under steam. The Turkish fleet did not come out to give battle, so the Italians were immobilized at the mouth of the Dardanelles. Italian commerce in the Black Sea and eastern Mediterranean was at a standstill. Upon Italian imports into Turkey had been placed a duty of one hundred per cent. Where, outside of Tripoli, was the pressure to be exercised?

Premier San Giuliano had promised before the war started that he would not disturb political conditions in the Balkan peninsula. The alliance with Austria-Hungary made impossible operations in the Adriatic. But it was clear that something must be done. Public opinion in Italy had been getting very restless. It did not seem to the Italians that the considerations of international diplomacy should stand in the way of finishing the war. Were they to burden themselves with heavy taxes in order to spare the feelings of the Great Powers? Had Russia hesitated in the Caucasus? Had Great Britain hesitated in Egypt? Had Austria hesitated in Bosnia-Herzegovina?

As a sop to public opinion, and also as a feeler to see how the move would be taken by the other Powers, the Cabinet decided upon direct action against Turkey. The fleet appeared before Beirut on February 24th, and sank two Turkish warships in the harbour. It was not exactly a bombardment of the city, but many shells did fall on the buildings and on the streets near the quay. Neither Turkey nor Europe paid much attention to this demonstration. In April, Italy had come to the point where she felt that she must cast all scruples to the winds. A direct attack upon Turkey was decided. Italy, at this writing the only neutral among the Great Powers of Europe, took the action which brought Balkan ambitions to a ferment, and caused the kindling of the European conflagration. Her declaration of war on Turkey and the annexation of Tripoli inevitably led to this. On April 18th Admiral Viala bombarded the forts of Kum Kale at the Dardanelles, and on the same day the port of Vathy in Samos. Four days later Italian marines disembarked on the island of Stampali. On May 4th, Rhodes was invaded, a battle occurred in the streets of the town, and the Turks withdrew to the interior of the island. They were pursued, and surrendered on the 17th. Ten other islands at the mouth of the Ægean Sea were occupied.

A demonstration at Patmos for union with Greece was vigorously repressed. Italy protested her good faith in regard to the islands. But the dismemberment of the Ottoman Empire, arrested at San Stefano in 1878, had begun again.

Turkey responded to the bombardment of Kum Kale by closing the Dardanelles, and to the occupation of Rhodes by attempting to expel from Turkey all Italian residents. The expulsion decree, however, was carried out with great humanity and consideration by the Turks. During the Italian War and also the Balkan War, Turkish treatment of subjects of hostile states living in Ottoman territory was highly praiseworthy. The Christian nations of Europe would today do well to follow their example!

The closing of the straits lasted for a month. It disturbed all Europe. Never before has the question of the straits been shown to be so vital to the world. From April 18th to May 18th, over two hundred merchant vessels of all nations were immobilized in Constantinople. It was a sight to be witness of once in a lifetime. For these ships were not lost in a maze of basins, docks, and piers. They lay in the stream of the Bosphorus and at the entrance to the Sea of Marmora. You could count them all from the Galata Tower. The loss to shipping was tremendous. Southern Russia is the bread basket of Europe. No European resident could remain unaffected by a closing of the only means of egress for these billions of bushels of wheat. Angry protests were in vain. Turkey reopened the straits only when assurance had been given to her that the attack of the Italian fleet would not be repeated.

Little had been gained by Italy as far as hastening peace was concerned. She had done all that she could. Turkey still remained passive and unresisting, because she knew well that any vital action, such as the bombardment of Salonika or Smyrna, or the invasion of European Turkey by way of Albania or Macedonia, would bring on a general European war. Italy could not take this responsibility before history. So for months longer it remained a war without battles. Many Italian warships had not fired a single shot.

During May, June, and July, the Italians pushed on painfully to the interior of Tripoli. There was no other way. In August, the Turkish resistance on the side of Tunis was finished. In September, a desperate attack of Enver bey against Derna was repulsed. The Italian forces were in a much better position than before. But the attacks of the Arabs were of such a character that they could not be suppressed by overwhelming numbers of trained men that the Italians could muster. It was a guerilla warfare with the oases of the desert as the background. The Italians felt that the Arabs, if left to themselves, would soon tire of the conflict. For they were, after all, traders, and were dependent upon the outlets for their caravan trade which was now completely in the hands of Italians. It was the mere handful of Turkish troops and Turkish officers who kept the Arabs stirred up to fight.

As early as June, Italian and Turkish representatives met informally at Ouchy on Lac Leman to discuss bases for a solution of the conflict which had degenerated into an odd *impasse*. Italy was anxious to conclude peace for several reasons. Her commerce was suffering. Her warships needed the drydock badly. While Turkey could no longer prevent the conquest of Tripoli and Benghazi, the absence of Turkish direction in keeping the tribesmen of the interior stirred up, and the cessation of the propaganda against the Italian occupation on the ground of religion, would help greatly in the pacification of the provinces. Since the Albanian revolution had assumed alarming proportions, Turkey also became anxious for peace. She was uncertain of Italy's attitude in case of an outbreak in the Balkans. Unofficially, Italy had let it be known that there was a limit to patience, and that the development of a hostile attitude by the Balkan States against Turkey would find her, in spite of Europe, in alliance with them against her. In reality, however, the Italian ministers at the Balkan courts had all along done their best to keep Greece and Bulgaria from being carried away by the temptation to take advantage of the situation. This had been especially true in April and May, during the period of Italian activity in the Ægean.

Turkey knew perfectly well, before the *pourparlers* at Ouchy, what were the Italian terms. In March, when the five other Powers had offered to mediate, Italy had laid down the following points: tacit recognition of the Italian conquest and withdrawal of the Turkish army from Africa; recognition by the Powers, if not by Turkey, of the decree of annexation. Italy promised, if this were done, to recognize the Sultan as Khalif in the African provinces (this meant purely religious sovereignty); to respect the religious liberty and customs of the Moslem populations; to accord an amnesty to the Arabs; to guarantee to the Ottoman Public Debt the obligations for which the customs-duties of Tripoli had been mortgaged; to buy the properties owned by the Ottoman Government; to guarantee, in accord with the other Powers, the (future!) "integrity of the Ottoman Empire." Turkey had refused these terms, in spite of the pressure of the Powers at the Sublime Porte. Then followed the loss of Rhodes and the other islands.

The first *pourparlers* at Ouchy had been interrupted by the fall of Saïd pasha. They were resumed on August 12th by duly accredited delegates. After six weeks an accord was prepared, and sent to Constantinople. The ministry, although facing a war with the Balkan States, tried to prolong the negotiations. Italy then addressed an ultimatum on October 12th. The Sublime Porte was doing its best to prevent war with the Balkan States. Italy was determined now to go to any length to wring peace from her stubborn opponent. For the Balkan storm was breaking, and she wanted to get her ambassador back to Constantinople to take part in the councils of the Great Powers. The continuance of a state of war with Turkey was never more clearly against her interests. When the ultimatum arrived, Turkey yielded. The preliminaries of Ouchy were signed on October 15th.

There were two distinct parts to the Treaty of Lausanne, as it is generally called. In order to save the pride of Turkey, nothing was said in the text of the treaty about a cession of territory. Turkey was not asked to recognize the Italian conquest. The unofficial portion of the treaty consisted of a *firman*, granting complete autonomy to the African *vilayet*, and appointing a personal religious representative of the Khalif, with functions purely nominal; and the promise of amnesty and good administration to the Ægean Islands.

The text of the treaty provided for the cessation of hostilities; the withdrawal of the Turkish army from Tripoli and Benghazi and the withdrawal of the Italian army from the islands of the Ægean; the resumption of commercial and diplomatic relations; and the assumption by Italy of Tripoli's share of the Ottoman Public Debt.

Italy had no intention of fulfilling the spirit of the second clause of this treaty, which was that the islands occupied by her be restored to Turkey. The text of the treaty provided that the recall of the Italian troops be subordinated to the recall of the Turkish troops from Tripoli. It was easy enough to quibble at a later time about the meaning of "Turkish." As long as there was opposition to the Italian pacification, the opponents could be called Turkish. Italy said that the holding of the Dodecanese was a guarantee of Turkish good faith in preventing the continuance secretly of armed opposition to her subjugation of the new African colonies. As long as an Arab held the field against the Italian army, it could still be claimed that Turkey had not fulfilled her side of the promise in Article 2. At the moment, Turkey was quite willing to see the Italians stay in the southern islands of the Ægean. For otherwise they would have inevitably fallen into the hands of the Greeks when the Balkan War broke out.

Since the Treaty of Lausanne was signed, the Italians have remained in the Dodecanese. Not only that, but they have used their position in Rhodes to begin a propaganda of Italian economic influence in south-western Asia Minor. Before the present European war, Italy might have found herself compelled to relinquish her hold on these islands. But now her advantageous neutrality has put into her hands the cards by which she can secure the acquiescence of Europe to the annexation of Rhodes.

The outbreak of indignation in Turkey against Italy at the beginning of the war was even more vehement than that against Austria-Hungary when she had annexed Bosnia-Herzegovina in 1908. Hussein Djahid bey, in the *Tanine*, wrote an editorial, in which he said: "Never shall we have any dealings with the Italians in the future. Never shall a ship bearing their flag find trade at an Ottoman port. And we shall teach our children, and tell them to teach their children, the reasons for the undying hatred between Osmanli and Italian as long as history lasts." Having read the same sort of a thing in 1908, I was interested in seeing just how long the hatred would last. Just a year from the day war was declared, and this editorial appeared, the

Italian ambassador returned on a warship to Constantinople, the Italian post offices opened, and all my Italian friends began to reappear. This is told here to illustrate the fact that cannot be too strongly emphasized: *there is no public opinion in Turkey.*

The chief importance of the year of "the war that was no war" is not in the loss of Tripoli. It is in the fact that the integrity of the Ottoman Empire, secure since 1878, had been attacked *by violence.* The example given by Italy was to be followed by the Balkan States. What Europe had feared had come. This war was the prelude to Europe in arms.

CHAPTER XIV
THE WAR BETWEEN THE BALKAN STATES AND TURKEY

During the year 1911 there had been a perceptible drawing together of the Balkan States in the effort to find a common ground for an offensive alliance against Turkey. The path of union was very difficult for the diplomats of the Balkan States to follow. It was clear to them in principle that they would never be able to oppose the policy of the Young Turks separately. They were not even sure whether their united armies could triumph over the large forces which the Ottoman Empire was able to put in the field, and which were reputed to be well trained and disciplined. This reputation was sustained by the unanimous opinion of the military *attachés* of the Great Powers at Constantinople. And then, there were the mutual antipathies to be healed, and the problem of the terrible rivalry in Macedonia, of which we have spoken before, to be solved. Most formidable of all, was the uncertainty as to the benefit to the different Balkan nations of a successful war against Turkey.

It is impossible to explain here all the diplomatic steps leading up to the Balkan alliance against Turkey. They have been set forth, with much divergency of opinion, by a number of writers who were in intimate touch with the diplomatic circles of the Balkan capitals during the years immediately preceding the formation of the alliance. We must confine ourselves to a statement of the general causes which induced the Balkan States, against the better judgment of many of their wisest leaders, to form the alliance, and to declare war upon Turkey. Both Bulgaria and Greece had sentimental reasons; the terrible persecution of the Christians of their own race in Macedonia seemed cause enough for war. But while Bulgaria had long held the thesis of Macedonian autonomy, which was sustained by the Bulgarian Macedonians themselves, Greece was afraid that the creation of such a *régime* would in the end prove an irrevocable blow to Hellenistic aspirations. It was well known to the Greeks that the population of Macedonia was not only largely Bulgarian, but aggressively so, and that its sense of nationality had been intelligently and skilfully awakened and fostered by the educational propaganda. Above all things Hellenism feared the Bulgarian schools. Under an autonomous *régime* their influence could not be combated.

The possibility of the Balkan alliance was really in the hands of Greece. For it was recognized that no matter how large and powerful an army

Bulgaria and Servia could raise, the co-operation of the Greek navy, which would prevent the use of the Ægean ports of the Macedonian littoral for disembarking troops from Asia, was absolutely essential to success. In spite of their fears for the future of Macedonia, the Greeks were converted to the idea of an alliance with the Slavic Balkan States to destroy the power of Turkey by the continual bullying of the Young Turks over Crete, and by the economic disasters from the boycott. It is not too much to say that the attitude of the Young Turks towards the Cretan questions, and their institution of the boycott, were two factors directly responsible for the downfall of the Empire.

The visit of three hundred Bulgarian students to Athens in Easter week, 1911, should have been a warning to Turkey of the danger which attended her policy of goading the Greeks to desperation. I was present on the Acropolis at the memorable reception given by the students of Athens to their guests from the University of Sofia, and remember well the peculiar political significance of the speeches of welcome addressed to them there. Later in the same year, Greece followed the example of the other Balkan States in sending her Crown Prince to Sofia to join in the festivities attendant upon the coming of age of Crown Prince Boris.

Bulgaria was drawn into the Balkan alliance, and reluctantly compelled to abandon the policy of Macedonian autonomy, by the attitude of the Young Turks toward Macedonians. The settlement of immigrants from Bosnia and Herzegovina, and the conscription for the Turkish army, led to reprisals on the part of Bulgarian bands. These were followed by massacres at Ishtib and elsewhere. In the first week of August, 1912, the massacre of Kotchana was for Bulgaria the last straw on the camel's back. I was in Sofia at the end of August when the national congress, called together wholly without the Government's co-operation, declared that war was a necessity. Seated one evening in the public garden at a café—if I remember rightly it was the 1st of September—I heard from the lips of one of the influential delegates at this congress that public opinion in Bulgaria was so wholly determined to force war, that the King and the Cabinet would have to yield.

In Servia and Montenegro, it had long been recognized that any opportunity to unite with Bulgaria and Greece to bring pressure to bear upon Turkey could not but be beneficial to these two kingdoms. There was the *sandjak* of Novi Bazar to be divided between Montenegro and Servia. There was the possibility of an outlet to the Adriatic. So far as Macedonia was concerned, if we believe that she was honest and sincere in the treaty of partition with Bulgaria, Servia was quite content with the idea of a possible annexation of Old Servia, and the opportunity to drive back the Moslem Albanians, who had been established on her frontiers under the

Young Turk *régime*, and were ruthlessly destroying Slavs wherever they got the opportunity.

One does not have any hesitation in declaring that the political leaders in power in the Balkan States at first hoped to avoid a war with Turkey. That they did not succeed in doing so was due to the pressure of public sentiment upon them. This public sentiment forced them to action. Every Balkan Cabinet would have fallen had the ministries remained advocates of peace. Over against the fear of the Turkish army, which (let me say it emphatically) was very strong among the military authorities in each of the Balkan States, was the feeling that the time was very favourable to act, and that chances of success in a common war against Turkey were greater in the autumn of 1912 than they would be later; for the Young Turks were spending tremendous sums of money on army reorganization. At that moment, they were coming to the end of a demoralizing war with Italy, and the Macedonian army had suffered greatly during the summer by the Albanian uprising.

Early in September, Bulgaria, Servia, Greece, and Montenegro decided that peace could be preserved only by the actual application, under sufficient guarantees, of sweeping reforms in Macedonia. They appealed to the Powers to sustain them in demanding for Macedonia a provincial assembly, a militia recruited within the limits of the province, and a Christian Governor. The Great Powers, as usual, tried to carry water on both shoulders. Blind to the fact that inaction and vague promises would no longer keep in check the neighbours of Turkey, they urged the Balkan States to refrain from "being insistent," and pointed out to Turkey the "advisability" of making concessions. The Turks did not believe in the reality of the union of the Balkan States. They could not conceive upon what grounds their neighbours had succeeded in forming an alliance. Neither the Balkan States nor Turkey had any respect for the threats or promises or offers of assistance of the Powers.

In order to convince the Balkan States that they had better think twice before making a direct ultimatum, the Turks organized autumn manoeuvres north of Adrianople, in which fifty thousand of the *élite* army corps were to take part. The answer of the Balkan States was an order for general mobilization issued simultaneously in the four capitals. This was on September 30th. The next day Turkey began to mobilize. All the Greek ships in the Bosphorus and the Dardanelles were seized. Munitions of war, disembarked at Salonika for Servia, were confiscated. It was not until then that it began to dawn upon Turkey and her sponsors, the Great Powers, that the Balkan States meant business. The questions of reforms in Macedonia had been so long the prerogative of the Powers that they did not realize that the moment had come when the little Balkan States, whom they called "troublesome," were no longer going to be put off with promises. The absolute failure of concerted European diplomacy to accomplish anything in the Ottoman Empire was demonstrated from the results in Macedonia, and also in Crete.

So the Balkan States were not in the proper frame of mind to receive the joint note on the *status quo*, which will remain famous in the annals of European diplomacy as a demonstration of the futility of concerted diplomatic action, when there is no genuine unity behind it. On the morning of October 8th, the ministers of Russia and Austria, acting in the name of the six "Great Powers," handed in at Sofia, Athens, Belgrade, and Cettinje, the following note:

"The Russian and Austro-Hungarian Governments declare to the Balkan States:

"1. That the Powers condemn energetically every measure capable of leading to a rupture of peace;

"2. That, supporting themselves on Article 23 of the Treaty of Berlin, they will take in hand, in the interest of the populations, the realization of the reforms in the administration of European Turkey, on the understanding that these reforms will not diminish the sovereignty of His Imperial Majesty the Sultan and the territorial integrity of the Ottoman Empire; this declaration reserves, also, the liberty of the Powers for the collective and ulterior study of the reforms;

"3. That if, in spite of this note, war does break out between the Balkan States and the Ottoman Empire, they will not admit, at the end of the conflict, any modification in the territorial *status quo* in European Turkey.

"The Powers will make collectively to the Sublime Porte the steps which the preceding declaration makes necessary."

The shades of San Stefano, Berlin, Cyprus, and Egypt, Armenian massacres, Mitylene and Mürszteg, Bagdad railway, Bosnia-Herzegovina, Tripoli, and Rhodes, haunted this declaration, and made it impotent, honest effort though it was to preserve the peace of Europe. It was thirty-six years too late.

For, one hour after it was delivered, the *chargé d'affaires* of the Montenegrin legation at Constantinople, evidently as a result of an anticipation of a joint note from the Powers, left at the Sublime Porte the following memorable declaration of war:.

"In conformity with the authorization of King Nicholas, I have the honour of informing you that I shall leave Constantinople to-day. The Government of Montenegro breaks off all relations with the Ottoman

Empire, leaving to the fortunes of arms of the Montenegrins the recognition of their rights and of the rights scorned through centuries of their brothers of the Ottoman Empire.

"I leave Constantinople.

"The royal government will give to the Ottoman representative at Cettinje his passports.

"October 8, 1912. PLAMENATZ."

There could no longer be any doubt of the trend of things. Inevitable result, this declaration of war, of the action of Italy one year before, just as the action of Italy harked back to Russian action in the Caucasus, British action in Egypt, Austrian action in Bosnia-Herzegovina, and French action in Morocco. Inevitable precursor, this declaration of war, of the European catastrophe of 1914. Who, then, is presumptuous enough to maintain that the cause is simple, and the blame all at one door? Europe is reaping in blood-lust what *all* the "Great Powers" have sown in land-lust.

The chancelleries made strenuous efforts to nullify what their inspired organs called the "blunder," or the "hasty and inconsiderate action," of King Nicholas. There was feverish activity in Constantinople, and a continual exchange of conferences between the embassies and the Sublime Porte. The ambassadors gravely handed in a common note, in which they offered to avert war by taking in hand themselves the long-delayed reforms. Had they forgotten the institution of the *gendarmerie* in 1903, and Hussein Hilmi pasha at Salonika?

On this same day, the Montenegrin ex-minister at Constantinople, whose declaration of war had been so theatrical, was reported as having said at Bukarest on his way home, "Montenegro wants territorial aggrandizements, and will not give back whatever conquests she makes. We do not fear to cross the will of the Great Powers, for they do not worry us." These words express exactly the sentiments of the other allies, both as regards their possible conquests and their attitude towards the *dictum* of the Powers.

Events moved rapidly during the next ten days. On October 13th, the Balkan States responded to the Russo-Austrian note, thanking the Powers for their generous offices, but declaring that they had come to the end of their patience in the matter of Turkish promises for Macedonian reform, and were going to request of the Ottoman Government that it accord "without delay the reforms that have been demanded, and that it promise to apply them in six months, with the help of the Great Powers, and of the Balkan States whose interests are involved." This response was not only a refusal of mediation. It was an assertion, as the last words show, that the time had come when the Balkan States felt strong enough to claim a part in the management of their own affairs.

Acting in accordance with this notification to the Powers, on October 14th, Servia, Greece, and Bulgaria demanded of Turkey the autonomy of the European provinces, under Christian governors; the occupation of the provinces by the allied armies while the reforms were being applied; the payment of an indemnity for the expenses of mobilization; the immediate demobilization of Turkey; and the promise that the reforms would be effected within six months. The demand was in the character of an ultimatum, and forty-eight hours were given for a response.

It was now evident that unless the Powers could compel the Balkan States to withdraw this sweeping claim, war would be inevitable. For no independent state could accept such a demand, and retain its self-respect. The representatives of Turkey at Belgrade and Athens were quite right in refusing to receive the note and transmit it to Constantinople.

The Sublime porte did not answer directly the ultimatum of the allies. An effort was made to anticipate the Balkan claims, and get the Powers to intervene, by reviving the law of reform for the *vilayets*, which provided for the organization of communes and schools, the building of roads, and the limitation of military service to the *vilayet* or recruitment. But the fact that this law had been on the statute books since 1880, and had remained throughout the Empire a dead letter, gave little hope that it would be seriously applied now.

On October 15th, fighting began on the Serbo-Turkish frontier. The war had already brought about Turkish reverses at the hands of the Montenegrins. Greece threw an additional defiance in the face of Turkey by admitting the Cretan deputies to the Greek legislative chamber.

To gain time, for she was unprepared, and her mobilization progressing very slowly, Turkey made desperate efforts to delay the declaration of war by offering to treat at Sofia, on the basis of a cessation of Moslem immigration into Macedonia, and the suspension of enrolment of Christians in Moslem regiments. These points, as we have already shown, were the two principal reasons why the Bulgarians of Macedonia had changed their policy from autonomy to independence. But Bulgaria, feeling that cause for hesitation over a war of liberation had been removed by her secret partition treaty with Servia, remained obdurate.

Then the Turkish diplomats turned their attention to Athens, and tried to detach the Greeks from the alliance by agreeing to recognize the annexation of Crete to Greece, and promising an autonomous government for some of the Ægean Islands. This failed. But, to the very last, the Turks believed that Greece might stay out of the war. For this reason her representative at Athens was instructed to do all in his power to remain at his post, even if war were declared by the Sublime Porte on Bulgaria and Servia.

Peace was hurriedly concluded with Italy at Ouchy on October 15th. On the 16th, when the forty-eight hours of the ultimatum had expired, and there was no answer from Turkey, every one expected a declaration of war from the allies. None came. On the 18th, to preserve her dignity, Turkey saw that she must be the one to act. It was no longer possible to wait until the allies were "good and ready"! She declared war on Bulgaria and Servia. Greece waited till afternoon to receive a similar declaration. None came. So Greece declared war on Turkey.

THE FIRST PERIOD OF THE WAR

While the diplomats were still agitating and blustering, while Turkey was procrastinating and trying to put off the evil day, and while the larger Balkan States were quietly completing their mobilization, Montenegro entered into action. On October 9th, the day following her declaration of war, the Montenegrins entered the *sandjak* of Novi Bazar, and surrounded the frontier fortress of Berana. This was captured after six days of fighting. On the same day, Biepolje fell. Nearly one thousand prisoners, fourteen cannon, and a large number of rifles and stores were captured by the Montenegrins. In the meantime, two other Montenegrin columns had marched southward, reached San Giovanni di Medua, at the mouth of the Boyana, and cut Scutari off from the sea. Scutari was invested, but the Montenegrins, who had been able to put into the field scarcely more than thirty thousand men, found themselves mobilized for the entire winter. The great fortress of Tarabosh, a high mountain, towering over the town of Scutari and the lower end of the lake, was too strong for their forces and for their artillery. Inside the city of Scutari, it was the Albanians fighting for their national life, and not the Turks, who organized and maintained the splendid and protracted resistance.

The mobilization in the other Balkan States was not completed until the 18th, when the declaration of war was made on both sides.

Most important of the foes of Turkey were the Bulgarians, whose military organization had for some years been attracting the admiration of all who had been privileged to see their manoeuvres and to visit their casernes. Bulgaria had been carefully and secretly preparing her mobilization long before the crisis became acute. I had the privilege of travelling in Bulgaria during the last two weeks of July, and of spending the month of August along the frontier between Thrace and Bulgaria. Everywhere one could see the accumulation of the soldiers of the standing army already on war footing, and of military stores, at a number of different places. During August and September, every detail of the mobilization had been carefully arranged. When war was declared, Bulgaria had four armies with a total effective of over three hundred thousand. Three of them were quickly massed on the frontier, fully equipped. No army has ever entered the field under better auspices.

On the day of the declaration of war, the Czar Ferdinand issued a proclamation to his troops which clearly defined the issue. It was to be a war of liberation, a crusade, undertaken to free the brothers of blood and faith from the yoke of Moslem oppression. In summing up, the Czar said: "In this struggle of the Cross against the Crescent, of liberty against tyranny, we shall have the sympathy of all those who love justice and progress." At the time, bitter criticism was directed against the Czar for having used words which brought out so sharply the religious issue. The proclamation of a *crusade* could bring forth on the other side the response of a *djehad* (holy war). This, above all things, was what the European Powers wished to avoid; for they feared not only that it would make the war more bitter and more cruel between the opponents in the field, but that it would awaken a wave of fanaticism among the Moslems living under European control in Asia and in Africa. How many lessons will it need to teach Europe that the political menace of Pan-Islamism is a phantom, a myth!

According to the plan adopted by the allied States, the offensive movement in Thrace, in which the bulk of the Turkish army would be met, was to be undertaken solely by Bulgaria. Only a Bulgarian army of secondary importance was to enter eastern Macedonia, to protect the flank of the main Bulgarian army from a sudden eastward march of the Turkish Macedonian army. Its objective point, though not actually agreed upon, was to be Serres.

The rôle of Servia and Greece, who in the general mobilization were expected to put about one hundred and fifty thousand troops each into the field, was to keep in check the Turkish army in Macedonia, and to prevent Albanian reinforcements from reaching the Turkish army in Thrace. In addition to this, Servia and Montenegro were expected to prevent the possible surprise of Austrian interference, while the fleet of Greece would perform the absolutely necessary service of preventing the passage of Turkish forces from Asia Minor to a Macedonian port.

The allies expected a bitter struggle and, in Macedonia and Thrace at least, the successful opposition of a Turkish offensive, rather than the destruction of the Turkish armies.

The mobilization in Turkey was described by many newspaper men who had come to Constantinople for the war in the most glowing terms. The efforts of Mahmud Shevket pasha to prepare the Turkish army for war were declared to be bearing splendid fruits in the first days of the mobilization. Wholly inaccurate accounts were written of the wonderful enthusiasm of the Turkish people for the war. Naturally, what even the residents of Constantinople saw at the beginning was the best foot front. We knew that tremendous sums had been expended for four years in bringing the army up to a footing of efficiency. We had seen with our own eyes the brilliant manoeuvres on the anniversary of the Sultan's accession in May, and on the anniversary of the Constitution in July. The work accomplished by the German mission had cast its spell over us. We saw what we were expecting to see during the first days of the mobilization. The "snap judgments" of special correspondents have little value, other than freshness and *naïveté*, except to readers even less informed than they are. But the East is a sphinx even to those who live there. After you have figured out, from what you call your "experience," what *ought* to happen, the chances are even that just the opposite comes true. In spite of the misgivings which had been awakened by a trip into the interior of Asia Minor, as far as Konia, during the third week of September, I believed that the Turkish army was going to give a good account of itself against the Bulgarians, whose spirit and whose organization I had had opportunity to see and admire during that very summer.

Every one was mistaken. There were large bodies of splendidly trained and well-equipped troops in Thrace. Spick and span regiments did come over from garrison towns in Asia. We saw them fill the trains at Stambul and at San Stefano. But we over-estimated their number. The truth of the matter is that the *trained* and *well-equipped* forces of the Thracian army, officered by capable men, did not amount to more than eighty thousand. In retrospect, after going over carefully the position of the forces which met the Bulgarians, I feel that these figures can be pretty accurately established. But even these eighty thousand soldiers of the *nizam* (active army) could have done wonders in the Thracian campaign, if they had been allowed to go ahead to meet the Bulgarians, and to form the first line of battle. But this was not done.

There are three time-honoured principles that cannot afford to be neglected at the beginning of a campaign. The army used for *initial* offensive action against the enemy should be composed *wholly* of soldiers in active service. The army should be concentrated to meet the attack, or to attack one opposing army first, leaving the others until later. Armies must be kept mobile, and not allow themselves to be trapped in fortresses. The fortresses in the portions of territory which may have to be abandoned temporarily to the invasion of the enemy may easily be overstocked with defenders, but never with provisions and munitions of war. In spite of the instructions of von der Goltz pasha, the Turks showed no regard for the first two, at least, of these elementary principles. The mobile army in Macedonia, outside of the fortresses, was not recalled to Thrace, and *redifs* (reservists) were mixed with *nizams* (actives) in the first line of battle. The neglect of these principles was the direct cause of the Turkish disasters.

After the *nizams*, most of whom were already in Thrace, came the *redifs* from Asia Minor. They arrived at Constantinople and at San Stefano in huge numbers, and without equipment. I saw many of them with their feet bound in rags. There were no tents over them or other shelter; there was no proper field equipment for them, and, even while they were patiently waiting for days to be forwarded to the front, they lacked (within sight of the minarets of Stambul!) bread to eat, shoes for their feet, and blankets to cover them at night. More than that, among them were many thousands who did not know how to use the rifles that were given to them, and who had not even a rudimentary military education. In defensive warfare, as they proved at Adrianople and at Tchatalja, they could fight like lions. But for an offensive movement in the field the great majority of the *redifs* were worse than useless.

The Turks were absolutely sure of victory. The press of the capital, on the day that war was declared, stated that the army of Thrace was composed of four hundred thousand soldiers, and that it was the intention to march direct to Sofia. Turkish officers of my acquaintance told me that they were all taking their dress uniforms in their baggage for this triumphal entry into Sofia, and that the invasion of Bulgaria would commence immediately.

On the 19th of October, the Bulgarian army appeared in force at Mustafa Pasha, the first railway station after passing the Turkish frontier on the line from Sofia to Constantinople, and about eighteen miles north-west of Adrianople. It was the announced intention of the Bulgarians to attack immediately the fortress of Adrianople, whose cannon commanded the sole railway line from Bulgaria into Thrace. Two of the Bulgarian armies were directed upon Adrianople, and the third army under General Dimitrieff received similar orders. In Bulgaria, as well as in Turkey, every one expected to see an attack upon Adrianople. Had not General Savoff declared openly that he would sacrifice fifty thousand men, if necessary, as the Japanese had done at Fort Arthur, in order to capture Adrianople?

A strict censorship was established in Bulgaria. No one, native or foreigner, who by chance saw just what the armies were doing, could have any hope of sending out the information. Postal and telegraphic communications were in the hands of the military authorities. No one, who happened to be in the region in which the troops were moving forward, was allowed to leave by train, automobile, bicycle, or even on foot. Never in history has the world been so completely in the dark as to the operations of the army. But the attacks of the outposts of Adrianople, and the commencement of the bombardment of the forts, seemed to indicate the common objective of the three Bulgarian armies. Adrianople had the reputation of being one of the strongest fortresses in the world. This reputation was well justified.

Some miles to the east of Adrianople, guarding the mountains of the south-eastern frontier of Bulgaria, was Kirk Kilissé, which was also supposed to be an impregnable position. Here the Ottoman military authorities had placed stores to form the base of supplies for the offensive military operation against Bulgaria. Shortly before the war, a branch railway from the sole line between Constantinople and Adrianople, going north from Lulé Burgas, was completed. It furnished direct means of communication between the capital and Kirk Kilissé.

The General Staff at Constantinople wisely decided to leave in Adrianople only a sufficient garrison to defend the forts and the city. It was their intention to send the bulk of their Thracian army north-west from Kirk Kilissé, using that fortress as a base, in order to cut off the Bulgarians from their supplies, and throw them back against the forts of Adrianople. In this way they intended to put the Bulgarians between two fires and crush them. Then they would commence the invasion of Bulgaria. The plan was excellent. If Turkey had actually had in the field a half million men well trained and well equipped, well officered and with a spirit of enthusiasm, and—most important of all—properly fed, it is probable that the Bulgarians could have been held in check. But this army did not exist. The millions spent for equipment had disappeared—who knows where? There were not enough horses, even with the requisitions in Constantinople, for the artillery, and for the cavalry reserves. That meant that there were no horses at all for the commissary department. The only means of communication with the front was a single railway track. Roads had never been made in Thrace since the conquest. The artillery and the waggons had to be drawn through deep mud.

Beyond the needs of the *nizam* (active) regiments, there were hardly any officers. The wretched masses of *redifs* (reservists) were without proper leadership. Not only was this all important factor for keeping up the *morale* of the soldiers lacking, but, from the moment they left Constantinople— even before that—there was insufficient food. Nor did the soldiers know why they were fighting. There was no enthusiasm for a cause. The great mass of the civil population, if not, like the Christians, hostile to the army, was wholly indifferent. I do not believe there were ten thousand people in the city of Constantinople, who really cared what happened in Thrace. Since I have been in the midst of a mobilization in France, and have seen how the French soldiers are equipped for war and fed, and how they have been made to feel that every man, woman, and child in the nation was ready to make any sacrifice—no matter how great—for "the little soldiers of France," I feel more deeply the tragedy of the Turkish *redifs*. My wonder is that they were able to fight as bravely as they did. The world has no use for the government—for the "system"—which caused them to suffer as they did, and to give their lives in a wholly useless sacrifice.

The story of the Thracian campaign I heard from the lips of many of those who had taken part in it, when the events were still fresh in their memory. It is fruitless to go into all the details, to discuss the strategy of the generals in command, and to give a technical description of the battles, and of the retreat. Turkish and Bulgarian officers, as well as a host of foreign correspondents, have published books on this campaign. Most of them hide the real causes of the defeat under a mass of unimportant detail, and seem to be written either to emphasize the writer's claim as a "first-hand" witness, to take to task certain generals, or to prove the superiority of French artillery, and the faultiness of German military instruction. When all these issues are cast to one side, the campaign can be briefly described.

We have already anticipated the *débâcle* of the military power of Turkey by giving the causes. This is not illogical. For these causes existed, and led to the inevitable result, before the first gun was fired.

On October 19th, the Bulgarians began the investment of Adrianople from the north and west. There was no serious opposition. The Turkish garrison naturally fell back to the protection of the forts, for the Turks had not planned to oppose, beyond Adrianople, the Bulgarian approach. The Ottoman advance-guard, composed of the corps of Constantinople and Rodosto, under the command of Abdullah and Mahmud Mukhtar pashas, was ordered to take the offensive north of Kirk Kilissé. They were to be followed by another army. This movement was intended to cut off the Bulgarians from their base of supplies, and throw them back on Adrianople. The remainder of the Turkish forces in Thrace were to wait the result of this movement. If the Bulgarians moved down the valley of the Maritza, leaving Adrianople, they would meet these imposing forces which covered Constantinople, and would have behind them the garrison of Adrianople, and the army of Abdullah and Mahmud Mukhtar threatening their communications. If they besieged Adrianople, the second army would take the offensive and the Bulgarians would be encircled.

The outposts of the Turkish army came into contact with the Bulgarians on October 20th. Believing that they had to do with the left of the army investing Adrianople, Mahmud and Abdullah decided to begin immediately their encircling movement. On the 21st and 22d, the two columns of the Turkish army were in fact engaged with the advance-guards of the first and second Bulgarian armies. But, in the meantime, General Dimitrieff and the third army (which they believed was on the extreme Bulgarian right, pressing down the Maritza to invest the southern forts of Adrianople) had quietly crossed the frontier almost directly north of Kirk Kilissé, and fell like a cyclone upon the Turks. The Turkish positions were excellent, and had to be taken at the point of the bayonet. From morning till night on October 23d, the Bulgarian third army captured position after position, without the help of their artillery, which was stuck in the mud some miles in the rear. In the evening, during a terrible storm, two fresh Bulgarian columns made an assault upon the Turkish positions. It was not until then that the Turks realized that they were fighting another army than that charged with the investment of Adrianople. A wild panic broke out among the *redifs*, who were mostly without officers. They started to retreat, and were soon followed by the remainder of the army. At Uskubdere, they met during the night reinforcements coming to their aid. Two regiments fired on each other, mutually mistaking the other for Bulgarians. The reinforcements joined in the disorderly retreat, which did not end until morning, when, exhausted and still crazed by fear, what remained of the Turkish army had reached Eski Baba and Bunar Hissar.

The army was saved from annihilation by the darkness and the storm. For not only were the Bulgarians ignorant of the abandonment of Kirk Kilissé, but, along the line where they knew the enemy were retreating, their cavalry could not advance in the darkness and mud, nor could their artillery shell the retreating columns. On the morning of the 24th, when General Dimitrieff was preparing to make the assault upon Kirk Kilissé, he learned that the Turkish army had fled, and that the fortress was undefended.

By the capture of Kirk Kilissé the Bulgarians gained enormous stores. They had a railway line open to them towards Constantinople. The only menace to a successful investment of Adrianople was removed. The victory, so easily purchased, was far beyond their dreams. But it would not have been possible had it not been for the willingness of the Bulgarian soldiers to charge without tiring or faltering at the point of the bayonet. The victory was earned, in spite of the Turkish panic. For the Bulgarian steel had much to do with that panic.

As soon as he realized the extent of the victory of Kirk Kilissé, General Savoff ordered a general advance of the three Bulgarian armies. Only enough troops were left around Adrianople to prevent a sortie of the garrison. Notwithstanding the unfavourable condition of the roads, the Bulgarian armies moved with great rapidity. The cavalry in two days made reconnaissances on the east as far as Midia, and on the south as far as Rodosto. The main—and sole—armies of the Turks were thus ascertained to be along the Ergene, and beyond in the direction of the capital. On the left, the third army of General Dimitrieff, not delaying at Kirk Kilissé, was in contact with the Turks at Eski Baba on the 28th. On the afternoon of the same day the Bulgarians drove the Turks out of the village of Lulé Burgas, on the railway to Constantinople, east of the point where the Dedeagatch-Salonika line branches off.

For three days, October 29-31, the Turkish armies made a stand along the Ergene from Bunar Hissar to Lulé Burgas. Since Gettysburg, Sadowa, and Sedan, no battle except that of Mukden has approached the battle of Lulé Burgas in importance, not only because of the numbers engaged, but also of the issue at stake. Three hundred and fifty thousand soldiers were in action, the forces being about evenly divided. For two days, in spite of the demonstration of Kirk Kilissé, the Turks fought with splendid courage and tenacity. Time and again the desperate charges of the Bulgarian infantry were hurled back with heavy loss. Not until the third day did the fighting seem to lean decisively to the advantage of the Bulgarians. Their artillery began to show marked superiority. From many points shells began to fall with deadly effect into the Turkish entrenchments. The Turks were unable to silence the murderous fire of the Bulgarian batteries. The soldiers, *because they were starving*, did not have it in them to attempt to take the most troublesome Bulgarian positions by assault.

The retreat began on the afternoon of the 31st. On November 1st, owing to lack of officers and of central direction, it became a disorderly flight, a *sauve qui peut*. Camp equipment was abandoned. The soldiers threw away their knapsacks and rifles, so that they could run more quickly. The artillery-men cut the traces of their gun-wagons and ammunition-wagons, and made off on horseback. Everything was abandoned to the enemy. Nazim pasha, generalissimo, and the general staff, who had been in headquarters at Tchorlu, without proper telegraphic or telephonic communication with the battle front, were drawn into the flight. The Turkish army did not stop until it had placed itself behind the Tchatalja line of forts, which protected the city of Constantinople.

The battle of Lulé Burgas marked more than the destruction of the Turkish military power and the loss of European Turkey to the Empire. It revealed the inefficiency of Turkish organization and administration to cope with modern conditions, even when in possession of modern instruction and modern tools. With the Turks, it is not a question of an ignorance or a backwardness which can be remedied. Total lack of organizing and administrative ability is a fault of their nature. Courage alone does not win battles in the twentieth century.

The Bulgarians were without sufficient cavalry and mounted machine-guns to follow up their victory. The defeat of the Turks, too, had not been gained without the expenditure of every ounce of energy in the army that had in those three days won undying fame. The problem of pursuit was difficult. There was only a single railway track. Food and munitions for the large army had to be brought up. The artillery advanced painfully through roads hub-deep in mud. It took two weeks for the Bulgarian army to move from the Ergene to Tchatalja, and prepare for the assault of the last line of Turkish defence.

An immediate offensive after Lulé Burgas would have found Constantinople at the mercy of the victorious army. The two weeks of respite changed the aspect of things. For in this time the forts across the peninsula from the Sea of Marmora to the Black Sea were hastily repaired. They were mounted with guns from the Bosphorus defences, the Servian Creusots detained at Salonika at the beginning of the war, and whatever artillery could be brought from Asia Minor. The army had been reformed, the worthless, untrained elements ruthlessly weeded out, and a hundred thousand of the best soldiers, among whom the only *redifs* were those who had come fresh from Asia Minor, and had not been contaminated by the demoralization of Kirk Kilissé and Lulé Burgas, were placed behind the forts. The Turkish cruisers whose guns were able to be fired were recalled from the Dardanelles, and anchored off the end of the line on either side.

On November 15th, the Bulgarians began to put their artillery in position all along the Tchatalja line from Buyuk-Tchekmedje on the Sea of Marmora to Derkos Lake, near the Black Sea. At the same time, they entrenched the artillery positions by earthworks and ditches, working with incredible rapidity. For they had to take every precaution against a sudden sortie of the enemy. In forty-eight hours they were ready.

The attack on the Tchatalja lines commenced at six o'clock on Sunday morning, November 17th, by machine-gun and rifle fire as well as by artillery. The forts and the Turkish cruisers responded. In the city and in the villages along the Bosphorus we could hear the firing distinctly. On the 17th and 18th, the Bulgarians delivered assaults in several places. Near Derkos they even got through the lines for a short while. These were merely for the purpose of testing the Turkish positions, however. Several of the assaults were repulsed. The Bulgarians suffered heavily on the 18th, when the first and only prisoners of the war were made. On the 19th, the artillery fire grew less and less, and there were no further attacks. Towards evening it was evident that the Bulgarians had abandoned their advanced lines, and did not intend to continue the attack. No general assault had been delivered.

It seems certain that General Savoff had in mind the capture of Constantinople on November 17th. Turkish overtures for peace, opened on the 15th, had been repulsed. Every preparation was made for the attempt to pierce Tchatalja. Why was the plan abandoned before it was actually proven impossible? Did General Savoff fear the risk of a reverse? Was he short of ammunition? Had the Turkish defence of the 17th and 18th been more determined than he had expected? Was it fear of a cholera epidemic among his soldiers? Or was the abandonment of the attempt to capture Constantinople for that is what a triumph at Tchatalja would have meant, dictated by political reasons?

Perhaps there was a shortage of ammunition. But it is impossible to believe that General Savoff ceased the attack because he feared a failure, or because he paused before the heavy sacrifice of life it would involve. The Bulgarians were too fresh from their sudden and overwhelming victories to be halted by the unimportant fighting of the 17th and 18th. They were not yet aware of the terrible danger from cholera.

At the time it was the common belief in Constantinople—I heard it expressed in a number of intelligent circles—that the Great Powers—in particular Russia—had informed Bulgaria that she should halt where she was. A second San Stefano! This seems improbable. Even in the moment of delirium over Lulé Burgas, the Bulgarians had no thought of occupying permanently Constantinople. They knew that this would be a task beyond their ability as a nation to undertake. If there was a thought of entering Constantinople, it was to satisfy military pride, and to be able to dictate more expeditiously and satisfactorily terms of peace.

The real reason for the halt of Tchatalja, and the willingness to conclude an armistice, must be found in the alarm awakened in Bulgaria by the Servian and Greek successes. Greece had settled herself in Salonika, and the King and royal family had come there to live. Is it merely a coincidence that *on November 18th* the Servians captured Monastir, *foyer* of Bulgarianism in western Macedonia, and *on the following day*, a telegram from Sofia caused the cessation of the Bulgarian attack upon Tchatalja?

At Adrianople, a combined Bulgarian and Servian army, under the command of General Ivanoff, which had been hampered during the first month of operations by the floods of the Maritza, and by daring sorties of the garrison, after receiving experienced reinforcements on November 22d, began a determined bombardment and narrow investment of the forts. Ten days later, a general attack was ordered, probably to hurry the Turks in the armistice negotiations. The investing army had made very little progress on December 2d and 3d, when the signing of the armistice caused a cessation of hostilities.

But while the Bulgarians were vigorously pressing the attack upon Adrianople, they were inactive at Tchatalja.

At the beginning of the Thracian campaign, a portion of the Turkish fleet started to attack the Bulgarian coast. The Bulgarians had only one small cruiser and six torpedo-boats of doubtful value. But their two ports, termini of railway lines, were well protected by forts. On October 19th, two Turkish battleships and four torpedo-boats appeared before Varna, and fired without effect upon the forts. Then they bombarded the small open port of Kavarna, near the Rumanian frontier. On the 21st, they succeeded in throwing a few shells into Varna, but did not risk approaching near enough to do serious damage. This was the extent of the offensive naval action against Bulgaria. A short time later, the *Hamidieh*, which was stationed on the Thracian coast of the Black Sea to protect the landing of *redifs* from Samsun, was surprised in the night by Bulgarian torpedo-boats. Two torpedoes tore holes in her bow. She was able to return to Constantinople under her own steam, but had to spend ten weeks in dry-dock. The only service rendered by the Turkish fleet against the Bulgarians was the safeguarding of the transport of troops from Black Sea ports of Asiatic Turkey, and the co-operation at the ends of the Tchatalja lines during the Bulgarian assaults of November 17th and 18th.

The Servian campaign was a good second to the astounding successes of the Bulgarians in Thrace. The third army entered the *sandjak* of Novi Bazar, so long coveted by Servia, and expelled the Turks in five days. A portion of this army next occupied Prisrend and Diakova, descended the valley of the Drin through the heart of northern Albania to Alessio, where it joined on November 19th the Montenegrins, who were already at San Giovanni di Medua. On the 28th, they occupied Durazzo. The Servians had reached the Adriatic!

While the third army was in the *sandjak* of Novi Bazar, the second Servian army crossed into Old Servia, passed through the plain of Kossova, where the Turks had destroyed the independence of Servia in 1389, and occupied Pristina on October 23d. This gave them control of the branch railway from Uskub to the confines of the *sandjak*.

The flower of the Servian fighting strength was reserved for the first army under the command of Crown Prince Alexander. This force, considerably larger than the two other armies combined, mustered over seventy thousand. Its objective point was Uskub, covering which was the strong Turkish army of Zekki pasha. Battle was joined outside of Kumanova on October 22d. After three days of fighting, during which the Turkish cavalry was annihilated by the Servian artillery and the Servian infantry took the Turkish artillery positions at the point of the bayonet, the army of Zekki Pasha evacuated Kumanova. No attempt was made to defend Uskub, which the Servians entered on October 26th. The Turkish army retreated to Küprülü on the Vardar, towards Salonika. When the Servians continued their march, Zekki pasha retreated to Prilip, where he occupied positions that could not well be shelled by artillery. After two days of continuous fighting, the Servians' bayonets dislodged the Turks. They withdrew to Monastir with the Servians hot upon their heels.

Together with Kumanova, in which the bulk of Prince Alexander's forces did not find it necessary to engage, the capture of Monastir is the most brilliant feat of an army whose intrepidity, agility, and intelligence deserve highest praise. Into Monastir had been thrown the army of Tahsin pasha, pushed northward by the Greeks, as well as that of Zekki pasha, harried southward by the Servians. The Servians did not hesitate to approach the defences of the city on one side up to their arm-pits in water, while on the other side they scaled the heights dominating Monastir—heights which ought to have been defended for weeks without great difficulty. The Turks were compelled to withdraw, for they were at the mercy of the Servian artillery. They tried to retreat to Okrida, but the Servian left wing anticipated this movement. Only ten thousand escaped into Epirus. Nearly forty thousand Turks surrendered to the Servians on November 18th. Monastir and Okrida were captured. The Turkish armies of Macedonia had ceased to exist.

The Greeks were eager to wipe out the shame of the war of 1897. Fifteen years had wrought a great difference in the *morale* of the Greek army. A new body of officers, who spent their time in learning their profession instead of in discussing politics at *café terrasses*, had been created. The French military mission, under General Eydoux, had been working for several years in the complete reorganization of the Greek army. I had the privilege at Athens of enjoying the hospitality of Greek officers in their casernes at several successive Easter festivals. Each year one could notice the progress. They were always ready to show you how the transformation of their artillery, and its equipment for mountain service as well as for field work, would make all the difference in the world in the "approaching" war with the Turks. The results were beyond expectations. What the Greeks had been working for was mobility. This they demonstrated that they had learned. They had also an *esprit de corps* which, in fighting, made up for what they lacked of Slavic dogged perseverance. Neither in actual combat, nor in strategy, with the exception of Janina, were the Greeks put to the test, or called upon to bear the burden, of the Bulgarians and Servians. But, especially when we take into consideration the invaluable service of their fleet, there is no reason to belittle their part in the downfall of Turkey. If the effort had been necessary, they probably would have been equal to it.

The Greeks sent a small army into Epirus. The bulk of their forces, following a sound military principle, were led into Thessaly by the Crown Prince Constantine. They crossed the frontier without resistance, fought a sharp combat at Elassona on the 19th, in which they stood admirably under fire, and broke down the last Turkish resistance at Servia. The army of Tahsin pasha was thrown back upon Monastir. The battles of the next ten days were hardly more than skirmishes, for the Turkish stand was never formidable. At Yanitza, the only real battle of the Greek campaign was fought. The Turks fled. The way to Salonika was open.

The battle of Yanitza (Yenidje-Vardar) was fought on November 3d. On October 30th, a Greek torpedo-boat had succeeded, in spite of the strong harbour fortifications, equipped with electric searchlights, and the mined channel, in coming right up to the jetty at Salonika during the night, and launching three torpedoes at an old Turkish cruiser which lay at anchor there. The cruiser sank. On his way out to open sea, the commander of the torpedo-boat did not hesitate to fire upon the forts!

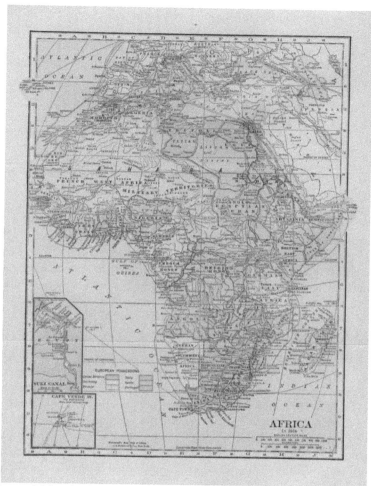

Map—Africa in 1914

This daring feat, and the approach of the Greek army, threw the city into a turmoil of excitement. The people had been fed for two weeks on false news, and telegrams had been printed from day to day, relating wonderful victories over the Servians, Bulgarians, and Greeks. But the coming of the refugees, fresh thousands from nearer places every day, and the presence in the streets of the city of deserters in uniform, gave the lie to the "official" news. When the German *stationnaire* arrived from Constantinople, and embarked the prisoner of the Villa Allatini, ex-Sultan Abdul Hamid, the most pessimistic suspicions were confirmed.

Although he had thirty thousand soldiers, and plenty of munitions, Tahsin pasha, commandant of Salonika, did not even attempt to defend the city. He began immediately to negotiate with the advancing Greek army. When the Crown Prince refused to accept any other than unconditional surrender, and moved upon the city, Tahsin pasha yielded. Not a shot was fired. On November 9th, without any opposition, the Greek army marched into Salonika.

In other places the Turks at least fought, even if they did not fight well. At Salonika their surrender demonstrated to what humiliation and degradation the arrogance of the Young Turks had brought a nation whose past was filled with glorious deeds of arms.

The Bulgarian expeditionary corps for Macedonia, under General Theodoroff, had crossed the frontier on October 18th. Joined to it were the notorious bands of *comitadjis* under the command of Sandansky, who afterwards related to me the story of this march. General Theodoroff's mission was to engage the portion of the Turkish Fifth Army Corps, which was stationed in the valleys of the Mesta and Struma, east of the Vardar, thus preventing it from assembling and making a flank movement against the main Servian or Bulgarian armies. The Bulgarians were greeted everywhere as liberators, and, although they were not in great numbers, the Turks did not try to oppose them. Soldiers and Moslem Macedonians together fled before them towards Salonika.

When General Theodoroff realized the demoralization of the Turks, and heard how the Greeks were approaching Salonika without any more serious opposition than that which confronted him, he hurried his column towards Salonika. The Bulgarian Princes Boris and Cyril joined him. They were not in time to take part in the negotiations for the surrender of the city. The cowardice of Tahsin pasha had brought matters to a climax on November 9th. But they were able to enter Salonika on the 10th, at the same time that Crown Prince Constantine was making his triumphal entry. Sandansky and his *comitadjis* hurried to the principal ancient church of the city, for over four hundred years the Saint Sophia of Salonika, and placed the Bulgarian flag in the minarets before the Greeks knew they had been outwitted. On the 12th, King George of Greece arrived to make his residence in the city that was to be his tomb.

After the capture of Monastir, the Servians pressed on to Okrida, on November 23d, and from there into Albania to Elbassan, which they reached five days later. It was their intention to join at Durazzo the other column of the third Servian army, of whose march down the Drin we have already spoken. But the threatening attitude of Austria-Hungary necessitated the recall of the bulk of the Servian forces to Nish. This is the reason they were not able, at that stage of the war, to give the Montenegrins effective assistance against Scutari.

The left wing of the Thessalian Greek army, after the capture of Monastir by the Servians, pursued towards Albania, the Turks who had escaped from Monastir. With great skill, they managed to prevent the Turks from turning north-west into the interior of Albania. After the brilliant and daring storming of the heights of Tchangan, what remained of the Turkish army was compelled to retreat into Epirus towards Janina.

On October 20th, the Greek fleet under Admiral Koundouriotis appeared at the Dardanelles to offer battle to the Turks. Under the cover of the protection of their fleet, the Greeks occupied Lemnos, Thasos, Imbros, Samothrace, Nikaria, and the smaller islands. The inhabitants of Samos had expelled the Turkish garrisons on their own initiative at the outbreak of the war. Mitylene was captured without great difficulty on November 21st. The Greeks landed at Chios on the 24th. Here the Turkish garrison of two thousand retired to the mountainous centre of the island, and succeeded in prolonging their resistance until January. When he saw that no help was coming from Asia Minor, whose shores had been in sight during all the weeks of combat and suffering, the heroic Turkish commander surrendered with one thousand eight hundred starving men on January 3d. It was only because Italy, by a clause of the Treaty of Ouchy, still held the Dodecanese, that all of the Ægean Islands were not "gathered into the fold" by Greece.

There had been less than six weeks of fighting. The Balkan allies had swept from the field all the Turkish forces in Europe. The Turkish armies were bottled up in Constantinople, Adrianople, Janma, and Scutari, with absolutely no hope of making successful sorties. Except at Constantinople, they were besieged, and could expect neither reinforcements nor food supplies. The Greek fleet was master of the Ægean Sea, and held the Turkish navy blocked in the Dardanelles. No new armies could come from Asiatic Turkey. This was the situation when the armistice was signed. The Ottoman Empire in Europe had ceased to exist. The military prestige of Turkey had received a mortal blow.

THE ARMISTICE AND THE FIRST CONFERENCE OF LONDON

The hopelessness of the outcome of the war with Italy, the dissatisfaction over the foolish and arbitrary rule of its secret committees had weakened the hold of the "Committee of Union and Progress" over the army. Despite its success in the spring elections of 1912, its position was precarious. In July, Mahmud Shevket pasha, who was suspected of planning a military *pronunciamento*, resigned the Ministry of War. The Grand Vizier, Saïd pasha, soon followed him into retirement. The Sultan declared that a ministry not under the control of a political party was a necessity.

Ghazi Mukhtar pasha, after much difficulty, succeeded in forming a ministry, in which a distinguished Armenian, Noradounghian effendi, was given the portfolio of Foreign Affairs. The Unionist majority in the lower house of Parliament proved intractable. Its obstructionist tactics won for the Chamber of Deputies the name of the "comic operahouse of Fundukli." (Fundukli was the Bosphorus quarter in which the House of Parliament was located.) With the help of the Senate, and the moral support of the army, the Sultan dissolved Parliament on August 5th. Only the menace of the Albanian revolution prevented the Committee from attempting to set up a rival Parliament at Salonika. This was the unenviable internal situation of Turkey at the opening of the Balkan War.

The disasters of the Thracian campaign led to the resignation of the Ghazi Mukhtar pasha Cabinet. The aged statesman of the old *régime*, Kiamil pasha, was called for the eighth time to the Grand Vizirate. He retained Nazim pasha, generalissimo of the Turkish army, and Noradounghian effendi, in the Ministries of War and Foreign Affairs. The most influential of the Young Turks, who had opposed bitterly the peace with Italy and were equally determined that no negotiations should be undertaken with the Balkan States, were exiled. Kiamil pasha saw clearly that peace was absolutely necessary. His long experience allowed him to have no illusions as to the possibility of continuing the struggle. Before the Bulgarian attack upon Tchatalja, he began *pourparlers* with General Savoff. After the repulse of November 17th and 18th, he was just as firm in his decision that the negotiations must be continued. He won over to his point of view the members of the Cabinet, and notably Nazim pasha.

The conditions of the armistice, signed on December 3d, were an acknowledgment of the complete *débâcle* of the Turkish army. Bulgaria forced the stipulation that her army in front of Tchatalja should be revictualled by the railway which passed under the guns of Adrianople, while that fortress remained without food! Greece, by an agreement with her allies, refused to sign the armistice, but was allowed to be represented in the peace conference. The allies felt that the state of war on sea must continue, in order that Turkey should be prevented during the armistice from bringing to the front her army corps from Syria and Mesopotamia and Arabia; while Greece, in particular, was determined to run no risk in connection with the Ægean Islands. The peace delegates were to meet in London.

Orientals, Christian as well as Moslem, are famous for bargaining. Nothing can be accomplished without an exchange of proposals and counter-proposals *ad infinitum*. In the Conference of London, the demands of the allies were the cession of all European Turkey, except Albania, whose boundaries were not defined, of Crete, and of the islands in the

Ægean Sea. A war indemnity was also demanded. Turkey was to be allowed to retain Constantinople, and a strip of territory from Midia on the Black Sea to Rodosto on the Sea of Marmora, and the peninsula of the Thracian Chersonese, which formed the European shore of the Dardanelles. The boundaries of Albania, and its future status, were to be decided by the Powers.

I had a long conversation with the Grand Vizier, Kiamil pasha, on the day the peace delegates left for London. He was frank and unhesitating in the statement of his belief that Turkey could not continue the war. He denounced unsparingly the visionaries who were clamouring for a continuance of the struggle. "It is because of them that we are in our present humiliating position," he said. "They cry out now that we must not accept peace, but they know well that we cannot hope to win back any portion of what we have lost."

There were a number of reasons why the position of Kiamil pasha was sound. First of all, the army organization was in hopeless confusion. Although the Bulgarians were checked at Tchatalja, the conditions on the Constantinople side of the forts was terrible. The general headquarters at Hademkeuy were buried in filth and mud. Although the army was but twenty-five miles from the city, there were days on end when not even bread arrived. Cholera was making great ravages. Soldiers, crazed from hunger, were shot dead for disobeying the order which forbade their eating raw vegetables. There were neither fuel, shelter, nor blankets. Winter was at hand. At San Stefano, one of the most beautiful suburbs of Stambul, in a concentration camp the soldiers died by the thousands of starvation fever. It was one of the most heart-rending tragedies of history.

All the while, in the cafés of Péra, Galata, and Stambul, Turkish officers sat the day long, sipping their coffee, and deciding that Adrianople must not be given up. Even while the fighting was going on, when the fate of the city hung in the balance, I saw these degenerate officers *by the hundreds*, feasting at Péra, while their soldiers were dying like dogs at Tchatalja and San Stefano. This is an awful statement to make, but it is the record of fact. Notices in the newspapers, declaring that officers found in Constantinople without permission would be immediately taken before the Court-Martial, had absolutely no effect.

The navy failed to give any account of itself to the Greeks, who were waiting outside of the Dardanelles. Finally, on December 16th, after the people of the vicinity had openly cursed and taunted them, the fleet sailed out to fight. An action at long range did little damage to either side. The Turkish vessels refused to go beyond the protection of their forts. They returned in the evening to anchor. The mastery of the sea remained to the Greeks.[1]

[1] In this connection, it would be forgetting to pay tribute to a remarkable exploit to omit mention of the raid of the *Hamidieh* during the late winter. One Ottoman officer at least chafed under the disgrace of the inaction of the Ottoman navy. With daring and skill, Captain Reouf bey slipped out into the Ægean Sea on the American-built cruiser, the *Hamidieh*. He evaded the Greek blockaders, bombarded some outposts on one of the islands, and sank the auxiliary cruiser, the *Makedonia*, in a Greek port. The *Hamidieh* next appeared in the Adriatic, where she sank several transports, and bombarded Greek positions on the coast of Albania. The cruiser was next heard of at Port Said. She passed through the Suez Canal into the Red Sea for a couple of weeks, and then returned boldly into the Mediterranean, although Greek torpedo-boats were lying in wait. Captain Reouf bey ran again the gauntlet of the Greek fleet, and got back to the Dardanelles without mishap. This venture, undertaken without permission from the Turkish admiral, had no effect upon the war. For it came too late. But it showed what a little enterprise and courage might have done to prevent the Turkish débâcle, if undertaken at the beginning of the war.

If the army and the navy were powerless, how about the people of the capital? From the very beginning of the war, the inhabitants of Constantinople, Moslem as well as Christian, displayed the most complete indifference concerning the fortunes of the battles. Even when the Bulgarians were attacking Tchatalja, the city took little interest. Buying and selling went on as usual. There were few volunteers for national defence, but the cafés were crowded and the theatres and dance-halls of Péra were going at full swing. The refugees came and camped in our streets and in the cemeteries outside of the walls. Those who did not die passed on to Asia. The wounded arrived, and crowded our hospitals and barracks. The cholera came. The soldiers starved to death at San Stefano. The spirit of Byzantium was over the city still. The year 1913 began as 1453 had begun.

The Government tried to raise money by a national loan. It could get none from Europe, unless it agreed to surrender Adrianople and make peace practically on the terms of the allies. An appeal must be made to the Osmanlis. For how could the war be resumed without money? There are many wealthy pashas at Constantinople. Their palaces line both shores of the Bosphorus. They spend money at Monte Carlo like water. They live at Nice, as they live at Constantinople, like princes—or like American millionaires! One of the sanest and wisest of Turkish patriots, a man whom I have known and admired, was appointed to head a committee to wait upon these pashas, many of them married to princesses of the imperial family, and solicit their contributions. The scheme was that the subscribers should advance five years of taxes on their properties for the purposes of national defence. The committee hired a small launch, and spent a day visiting the homes of the pashas. On their return, after paying the rental of the launch, they had about forty pounds sterling! Was it not two million pounds that was raised for the Prince of Wales Fund recently in London? Was not the French loan "for national defence," issued just before the present war, subscribed in a few hours *forty-three times* over the large amount of thirty-two million pounds asked for?

In the face of these facts, the Young Turks were vociferous in their demand that the war be continued. Adrianople must not be surrendered! Kiamil pasha decided to call a "Divan," or National Assembly, of the most important men in Turkey. They were summoned by the Sultan to meet at the palace of Dolma-Baghtche on January 22, 1913. I went to see what would happen there. One would expect that the whole of Constantinople would be hanging on the words of this council, whose decision the Cabinet had agreed to accept. A half-dozen policemen at the palace gate, a vendor of lemonade, two street-sweepers, an Italian cinematograph photographer, and a dozen foreign newspaper men—that was the extent of the crowd.

The Divan, after hearing the *exposés* of the Ministers of War, Finance, and Foreign Affairs, decided that there was nothing to discuss. The decision was inevitable. Peace must be signed. That night Kiamil pasha telegraphed to London to the Turkish commissioners, directing them to consent to the reddition of Adrianople; and, the other fortresses which were still holding out, and to make peace at the price of ceding all the Ottoman territories in Europe beyond a line running from Enos on the Ægean Sea, at the mouth of the Maritza River, to Midia on the Black Sea.

On the following day, January 23d, a *coup d'état* was successfully carried out.

Enver bey, the former "hero of liberty," who had taken a daring and praiseworthy part in the revolution of 1908, had been ruined afterwards by being appointed military *attaché* of the Ottoman Embassy at Berlin. There was much that was admirable and winning in Enver bey, much that was what the French call "elevation of soul." He was a sincere patriot. But the years at Berlin, and the deadening influence of militarism and party politics mixed together, had changed him from a patriot to a politician. He went to Tripoli during the Italian War, and organized a resistance in Benghazi, which he announced would be "as long as he lived." But it was a decision *à la Turque*. The Balkan War found him again at Constantinople—not at the front leading a company against the enemy—but at Constantinople, plotting with the other Young Turks how they could once more get the reins of government in their hands. The decision of the Divan was the opportunity. Enver bey led a small band of followers into the Sublime Porte, and shot Nazim pasha and his *aide-de-camp* dead. The other members of the Cabinet were imprisoned, and the telephone to the palace cut. Enver bey was driven at full speed in an automobile to the palace. He secured from the Sultan a *firman* calling on Mahmud Shevket pasha to form a new Cabinet. The Young Turks were again in power.

The bodies of Nazim pasha and the *aide-de-camp* were buried quickly and secretly. For one of Enver's companions, a man of absolutely no importance, who had been killed by defenders of Nazim, a great military funeral was held.

Mahmud Shevket pasha, who had been living in retirement at Scutari since the war began, accepted the position of Grand Vizier. I heard him, on the steps of the Sublime Porte, justify the murder of Nazim pasha, on the ground that there had been the intention to give up Adrianople. The new Cabinet was going to redeem the country, and save it from a shameful peace.

When the news of the *coup d'état* reached London, it was recognized that further negotiations were useless. The peace conference had failed.

THE SECOND PERIOD OF THE WAR

It is very doubtful if Mahmud Shevket, Enver, and their accomplices had any hope whatever of retrieving the fortunes of Turkish arms. They had prepared the *coup d'état* to get back again into office. This could not be done without the tacit consent of the army. At the moment of the Divan the army was stirred up over the surrender of Adrianople. It was the moment to act. At any other time the army would not have acquiesced in the murder of its generalissimo. The Sultan's part in the plot was not clear. His assent was, however, immediately given. Living in seclusion, and knowing practically nothing of what was going on, he signed the *firmans*, accepting the resignation of the Kiamil pasha Cabinet and charging Mahmud Shevket with the formation of a new Cabinet, either by force or by playing upon his fears of what might be his own fate, should the agreement to surrender Adrianople lead to a revolution.

On January 29th, the allies denounced the armistice, and hostilities reopened. The Bulgarians at Tchatalja had strongly entrenched themselves, and were content to rest on the defensive. They did not desire to capture Constantinople. But the Turks wanted to relieve Adrianople. The offensive movement must come from them. The Young Turks had killed Nazim pasha, they said, because they believed Adrianople could be saved. The word was now to Mahmud Shevket and Enver. Let them justify their action.

Enthusiastic speeches were made at Constantinople. We were told that the army at Tchatalja had moved forward, and was going to drive the Bulgarians out of Thrace. The Turks did advance some kilometres, but, like their fleet at the Dardanelles, not beyond the protection of the forts! They did not dare to make a general assault upon the Bulgarian positions. The renewal of the war, as far as Tchatalja was concerned, was a perfect farce. Every one in Constantinople knew that the army was not even trying to relieve Adrianople by a forward march from Constantinople.

Enver bey, who realized that he must make some move to justify the *coup d'état* of January 23d, gathered two army corps on the small boats which serve the Bosphorus villages and the Isles of Princes. It was his intention to land on the European shore of the Dardanelles, and take the Bulgarians in the rear. A few of his troops—the first that were sent—disembarked at Gallipoli, and, co-operating with the Dardanelles garrison, attempted an offensive movement against the Bulgarian positions at Bulair, which were bottling the peninsula. The attack failed ignominiously. For the Bulgarians, after dispersing the first bayonet charge by their machine-guns, were not content to wait for another attack. They scrambled over their trenches, and attacked the Turks at the point of the bayonet. The army broke, and fled. Some six thousand Turks were left on the field. The Bulgarian losses were trifling. On the same day, February 8th, and the following day, the rest of Enver bey's forces tried to land at several places on the European shore of the Sea of Marmora. For some reason that has never been explained, the Turkish fleet did not co-operate with Enver bey's attempted landings. Naturally the Turks were mowed down. At Sharkeuy it was simply slaughter. Three divisions were butchered. Those few who succeeded in getting foot on shore were driven into the sea and bayoneted. The two corps were practically annihilated.

After this exploit, Enver bey returned to Constantinople, and received the congratulations of the Grand Vizier whom he had created, by a murder, *to redeem Turkey and recover Adrianople.*

The inability to advance at Tchatalja and at Bulair, and the failure to land troops on the coasts of Thrace, entirely immobilized the Turkish armies during the second period of the war. They were content to sit and watch the fall of the three fortresses of Janina, Adrianople, and Scutari. At the moment of the *coup d'état*, I telegraphed that the whole miserable affair was nothing more than a party move of the "outs" to oust the "ins." The events confirmed this judgment. Mahmud Shevket pasha had no other policy than that of Kiamil pasha and Nazim pasha. He, and the Young Turk party, did absolutely nothing to relieve the situation. As soon as they thought they were safe from those who swore to avenge Nazim's death, they began again negotiations for peace, and on exactly the same terms.

In the meantime, the Greeks, who had not signed the armistice, decided that they must take Janina by assault. The worst of the winter was not yet over, but plans were made to increase the small Greek forces which had been practically inactive since the siege began. Janina had never been completely invested. When the Crown Prince arrived, he planned to capture the most troublesome forts, and from them to make untenable the formidable hills which commanded the city. The Greeks followed the plan with great skill and courage. Position after position was taken until the city was at the mercy of their artillery. During the night of March 5th, Essad pasha sent to Prince Constantino emissaries to surrender the city, garrison, and munitions of war without conditions.

The Crown Prince returned to Salonika in triumph. A few days later, the assassination of King George made him King. From this time on, the diplomatic position of Premier Venizelos, in his endeavour to keep within bounds the military party which had the ear of the new King, became most difficult. Even his great genius could not prevent the rupture with Bulgaria.

After the fall of Janina, the Bulgarian general staff realized that it was essential for them to force the capitulation of Adrianople, or to take the city by assault. As they had to keep a large portion of their army before Tchatalja and Bulair, it was decided that forty-five thousand Servians, with their siege cannon, should co-operate in the attack upon Adrianople. It was afterwards given by the Servians as an excuse for breaking their treaty with Bulgaria, that they had helped in the fall of Adrianople. But it must be remembered that the Bulgarian army, by its maintenance of the positions at Tchatalja and Bulair, was rendering service not to herself alone but to the common cause of the allies. Greece and Servia will never be able to get away from the fact that Bulgaria bore the brunt of the burden in the first Balkan War, and that her services in the common cause were far greater than those of either of her allies. One cannot too strongly emphasize the point, also, that the capture and possession of Adrianople did not mean to Bulgaria either from the practical or from the sentimental standpoint what Salonika meant to the Greeks and Uskub to the Servians. The Servian contingent before Adrianople was not helping Bulgaria to do what was to be wholly to the benefit of Bulgaria. The Servians were co-operating in an enterprise that was to contribute to the success of their common cause.

Adrianople had been closely invested ever since the battle of Kirk Kilissé. No army came to the relief of the garrison after the fatal retreat of October 24th. The Bulgarians had not made a serious effort to capture the city during the first period of the war. The armistice served their ends well, because each day lessened the provisions of the besieged. Inside the city Shukri pasha had done all he could to keep up the courage of the inhabitants. He himself was ignorant of the real situation at Constantinople. Perhaps it was in good faith that he assured the garrison continually that the hour of deliverance was at hand. By wireless, the authorities at Constantinople, after the *coup d'état* especially, kept assuring him that the army was advancing, and that it was a question only of days. So, in spite of starvation and of the continual rain of shells upon the city, he managed to maintain the *morale* of his garrison. The allies finally decided upon a systematic assault of the forts on all sides of the city at once. In this way, the Turks were not able to use their heavy artillery to best advantage. Advancing with scissors, the Bulgarians and Servians cut their way through the tangle of barbed wire. On the 24th and 25th, the forts fell one after the other. Czar Ferdinand entered the city with his troops on March 26th.

It was at the moment of this heroic capture, in which there was glory enough for all, that the clouds of trouble between Bulgaria and Servia began to appear on the horizon. Shukri pasha, following the old policy of the Turks, which had been so successful for centuries in the Balkan Peninsula, tried to surrender to the Servian general, who was too loyal to discipline to fall into this trap. But the Servian newspapers began to say that it was really the Servian army who had captured the city, and that Shukri pasha recognized this fact when he sent to find the Servian commander. There was an unedifying duel of newspapers between Belgrade and Sofia, which showed that the material for conflagration was ready.

In the second period of the war, the Servians gave substantial aid, especially in artillery, to the Montenegrins, who had been besieging Scutari ever since October 15th. I went over the mountain of Tarabosh on horse with an Albanian who had been one of its defenders. He related graphically the story of the repeated assaults of the Montenegrins and Servians. Each time they were driven back before they reached those batteries that dominated Scutari and made impossible the entry to the city without their capture. The loss of life was tremendous. The bravery of the assailants could do nothing against the miles and miles of barbed wire. No means of stopping assault has ever proved more efficacious. The besiegers were unable to capture Tarabosh. So they could not enter the city.

At the beginning of the war, Scutari was under the command of Hassan Riza pasha. In February, he was assassinated by his subordinate, Essad pasha, an Albanian of the Toptani family, who had been a favourite of Abdul Hamid, and had had a rather questionable career in the *gendarmerie* during the days of despotism. After the assassination of the Turkish commandant, it was for Albania and not for Turkey that Essad pasha continued the resistance. In March, Austria began to threaten the Montenegrins, and assure them that they could not keep the city. The story of how she secured the agreement of the Great Powers in coercing Montenegro is told in another chapter. Montenegro was defiant, and paid no attention to an international blockade. But on April 13th, the Servians, fearing international complications, withdrew from the siege. It was astonishing news to the world that after this, on April 22d, Essad pasha surrendered Scutari to the King of Montenegro, with the stipulation that he could withdraw with his garrison, his light artillery, and whatever munitions he might be able to take with him.

The Ottoman flag had ceased to wave in any part of Europe except Constantinople and the Dardanelles. The war was over, whether the Young Turks would have it so or not. Facts are facts.

THE TREATY OF LONDON

Nazim pasha was assassinated on January 23d. The armistice was denounced on the 29th. On February 10th, Mahmud Shevket pasha began to sound the Great Powers for their intervention in securing peace. It was necessary, however, now that the war had been resumed, that the impossibility of relieving Adrianople be demonstrated, so that it might not continue to be a stumbling-block in reopening the negotiations. The Great

Powers were willing to act as mediators, but could not make any acceptable overture until after the fall of Janina and Adrianople.

On March 23d, they proposed the following as basis for the renewal of the negotiations at London:

"1. A frontier line from Enos to Midia, which would follow the course of the Maritza, and the cession to the Allies of all the territories west of that line, with the exception of Albania, whose status and frontiers would be decided upon by the Powers.

"2. Decision by the Powers of the question of the Ægean Islands.

"3. Abandonment of Crete by Turkey.

"4. Arrangement of all financial questions at Paris, by an international commission, in which the representatives of Turkey and the allies would be allowed to sit. Participation of the allies in the Ottoman Debt, and in the financial obligations of the territories newly acquired. No indemnity of war, in principle.

"5. End of hostilities immediately after the acceptance of this basis of negotiations."

Turkey agreed to these stipulations. The Balkan States, however, did not want to commit themselves to the Enos-Midia line "as definitely agreed upon," but only as a base of *pourparlers*. They insisted that the Ægean Islands must be ceded directly to them. They wanted to know what the Powers had in mind in regard to the frontiers of Albania. In the last place, they refused to relinquish the possibility of an indemnity of war.

Notes were exchanged back and forth among the chancelleries until April 20th, when the Balkan States finally agreed to accept the mediation of the Powers. They had practically carried all their points, however, except that of the communication of the Albanian frontier. Hostilities ceased. There really was not much more to fight about, at least as far as Turkey was concerned.

It was a whole month before the second conference at London opened. The only gleam of hope that the Turks were justified in entertaining, when they decided to renew the war, had been the possible outbreak of a war between the Allies. If only the quarrel over Macedonia had come, for which they looked from week to week, they might have been able to put pressure on Bulgaria for the return of Adrianople, and on Greece for the return of the Ægean Islands. But the rupture between the Allies did not take place until after they had settled with Turkey. Why fight over the bear's skin until it was actually in their hands?

The negotiations were reopened in London on May 20th. On May 30th, the peace preliminaries were signed. The Sultan of Turkey ceded to the Kings of the allied states his dominions in Europe beyond the Enos-Midia line. Albania, its status and frontiers, were intrusted by the Sultan to the sovereigns of the Great Powers. He ceded Crete to the allied sovereigns, but left the decision as to the islands in the Ægean Sea, and the status of Mount Athos, to the Great Powers.

The war between the allies enabled Turkey to violate this treaty. They won back from Bulgaria, without opposition, most of Thrace, including Adrianople and Kirk Kilissé. Later, treaties were made separately with each of the Balkan States. But, as it seems to be a principle of history that no territories that have once passed from the shadow of the Crescent return, it is probable that the Treaty of London will, in the end, represent the *minimum* of what Turkey's former subjects have wrested from her.

CHAPTER XV
THE RUPTURE BETWEEN THE ALLIES

To those who knew the centuries-old hatred and race rivalry between Greece and Servia and Bulgaria in the Balkan Peninsula, an alliance for the purpose of liberating Macedonia seemed impossible. The Ottoman Government had a sense of security which seemed to be justifiable. They had known how to keep alive and intensify racial hatred in European Turkey, and believed that they were immune from concerted attack because the Balkan States would never be able to agree as to the division of spoils after a successful war.

The history of the ten years of rivalry between bands, which had nullified the efforts of the Powers to "reform" Macedonia by installing a *gendarmerie* under European control, had taught the diplomats that they had working against the pacification of Macedonia not only the Ottoman authorities, but also the native Christian population and the neighbouring emancipated countries. They were ready to believe the astute Hussein Hilmy pasha, Vali of Macedonia, when he said: "I am ruling over an insane asylum. Were the Turkish flag withdrawn, they would fly at each other's throats, and instead of reform, you would have anarchy."

If the Balkan States had realized how completely and how easily they were going to overthrow the military power of Turkey, they probably would not have attempted it. This seems paradoxical, but it is true all the same.

The Allies did not anticipate more than the holding of the Ottoman forces in check and the occupation of the frontiers and of the upper valleys of the Vardar and Struma. Greece felt that she would be rewarded by a slight rectification of boundary in Thessaly and Epirus, if only the war would settle the status of Crete and result in an autonomous *régime* for the Ægean Islands. At the most, the Balkan States hoped to force upon Turkey the autonomy of Macedonia under a Christian governor. So jealous was each of the possibility of another's gaining control of Macedonia that this solution would have satisfied them more than the complete disappearance of Turkish rule. Both hopes and fears as to Macedonia were envisaged rather in connection with each other than in connection with the Turks.

Between Servia and Bulgaria there was a definite treaty, signed on March 13, 1912, which defined future spheres of influence in upper Macedonia. But Greece had no agreement either with Bulgaria or Servia.

The events of October, 1912, astonished the whole world. No such sudden and complete collapse of the Ottoman power in Europe was dreamed of. I have already spoken of how fearful the European Chancelleries were of an Ottoman victory. Had they not been so morally certain of Turkey's triumph they would never have sent to the belligerents their famous—and in the light of subsequent events ridiculous—joint note concerning the *status quo*.

But if the Great Powers were unprepared for the succession of Balkan triumphs, the allies were much more astonished at what they were able to accomplish. Kirk Kilissé and Lulé Burgas gave Thrace to Bulgaria. Kumanovo opened up the valley of the Vardar to the Servians, while the Greeks marched straight to Salonika without serious opposition.

The victories of the Servians and Greeks, so easily won, were to the Bulgarians a calamity which overshadowed their own striking military successes. They had spilled much blood and wasted their strength in the conquest of Thrace which they did not want, while their allies—but rivals for all that—were in possession of Macedonia, the *Bulgaria irredenta*. To be encircling Adrianople and besieging Constantinople, cities in which they had only secondary interest, while the Servians attacked Monastir and the Greeks were settling themselves comfortably in Salonika, was the irony of fate for those who felt that others were reaping the fruits for which they had made so great and so admirable a sacrifice.

When we come to judge dispassionately the folly of Bulgaria in provoking a war with her comrades in arms, and the seemingly amazing greed for land which it revealed, we must remember that the Bulgarians felt that they had accomplished everything to receive nothing. Salonika and not Adrianople was the city of their dreams. Macedonia and not Thrace was the country which they had taken arms to liberate. The Ægean Sea and not the extension of their Black Sea littoral formed the substantial and logical economic background to the appeal of race which led them to insist so strongly in gathering under their sovereignty all the elements of the Bulgarian people. European writers have not been able to understand how little importance the Bulgarians attached to their territorial acquisitions in Thrace, and of how little interest it was for them to acquire new possessions in which there were so few Bulgarians.

Then, too, the powerful elements which had pushed Bulgaria into the war with Turkey, and had contributed so greatly to her successes, were of Macedonian origin. In Sofia, the Macedonians are numerically, as well as financially and politically, very strong. I had a revelation of this, such as the compilation of statistics cannot give, on the day after the massacre of Kotchana. The newspapers called upon all the Macedonians in Sofia to put out flags tied with crêpe. In the main streets of the city, it seemed as if every second house was that of a Macedonian. To these people, ardent and powerful patriots, Macedonia was home. It had been the dream of their lives to unite the regions from which they had come—once emancipated from the Turks—to the mother country. From childhood, they had been taught to look towards the Rhodope Mountains as the hills from which should come their help. Is it any wonder then, that, after the striking victories of their arms, there should be a feeling of insanity—for it was that—when they saw the dreams of a lifetime about to vanish?

But the mischief of the matter, as a Scotchman would say, was that Greeks and Servians felt the same way about the same places. Populations had been mixed for centuries. At some time or other in past history each of the three peoples had had successful dynasties to spread their sovereignty over exactly the same territories. Each then could evoke the same historical memories, each the same past of suffering, each the same present of hopes, and the same prayers of the emancipated towards Sofia and Athens and Belgrade.

After the occupation of Salonika by the Greeks, the Bulgarian ambitions to break the power of Turkey were not the same as they had been before. Had Salonika been occupied two weeks earlier, there might not have been a Lulé Burgas. An armistice was hurriedly concluded. During the trying period of negotiations in London, and during the whole of the second part of the war, the jealousies of the allies had been awakened one against the other. Between Greeks and Bulgarians, it had been keen since the very first moment that the Greek army entered Macedonia. The crisis between Servia and Bulgaria did not become acute until Servia saw her way blocked to the Adriatic by the absurd attempt to create a free Albania. Then she naturally began to insist that the treaty of partition which she had signed with Bulgaria could not be carried out by her. In vain she appealed to the sense of justice of the Bulgarians. The treaty had been signed on the understanding that Albania would fall under the sphere of Servian aggrandizement. Nor, on the other hand, had it been contested that Thrace would belong to Bulgaria. If the treaty were carried out, Bulgaria would get everything and Servia nothing. Servia also reminded the Bulgarians of the loyal aid that had been given them in the reduction of Adrianople. But Bulgaria held to her pound of flesh.

Under the circumstances of the division of territory, Bulgaria's claim to cross the Vardar and go as far as Monastir and Okrida, would not only have given her possession of a fortress from which she could dominate both

Servia and Greece, but would have put another state between Servia and Salonika. Bulgaria was, in fact, demanding everything as far as Servia was concerned. Servia cannot be blamed then for coming to an understanding with Greece, even if it were for support in the violation of a treaty. For where does history give us the example of a nation holding to a treaty when it was against her interest to do so?

After their return from London, the Premiers Venizelos and Pasitch made an offensive and defensive alliance for ten years against the Bulgarian aspirations. In this alliance, concluded at Athens shortly after King George's death, the frontiers were definitely settled. In the negotiations, Greece showed the same desire to have everything for herself which Bulgaria was displaying. Finally she agreed to allow Servia to keep Monastir. Without this concession, Servia would have fared as badly at the hands of Greece as at the hands of Bulgaria. It is only because Greece feared that Servia might be driven to combine with Bulgaria against her, that the frontier in this agreement was drawn south of Monastir. The Greek army officers opposed strongly this concession, but Venizelos was wise enough to see that the maintenance of Greek claims to Monastir might result in the loss of Salonika. The Serbo-Greek alliance was not made public until the middle of June. Bulgaria had also been making overtures to Greece, and at the end of May had expressed her willingness to waive her claim to Salonika in return for Greek support against Servia. Venizelos, already bound to Servia, was honourable enough to refuse this proposition.

But the military reputation of Bulgaria was still so strong in Bulgarian diplomacy that Servia and Greece were anxious to arrive, if possible, at an arrangement without war. Venizelos proposed a meeting at Salonika. Bulgaria declined. Then Venizelos and Pasitch together proposed the arbitration of the Czar. Bulgaria at the first seemed to receive this proposition favourably, but stipulated that it would be only for the disputed matter in her treaty with Servia. At this moment, the Russian Czar sent a moving appeal to the Balkan States to avoid the horrors of a fratricidal war. Bulgaria then agreed to send, together with her Allies, delegates to a conference at Petrograd.

All the while, Premier Gueshoff of Bulgaria had been struggling for peace against the pressure and the intrigues of the Macedonian party at Sofia. They looked upon the idea of a Petrograd conference as the betrayal of Macedonians and Bulgarians by the mother country. Unable to maintain his position, Gueshoff resigned. His withdrawal ruined Bulgaria, for he was replaced by M. Daneff, who was heart and soul with the Macedonian party. A period of waiting followed. But from this moment war seemed inevitable to those who knew the feeling on both sides. Daneff and his friends did not hesitate. They would not listen to reason. They believed that they had the power to force Greece and Servia to a peace very nearly on their own terms. Public opinion was behind them, for news was continually coming to Sofia of Greek and Servian oppression of Bulgarians in the region between Monastir and Salonika. These stories of unspeakable cruelty, which were afterwards established to be true by the Carnegie Commission, had much to do with making possible the second war.

It was not difficult for the Macedonian party at Sofia to precipitate hostilities. The Bulgarian general staff, in spite of the caution that should have imposed itself upon them by the consideration of the exhausting campaign in the winter, felt certain of their ability to defeat the Servians and Greeks combined. Then, too, the army on the frontiers, in which there was a large element—perhaps twenty per cent.—of Macedonians, had already engaged in serious conflicts with the Greeks.

In fact, frontier skirmishes had begun in April. The affair of Nigrita was really a battle. After these outbreaks, Bulgarian and Greek officers had been compelled to establish a neutral zone in order to prevent the new war from beginning of itself. At the end of May, there had been fighting in the Panghaeon district, east of the river Strymon. The Bulgarian staff had wanted to prevent the Greeks from being in a position to cut the railway from Serres to Drama. In the beginning of June, Bulgarian coast patrols had fired on the *Averoff.* By the end of June, the Bulgarian outposts were not far from Salonika.

The first Bulgarian plan was to seize suddenly Salonika, which would thus cut off the Greek army from its base of supplies and its advantageous communication by sea with Greece. There were nearly one thousand five hundred Bulgarian soldiers in Salonika under the command of General Hassapsieff. How many *comitadjis* had been introduced into the city no one knows. I was there during the last week of June, and saw many Bulgarian peasants, big strapping fellows, who seemed to have no occupation. When I visited the Bulgarian company, which was quartered in the historic mosque of St. Sophia, two days before their destruction, they seemed to me to be absolutely sure of their position. At this moment, the atmosphere among the few Bulgarians in Salonika was that of complete confidence.

Among the Greeks, a spirit of excitement and of apprehension made them realize the gravity and the dangers of the events which were so soon to follow. Perfect confidence, while highly recommended by the theorists, does not seem to win wars. Nervousness, on the other hand, makes an army alert, and ready to exert all the greater effort, from the fact that it feels it needs that effort. In all the wars with which this book deals this has been true,—Italian confidence in 1911, Turkish confidence in 1912, Bulgarian confidence in 1913, and German confidence in 1914.

On the 29th of June, when I left Salonika to go to Albania, it was the opinion of the Greek officers in Salonika that the war—which they viewed with apprehension—would be averted by the conference at Petrograd. When I got on my steamship, the first man I met was Sandansky, who had become famous a decade before by the capture of Miss Stone, an American missionary. He had embarked on this Austrian Lloyd steamer at Kavalla, with the expectation of slipping ashore at Salonika, if possible, to prepare the way for the triumphal entry of the Bulgarian army. But he was only able to look sorrowfully out on the city, for the police were waiting to arrest him. What bitter thoughts he must have had when he saw the Bulgarian flag, which he had planted there with his own hands, waving from the minaret of St. Sophia, and he unable to organize its defence! A week later I saw Sandansky at a café in Valona. The war had then started, and he was probably trying to persuade the Albanians to enter the struggle and to take the Servians in the rear.

Up to June 29th, Servians and Bulgarians were fraternizing at their outposts, and joking about how soon they would be getting back to their everyday occupations, for which months of war and excitement had begun to unfit them. In several places Servians and Bulgarians ate together. I know of one outpost where the patrols were photographed together on a bridge. Little did they realize the horrible plot that was being coolly planned at Sofia,

CHAPTER XVI
THE WAR BETWEEN THE BALKAN ALLIES

On Sunday night, June 29th, without any declaration of war or even warning, General Savoff ordered a general attack all along the Greek and Servian lines. There was no direct provocation on the part of Bulgaria's allies.

The responsibility for precipitating the war which brought about the humiliation of Bulgaria can be directly fixed. Two general orders, dated from the military headquarters at Sofia on June 29th, have been published. They set forth an amazing and devilish scheme, which stands out as a most cold and bloody calculation, even among all the horrors of Balkan history. General Savoff stated positively that this energetic action was not the commencement of a war. It was merely for the purpose of occupying as much territory as possible in the contested regions before the intervention of the Powers. It had a two-fold object: to cut the communications between the Greeks and Servians at Veles (Küprülü) on the Vardar, and to throw an army suddenly into Salonika. The fighting began in the night-time. The Bulgarians naturally were able to advance into a number of important positions.

When the news became known at Salonika on the morning of the 30th, General Hassapsieff, on the ground that he was a diplomatic agent, was allowed to leave. Before his departure he gave an order to his forces to resist, if they were attacked, as he would return with the Bulgarian army in twenty-four hours.

Early in the afternoon the Greeks sent an ultimatum ordering the Bulgarians in Salonika to surrender by six o'clock. Their refusal led to all-night street fighting. Barricaded in St. Sophia and several other buildings, they were able to defend themselves until the Greeks turned artillery upon their places of refuge. Not many were killed on either side. Salonika was calm again the next day. One thousand three hundred Bulgarian soldiers and a number of prominent Bulgarian residents of Salonika, under conditions of exceptional cruelty and barbarism, were sent to Crete. The Greek forces in Salonika, among whom were some twenty thousand from America, were hurried to the outposts for the defence of the city.

There was no diplomatic action following the treachery of the Bulgarians towards their allies. The Greek Foreign Minister stated that Greece considered the Bulgarian attack an act of war, and that the Greek army had been ordered to advance immediately to retake the positions which the Bulgarians had captured. Nor did Servia show any disposition to treat with Bulgaria. No official communications reached Sofia from a Great Power. There had been a miscalculation. Bulgaria was compelled, as a consequence of her ill-considered act, to face a new war. There was no withdrawal possible.

From a purely military point of view, it seems hard to believe that the Bulgarians really thought that their night attack would bring about war. Their army had borne the brunt of the campaign against the Turks, and had suffered terribly during the winter spent in the trenches before Tchatalja. They were not in a good strategic position, for the army was spread out over a long line, and the character of the country made concentration difficult. Adequate railway communication with the bases of supplies was lacking. The Greeks and Servians, on the other hand, held not only the railway from Salonika to Nish through the valley of the Vardar, but even were it successfully cut, had communication by railway with their bases at Salonika, Monastir, Mitrovitza, Uskub, and Nish.

General Ivanoff, in command of the second Bulgarian army, was charged with confronting the whole of the Greek forces, in a line passing from the Ægean Sea to Demir-Hissar on the Vardar, between Serres and Salonika. When we realize that General Ivanoff had less than fifty thousand men, a portion of whom were recruits from the region of Serres, and that he had to guard against an attack on his right flank from the Servians, we cannot help wondering what the Bulgarian general staff had counted upon in provoking their allies to battle. Did they expect that the Greeks and Servians would be intimidated by the night attack of June 29th, and would agree to continue the project of a conference at Petrograd? Or did they think that the Greek army was of so little value that they could brush it aside, and enter Salonika, just as the Greeks had been able to enter in November? Whatever hypothesis we adopt, it shows contempt for their opponents and belief in their own star. The proof of the fact that the Bulgarians never dreamed of anything but the success of their "bluff," or, if there was resistance, of an easy victory, is found in the few troops at the disposal of General Ivanoff, and in the choice of Doiran, so near the front of battle, as the base of supplies. At Doiran everything that the second army needed in provisions and munitions of war was stored. From the financial standpoint alone, Bulgaria could not afford to risk the loss of these supplies.

On July 2d, the Greek army, under the command of Crown Prince Constantine, took the offensive against the Bulgarians, who had occupied on the previous day the crest of Beshikdag, from the mouth of the Struma to the plateau of Lahana, across the road from Salonika to Serres, and the heights north of Lake Ardzan, commanding the left bank of the Vardar. The positions were strong. If the Greek army had been of the calibre that the Bulgarians evidently expected, or if General Ivanoff had had sufficient forces to hold the positions against the Greek attack, there would undoubtedly have been *pourparlers*, and a probable cessation of hostilities just as the Bulgarians counted upon.

But the Greeks soon proved that they were as brave and as determined as their opponents. Their artillery fire was excellent. There was no wavering before the deadly resistance of the entrenched Bulgarians. After five days of struggle, in which both sides showed equal courage, the forces of General Ivanoff yielded to superior numbers. The Bulgarians were compelled to retreat, on July 6th, in two columns, towards Demir-Hissar and Strumitza. The retreat was effected in good order, and the Greeks, though in possession of mobile artillery, could not surround either column. Victory had been purchased at a terrible price. The Greek losses in five days were greater than during the whole war with Turkey. They admitted ten thousand *hors du combat*. The Greeks had received their first serious baptism of fire, and had demonstrated that they could fight. The Turks had never given them the opportunity to wipe out the disgrace of 1897.

It is a tribute to the quickness of decision of the Crown Prince Constantine and his general staff, and to the spirit of his soldiers, that this severe trial of five days of continuous fighting and fearful loss of life was not followed by a respite. The Greek headquarters were moved to Doiran on the 7th. It was decided to maintain the offensive as long as the army had strength to march and men to fill the gaps made by the fall of thousands every day. The Bulgarians, although they contested desperately every step, were kept on the move. On the right, the Greeks pushed through to Serres, joining there, on July 11th, the advance-guard of the detachments which the Greek fleet had landed at Kavalla on the 9th.

The advance of the Greek armies was along the Vardar, the Struma, and the Mesta. On the Vardar, the Bulgarian abandonment of Demir-Hissar, on the 10th, enabled the Greeks to repair the railway, and establish communication with the Servian army. The right wing, advancing by the Mesta, occupied Drama. On July 19th, the Bulgarian resistance was concentrated at Nevrokop. When it broke here, the Greek right wing was able to send its outposts to the foothills of the Rhodope Mountains, on the Bulgarian frontier.

The Greeks began to speak of the invasion of Bulgaria, and of making peace at Sofia. But the bulk of their forces met an invincible resistance at Simitli. From the 23d to the 26th, they attacked the Bulgarian positions, and believed that the advantage was theirs. But on the 27th the Bulgarians began a counter-attack against both wings of the Greek army at once. On the 29th, the Greeks began to plan their retreat. On the 30th, they realized that the retreat was no longer possible. The Bulgarians were on both their flanks. It was then that the armistice saved them.

While the Greek army was gaining its victories in the *hinterland* of Macedonia, the ports of the Ægean coast, Kavalla, Makri, Porto-Lagos, and Dedeagatch were occupied without resistance by the Greek fleet. Detachments withdrawn from Epirus were brought to these ports. Some went to Serres and Drama. Others garrisoned the ports, and occupied Xanthi and other nearby inland towns.

The Bulgarians may have had some reason to discount the value of the Greek army. For it had not yet been tried. But the Servians had shown from the very first day of the war with Turkey that they possessed high military qualities. The courage of their troops was coupled with agility. They had had more experience than the Bulgarians and Greeks in quick marches, and in breaking up their forces into numerous columns. There is probably no army in Europe to-day which can equal the Servians in mobility. It is incredible that the Bulgarians could have hoped to surprise the Servians, and find a weak place anywhere along their lines. On the defensive, in localities which they had come to know intimately by nine months in the field, it would have taken a larger force than the Bulgarians could muster to get the better of soldiers such as the Servians had proved themselves to be.

Whether it was by scorn for the Greeks, or by appreciation of the Servian concentration, the Bulgarians had planned to confront the Servians with four of their five armies. We have already seen that General Ivanoff had the second army alone to oppose to the Greeks, and that even a few battalions of his troops were needed on the Servian flank.

The engagements between the Bulgarians and the Servians had two distinct fields of action, one in Macedonia, and the other on the Bulgaro-Servian frontier.

In Macedonia, the Bulgarians experienced the same surprise in regard to the Servians as in regard to the Greeks. Their sudden attack of June 30th did not strike terror to the hearts of their opponents. Instead of gaining for them a favourable diplomatic position, they found that the Servians did not even suggest a parley. On July 1st, the Servians started a counter-attack, and kept a steady offensive against their former allies for eight days. Gradually the Bulgarians, along the Bregalnitza, gave ground, retreating from position to position, always with their face towards the enemy. The battle, after the first day, was for the Bulgarians a defensive action all along the line.

On July 4th, General Dimitrieff assumed the functions of generalissimo of the Bulgarian forces. He tried his best to check the Servian offensive. But the aggressive spirit had gone out of the Bulgarian army. Lulé Burgas could not be repeated. It was incapable of more than a stubborn resistance to the Servian advance. By July 8th, the Servians were masters of the approaches to Istip, and had cleared the Bulgarians out of the territory which led down into the valley of the Vardar. Then they stopped. From this time on to the signing of the armistice, the Macedonian Servian army was content with the victories of the first week.

Along the Servian-Bulgarian frontier, the Bulgarian army had some initial success. But General Kutincheff did not dispose of enough men to make possible a successful aggressive movement towards Nish. From the very first, when the Macedonian army failed to advance, the Bulgarian plans for an invasion of Servia fell to the ground. They had based everything upon an advance in Macedonia to the Vardar. So the forward movement wavered. The Servians, now sure of Rumanian co-operation, advanced in turn towards Widin. General Kutincheff was compelled to fall back on Sofia by the Rumanian invasion. Widin was invested by the Servians on July 23d.

Rumania had watched with alarm the rise of the military power of Bulgaria. She could not intervene in the first Balkan war on the side of the Turks. The civilized world would not have countenanced such a move, nor would it have had the support of Rumanian public opinion. Whatever the menace of Bulgarian hegemony in the Balkan Peninsula, Rumania had to wait until peace had been signed between the allies and the Turks. But, as we have already seen, during the first negotiations at London, her Minister to Great Britain had been instructed to treat with Bulgaria for a cession of territory from the Danube at Silistria to the Black Sea, in order that Rumania might have the strategic frontier which the Congress of Berlin ought to have given her, when the Dobrudja was awarded to her, without her consent, in exchange for Bessarabia. As Rumania had helped to free Bulgaria in 1877-78, and had never received any reward for her great sacrifices, while the Bulgarians had done little to win their own independence, the demand of a rectification of frontier was historically reasonable. Since Rumania had so admirably developed the Dobrudja, and had constructed the port of Constanza, it was justified from the economic standpoint. For the possession of Silivria, and a change of frontier on the Dobrudja, was the only means by which Rumania could hope to defend her southern frontier from attack.

At first, the Bulgarians bitterly opposed any compensation to Rumania. They discounted the importance of her neutrality, for they knew that she could not act against them as long as they were at war with Turkey. They denounced the demands of Rumania, perfectly reasonable as they were, as "blackmail." They were too blinded with the dazzling glory of their unexpected victories against the Turks to realize how essential the friendship of Rumania—at least, the neutrality of Rumania—was to their schemes for taking all Macedonia to themselves. When, in April, they signed with very ill grace the cession of Silivria, as a compromise, and refused to yield the small strip of territory from Silivria to Kavarna on the Black Sea, the Bulgarians made a fatal political mistake. It was madness enough to go into the second Balkan war in the belief that they could frighten, or, if that failed, overwhelm the Servians and Greeks. What shall we call the failure to take into their political calculations the possibility of a Rumanian intervention? Even if there were not the question of the frontier in the Dobrudja, would not Rumanian intervention still be justified by the consideration of preserving the balance of power in the Balkans? By intervening, Rumania would be acting, in her small corner of the world, just as the larger nations of Europe had acted time and again since the sixteenth century.

The Rumanian mobilization commenced on July 3d. On July 10th, Rumania declared war, and crossed the Danube. The Bulgarians decided that they would not oppose the Rumanian invasion. How could they? Already their armies were on the defensive, and hard pressed, by Greeks and Servians. There is a limit to what a few hundred thousand men could do. It is possible, though not probable, that the Bulgarian armies might have gained the upper hand in the end against their former allies in Macedonia. But with Rumania bringing into the field a fresh army, larger than that of any other Balkan States, Bulgaria's case was hopeless. The Rumanians advanced without opposition, and began to march upon Sofia. They occupied, on July 15th, the seaport of Varna, from which the Bulgarian fleet had withdrawn to Sebastopol.

It would have been easy for the Rumanians to have occupied Sofia, and waited there for the Servian and Greek armies to arrive. The humiliation of Bulgaria could have been made complete. Why, then, the armistice of July 30th? Why the assembling hastily of a peace conference at Bukarest? Political and financial, as well as military, considerations dictated the wisdom of granting to Bulgaria an armistice.

Greece and Servia were exhausted financially, and their armies could gain little more than glory by continuing the war. The Greek army, in fact, was in a critical position, and ran the risk of being surrounded and crushed by the Bulgarians. The Servians had not shown much hurry to come to the aid of the Greeks. The truth of the matter is that, after the battle of the Bregalnitza, which ended on July 10th, the Servians began to get very nervous about the successes of their Greek allies. They knew well the Greek character, and feared that too easy victories over the Bulgarians might necessitate a third war with Greece over Monastir. So, on July 11th, with the ostensible reason that such a measure was necessary to protect their rear against the Albanians, the Servian general staff withdrew from the front a number of the best regiments, and placed them in a position where they could act, if the Greeks tried to seize Monastir. On the other hand, Rumania gave both Greece and Servia to understand that she had entered the war, not from any altruistic desire to help them, but for her own interests. To see Bulgaria too greatly humiliated and weakened was decidedly no more to the interest of Rumania than to see her triumphant.

As for Montenegro, she had entered the second Balkan war to give loyal support to Servia, from whom she expected in return a generous spirit in dividing the *sandjak* of Novi Bazar. Her co-operation, however, as I am able to state from having been in Cettinje when the decision was taken to send ten thousand men against Bulgaria, was not made the subject of any bargain. So, when Servia thought best to sign the armistice, Montenegro was in thorough accord.

After a month of fighting, in which the losses had been far greater than during the war with Turkey, and the treatment of non-combatants by all the armies horrible beyond description, the scene of battle shifted from the blood-stained mountains and valleys of Macedonia to the council chamber at Bukarest. Rumania was to preside over a Balkan Congress of Berlin!

CHAPTER XVII
THE TREATY OF BUKAREST

When the delegates from the various important capitals reached Bukarest on July 30th, the armies were still fighting. Everyone, however, seemed anxious to come to an understanding as soon as possible. The first session of the delegates was held on the afternoon of July 30th. Premier Pasitch for Servia and Premier Venizelos for Greece were present. But Premier Daneff, who had so wanted the war, did not have the manhood to face its consequences. The Bulgarians were represented in Bukarest by no outstanding leader, either political or military. Premier Majoresco of Rumania presided over the conference. The first necessity was the decision for an armistice. A suspension of arms was agreed upon to begin upon August 1st at noon. On August 4th the armistice was extended for three days to August 8th.

In the conference of Bukarest, Bulgaria, naturally, stood by herself. It was necessary, if there was to be peace, that her delegates should come to an understanding as to the sacrifices she was willing to make with each of her neighbours separately. Consequently the important decisions were made in committee meetings. The general assembly of delegates had little else to do than to ratify the concessions wrung from Bulgaria in turn by each of the opponents.

Rarely have peace delegates been put in a more painful position than the men whom Bulgaria sent to Bukarest. It will always be an open question as to whether the military situation of Bulgaria on the 31st of July, as regards Servia and Greece, was retrievable. But the presence of a Rumanian army in Bulgaria made absolutely impossible the continuance of the war. Consequently there was nothing for Bulgaria to do but to yield to the demands of Greece and Servia. The only check upon the Servian and Greek delegates was the determination of Rumania not to see Bulgaria too greatly weakened. She had entered into line to gain her bit of territory in the south of the Dobrudja. But she had also in mind the prevention of Bulgarian hegemony in the Balkan Peninsula, and she did not propose to see this hegemony go elsewhere. This explains the favourable terms which Bulgaria received.

The Bulgarian and Rumanian delegates quickly agreed upon a frontier to present to the meeting of August 4th. By this, the first of the protocols, Bulgaria ceded to Rumania all her territory north of a line from the Danube, above Turtukaia, to the end of the Black Sea, south of Ekrene. In addition, she bound herself to dismantle the present fortresses and promised not to construct forts at Rustchuk, Schumla, and the country between and for twenty kilometres around Baltchik.

On August 6th, the protocol with Servia was presented. The Servian frontier was to start at a line drawn from the summit of Patarika on the old frontier, and to follow the watershed between the Vardar and the Struma to the Greek-Bulgarian frontier, with the exception of the upper valley of the Strumnitza which remained Servian territory.

The following day the protocol with Greece was presented. The Greek-Bulgarian frontier was to run from the crest of Belashitcha to the mouth of the River Mesta on the Ægean Sea. Bulgaria formally agreed to waive all pretensions to Crete. The protocol with the Greeks was the only one over which the Bulgarians made a resolute stand. When they signed this protocol, they stated that the accord was only because they had taken notice of the notes which Austria-Hungary and Russia presented to the conference, to the effect that in their ratification they would reserve for future discussion the inclusion of Kavalla in Greek territory.

The Bulgarians insisted on a clause guaranteeing autonomy for churches and schools in the condominium of liberated territories. Servia opposed this demand mildly, and Greece strongly. They were right. The question of national propaganda through churches and schools had done more to arouse and keep alive racial hatred in Macedonia than any other cause. If there were to be a lasting peace, nothing could be more unwise than the continuance of the propaganda which had plunged Macedonia into such terrible confusion.

Rumania, however, secured in the Treaty of Bukarest from each of the States what they had been unwilling to grant each other. Rumania imposed upon Bulgaria, Greece, and Servia, the obligation of granting autonomy to the Kutzo-Wallachian churches, and assent to the creation of bishoprics subsidized by the Rumanian Government.

A rather amusing incident occurred on August 5th by the proposition of the United States Government through its Minister at Bukarest, that a provision be embodied in the treaty according full religious liberties in transferred territories. The ignorance of American diplomacy, so frequently to be deplored, never made a greater blunder than this. It showed how completely the American State Department and its advisors on Near Eastern affairs had misunderstood the Macedonian question. Quite rightly, the consideration even of this request was rejected as superfluous. Mr. Venizelos administered a well-deserved rebuke when he said that religious liberty, in the right sense of the word, was understood through the extension of each country's constitution over the territories acquired.

Much has been written concerning the intrigues of European Powers at Bukarest during the ten days of the conference which made a new map for the Balkan Peninsula. It will be many years, if ever, before these intrigues are brought to light. Therefore we cannot discuss the question of the pressure which was brought to bear upon Rumania, upon Bulgaria, and upon Servia and Greece to determine the partition of territories. Germany looked with alarm upon the possibility of a durable settlement. Austria was determined that Bulgaria and Servia should not become reconciled.

Austria-Hungary and Russia, though for different reasons, were right in their attitude toward the matter of Greece's claim upon Kavalla. Greece would have done well had she been content to leave to Bulgaria a larger littoral on the Ægean Sea, and the port which is absolutely essential for the proper economic development of the *hinterland* attributed to her. By taking her pound of flesh, the Greeks only exposed themselves to future dangers. The laws of economics are inexorable. Bulgaria cannot allow herself to think sincerely about peace until her portion of Macedonia, by the inclusion of Kavalla, is logically complete. It would have been better politics for Greece to have shown herself magnanimous on this point. As George Sand has so aptly said: "It is not philanthropy, but our own interest, which leads us sometimes to do good to men in order that they may be prevented in the future from doing harm to us."

When we come to look back upon the second Balkan war, and have traced out the sad consequences and the continued unrest which followed the Treaty of Bukarest, it is possible that Servia's responsibility may be considered as great, if not greater, than that of Bulgaria in bringing about the strife between the allies. In our sympathy with the inherent justice of Servia's claim for adequate territorial compensation for what she had suffered for, and what she had contributed to, the Turkish *débâcle* in Europe, we are apt to overlook three indisputable facts: that Servia repudiated a solemn treaty with Bulgaria, on the basis of which Bulgaria had agreed to the alliance against Turkey; that the territories granted to Servia, *south of the line which she had sworn not to pass in her territorial claims*, and a portion of those in the "contested zone" of her treaty with Bulgaria, were beyond any shadow of doubt inhabited by Bulgarians; and that since these territories were ceded to her she has not, as was tacitly understood at Bukarest, extended to them the guarantees and privileges of the Servian constitution.

The Treaty of Bukarest, so far as the disputed territories allotted to Servia are concerned, has created a situation analogous to that of Alsace and

Lorraine after the Treaty of Frankfort. And Servia started in to cope with it by following Prussian methods. What Servians of Bosnia and Herzegovina and Dalmatia have suffered from Austrian rule, free Servia is inflicting upon the Bulgarians who became her subjects after the second Balkan war.

It would not be an exaggeration to say that the population of Macedonia, as a whole, of whatever race or creed, would welcome to-day a return to the Ottoman rule of Abdul Hamid. The Turkish "constitutional *régime*" was worse than Abdul Hamid, the war of "liberation" worse than the Young Turks, and the present disposition of territories satisfies none. Poor Macedonia!

After the disastrous and humiliating losses at Bukarest, Bulgaria still had her former vanquished foe to reckon with. The Turks were again at Adrianople and Kirk Kilissé. Thrace was once more in her power. The Treaty of Bukarest, while attributing Thrace to Bulgaria on the basis of the Treaty of London, actually said nothing whatever about it. Nor were there any promises of aid in helping Bulgaria to get back again what she had lost, without a struggle, by her folly and treachery.

A new war by Bulgaria alone in her weakened military condition and with her empty treasury, to drive once more the Turks back south of the Enos-Midia line, was impossible. Bulgaria appealed to the chancelleries of Europe to help her in taking possession of the Thracian territory ceded to her at London. The Powers made one of their futile overtures to Turkey, requesting that she accept the treaty which she had signed a few months before.

But no one could blame the Turks for having taken advantage of Bulgarian folly. Who could expect them to meekly withdraw behind the Enos-Midia line? Bulgaria could get no support in applying the argument of force.

In the end, the victors of Lulé Burgas had to go to Constantinople and make overtures directly to the Sublime Porte. They fared very badly. The Enos-Midia line was drawn, but it took a curve northward from the Black Sea and westward across the Maritza in such a way that the Turks obtained not only Adrianople, but also Kirk Kilissé and Demotica. The Bulgarians were not even masters of the one railway leading to Dedeagatch, their sole port on the Ægean Sea.

The year 1913 for Bulgaria will remain the most bitter one of her history. She had to learn the lesson that the life of nations, as well as of individuals, is one of give as well as take, and that compromise is the basis of sound statesmanship. Who wants all, generally gets nothing.

CHAPTER XVIII
THE ALBANIAN FIASCO

The world has not known just what to do with the mountainous country which comes out in a bend on the upper western side of the Balkan Peninsula directly opposite the heel of Italy. It caused trouble to the Romans from the very moment that they became an extra-Italian power. Inherited from them by the Byzantines, fought for with the varying fortunes by the Frankish princes, the Venetians, and the Turks, Albania has remained a country which cannot be said to have ever been wholly subjected. Nor can it be said to have ever had a national entity. Its present mediæval condition is due to the fact that, owing to its high mountains and its being on the road to nowhere, it has not, since the Roman days at least, undergone the influences of a contemporary civilization.

Venice recognized the importance of Albania during the days of her commercial prosperity. For the Albanian coast, with its two splendid harbours, of Valona and Durazzo, effectively guards the entrance of the Adriatic into the Mediterranean Sea.

But Albania did not demand attention a hundred years ago when the last map of Europe was being made by the Congress of Vienna. The reason for this is simple. Italy was not a political whole. The head of the Adriatic was entirely in the hands of Austria. There was no thought at that time of our modern navies, and of the importance of keeping open the Straits of Otranto. It was the Dalmatian coast, north of Albania, which Austria considered essential to her commercial supremacy. Then, too, Greece had not yet received her freedom, and the Servians had not risen in rebellion against the Ottoman Empire. There were no Slavic, Hellenic, and Italian questions to disturb Austria in her peaceful possession of the Adriatic Sea.

It was not until the union of Italy had been accomplished, and the south Slavic nationalities had formed themselves into political units, that Albania became a "question" in the chancelleries of Europe.

Austria-Hungary determined that Italy should not get a foothold in Albania. Italy had the same determination in regard to Austria-Hungary. Since the last Russo-Turkish War, Austria-Hungary and Italy have had the united determination to keep the Slavs from reaching the Adriatic. For the past generation, feeling certain that the end of the Ottoman Empire was at hand, Austria and Italy through their missionaries, their schools, and their consular and commercial agents, have struggled hard against each other to secure the ascendancy in Albania. Their intrigues have not ceased up to this day.

When Austria-Hungary annexed Bosnia-Herzegovina, and the Young Turk oppression of the Albanians aroused the first expression of what might possibly be called national feeling since the time of Skander bey's resistance to the Ottoman conquest, the rival Powers, instead of following in the line of Russia and Great Britain in Persia, and establishing spheres of interest, agreed to support the Albanian national movement as the best possible check upon Servian and Greek national aspirations. This was the status of Albania in her relationship to the Adriatic Powers, when the war of the Balkan States against Turkey broke out. The accord between Austria and Italy had stood the strain of Italy's war with Turkey. Largely owing to their fear of Russia and to the pressure of Germany, it stood the strain of the Balkan War. But both Italy and Austria let it be known to the other Powers that if the Turkish Empire in Europe disappeared, there must be an independent Albania.

This dictum was accepted in principle by the other four Powers, who saw in it the only possible chance of preventing the outbreak of a conflict between Austria and Russia which would be bound to involve all Europe in war. No nation wanted to fight over the question of Albania. Russia could not hope to have support from Great Britain and France to impose upon the Triple Alliance her desire for a Slavic outlet to the Adriatic. For neither France nor Great Britain was anxious for the Russian to get to the Mediterranean. The accord between the Powers was shown in the warning given to Greece and Servia that the solution of the Albanian question must be reserved for the Powers when a treaty of peace was signed with Turkey. The accord weathered the severe test put upon it by the bold defiance of the Montenegrin occupation of Scutari.

We have spoken elsewhere of the policy of the Young Turks towards Albania. This most useful and loyal corner of the Sultan's dominions was turned into a country of perennial revolutions, which started soon after the inauguration of the constitutional *régime*. In the winter of 1911-1912, when the group of Albanian deputies in the Ottoman Parliament saw their demands for reforms rejected by the Cabinet, and even the right of discussion of their complaints refused on the floor of Parliament, the Albanians north and south, Catholic and Moslem, united in a resistance to the Turkish authorities that extended to Uskub and Monastir. After the spring elections of 1912, the resistance became a formidable revolt. For the Young Turks had rashly manoeuvred the balloting with more than Tammany skill. The Albanians were left without representatives in Parliament! Former deputies, such as Ismail Kemal bey, Hassan bey, and chiefs such as Isa Boletinatz, Idris Sefer, and Ali Riza joined in a determination to demand autonomy by force of arms.

When, in July, the Cabinet decided to move an army against the Albanians, there were wholesale desertions from the garrison of Monastir, and of Albanian officers from all parts of European Turkey. Mahmoud Shevket pasha was compelled to resign the Ministry of War, and was followed by Saïd pasha and the whole Cabinet. The Albanians demanded as a *sine qua non* the dissolution of Parliament. The Mukhtar Cabinet agreed to the dissolution, and accepted almost all the demands of the rebels in a conference at Pristina.

For the tables had now been turned. Instead of a Turkish invasion of Albania for "pacification," as in previous summers, it was a question now of an Albanian invasion of Turkey. In spite of the conciliatory spirit of the new Cabinet, the agitation persisted. It was rumoured that the Malissores and the Mirdites were planning a campaign against Scutari and Durazzo. I was in Uskub in the early part of September. Isa Boletinatz and his band were practically in possession of the city. A truce for Ramazan, the Moslem fast month, had been arranged between Turks and Albanians. But the Albanians said they would not lay down their arms until a new and honestly constitutional election was held.

Immediately after Ramazan came the Balkan War. Albania found herself separated from Turkey, and in a position to have more than autonomy without having to deal further with the Turks.

During the Balkan War, the attitude of the Albanians was a tremendous disappointment to the Turks. One marvels that loyalty to the Empire could have been expected, even from the Moslem element, in Albania. And yet the Turks did expect that a Pan-Islamic feeling would draw the Albanian *beys* to fight for the Sultan, just as they had expected a similar phenomenon on the part of the rebellious Arabs of the Arabic peninsula during the war with Italy.

From the very beginning the Albanians adopted an attitude of opportunism. They did not lift a hand directly to help the Turks. Had they so desired, they might have made impossible the investment of Janina by the Greeks. But nowhere, save in Scutari, did the Albanians make a stubborn stand against the military operations of the Balkan allies. Almost from the beginning, they had understood that the Powers would not allow the partition of Albania. They knew that the retention of Janina was hopeless after the successes of the allies during October. But they received encouragement from both Austria-Hungary and Italy to fight for Scutari.

The heroic defence of Scutari, which lasted longer than that of any of the other fortified towns in the Balkan Peninsula, cannot be regarded as a feat of the Turkish army. During the siege, the general commanding Scutari had been assassinated by order of Essad pasha, who was his second in command. Essad then assumed charge of the defence as purely Albanian in character. He refused to accept the armistice, and continued the struggle throughout the debates in London. Scutari is at the south end of a lake which is shared between Albania and Montenegro. Commanding the city is a steep barren hill called Tarabosh. With their heavy artillery on this hill, the Albanians were able to prevent indefinitely the capture of their city. Servians and Montenegrins found themselves confronted with the task of taking Tarabosh by assault, if they hoped to occupy Scutari. This was a feat beyond the strength of a Balkan army. On the steep slopes of this hill were placed miles of barbed wire. The assailants were mowed down each time they tried to reach the batteries at the top. As Tarabosh commanded the four corners of the horizon, its cannon could prevent an assault or bombardment of the city from the plain. The allies were unable to silence the batteries on the crest of this hill.

During the winter, the principal question before the concert of European Powers was that of Scutari. Austria-Hungary was so determined that Scutari should not fall into the hands of the Montenegrins and Servians that she mobilized several army corps in Bosnia-Herzegovina and on the Russian frontier of Galicia, at Christmas time, 1912. The New Year brought with it ominous forebodings for the peace of Europe. Diplomacy worked busily to bring about an accord between the Powers, and pressure upon the besiegers of Scutari. In the middle of March, it was unanimously agreed that Scutari should remain to Albania, and that Servia should receive Prizrend, Ipek, Dibra, and Diakova as compensation for not reaching the Adriatic, and the assurance of an economic outlet for a railroad at some Albanian port. The European concert then decided to demand at Belgrade and Cettinje the lifting of the siege of Scutari.

Servia, yielding to the warning of Russia that nothing further could be done for her, consented to withdraw her troops from before Scutari, and to abandon the points in Albanian territory which had been allotted by the Powers to the independent Albanian State which they intended to create. Servia had another reason for doing this. Seeing the hopelessness of territorial aggrandizement in Albania, she decided to denounce her treaty of partition, concluded before the war, with Bulgaria. To realize this act of faithlessness and treachery, she had need of the sympathetic support of the Powers in the quarrel which was bound to ensue. We see here how the blocking of Servia's outlet to the Adriatic led inevitably to a war between the Balkan Allies.

But with Montenegro the situation was entirely different. She had sacrificed one-fifth of her army in the attacks upon Tarabosh, and Scutari seemed to her the only thing that she was to get out of the war with Turkey. Perched up in her mountains, there was little harm that the Powers could do to her. Just as King Nicholas had precipitated the Balkan War against the advice of the Powers the previous October, he decided on April 1st to refuse to obey the command of the Powers to lift the siege of Scutari. From what I have gathered myself from conversations in the Montenegrin capital two months later, I feel that the King of Montenegro can hardly be condemned for what the newspapers of Europe called his "audacious folly" in refusing to give a favourable response to the joint note presented to him by the European Ministers at Cettinje. The Montenegrins are illiterate mountaineers, who know nothing whatever about considerations of international diplomacy. If their King had listened to words written on a piece of paper, and had ordered the Montenegrin troops to withdraw from before Scutari, he would probably have lost his throne.

So the Powers were compelled to make a show of force. Little Montenegro, with its one port, and its total population not equal to a single *arrondissement* of the city of Paris, received the signal honour of an international blockade. On April 7th, an international fleet, under the command of the British Admiral Burney, blockaded the coast from Antivari to Durazzo. While all Europe was showing its displeasure in the Adriatic, the Montenegrins kept on, although deserted by the Servians, sitting in a circle around Scutari, only twenty-five miles inland from the blockading fleet. On April 23d, after the Balkan War was all finished, Europe was electrified by the news that the Albanians had surrendered Scutari to Montenegro. The worst was to be feared, for Austria announced her determination to send her troops across the border from Bosnia into Montenegro. Such an action would certainly have brought on a great European war. For neither at Rome nor at Petrograd could Austrian intervention have been tolerated.

No Power in Europe was at that moment ready for war. Largely through pressure brought to bear at Cettinje by his son-in-law, the King of Italy, King Nicholas decided on May 5th to deliver Scutari to the Powers. The Montenegrins withdrew, and ten days later Scutari was occupied by detachments of marines from the international squadron. The blockade was lifted. The peace of Europe was saved.

The Treaty of London, signed on May 30, 1913, put Albania into the hands of the Powers. The northern and eastern frontiers had been arranged by the promise made to Servia in return for her withdrawal from the siege of Scutari. But the southern frontier was still an open question. Here Italy was as much interested as was Austria in the north. With Corfu in the possession of Greece, Italy would not agree that the coast of the mainland opposite should also be Hellenic. The Greeks, on the contrary, declared that the littoral and *hinterland*, up beyond Santi Quaranta, was part of ancient Epirus, and inhabited principally by Greeks. It should therefore revert logically to greater Greece. Athens lifted again the old cry, "Where there are Hellenes, there is Hellas." The Greeks were occupying Santi Quaranta. They claimed as far north as Argyrokastron. But they consented to withdraw from the Adriatic, north of and opposite Corfu, if interior points equally far to the north were left to them. An international commission was formed to make a southern boundary for Albania. Its task has is still open.

What was to be done with this new state, foster child of all Europe, with indefinite boundaries, with guardians each jealous of the other, and neighbours waiting only for a favourable moment to throw themselves upon her and extinguish her life?

I visited Albania in July, 1913, during the second Balkan War. At Valona, in the south, I found a provisional government, self-constituted during the previous winter, whose authority was problematical outside of Valona itself. At the head of the government was Ismail Kemal, whom I had known as the champion of Albanian autonomy in the Ottoman Parliament at Constantinople. He talked passionately of Albania, the new State in Europe, with its *united* population and its *national* aspirations. He was eager to have the claims of Albania to a generous southern frontier presented at London. He assured me that I could write with perfect confidence in glowing terms concerning the future of Albania, that a spirit of harmony reigned throughout the country, and that the Albanians of all creeds, freed from Turkish oppression, were looking eagerly to their new life as an independent nation. When I expressed misgivings as to the rôle of Essad pasha, the provisional president asserted that the former commander of Scutari was wholly in accord with him, and cited as proof the fact that he had that very day received from Essad pasha his acceptance of the portfolio of Minister of the Interior.

But that indefinable feeling of misgiving, which one always has over the enthusiasm of Orientals, caused me to withhold judgment as to the liability of Albania until I had seen how things were going in other portions of the new kingdom.

At Durazzo, the northern port of Albania, the friends of Essad pasha were in control of the government. Things were still being done *à la turque*, and there was a feeling of great uncertainty concerning the future. Few had any faith whatever in the provisional government at Valona, and it was declared that the influence of Essad pasha would decide the attitude of the Albanians in Durazzo, Tirana, and Elbassan. Essad was chief of the Toptanis, the most influential family in the neighbourhood of Durazzo. He had "made his career" in the *gendarmerie*, and had risen rapidly through the approval and admiration of Abdul Hamid. This is an indication of his character. He was credited with the ambition of ruling Albania. To withdraw his forces and his munitions of war intact, so that he could press these claims, is the only explanation of his "deal" with King Nicholas of Montenegro to surrender Scutari. Essad had sacrificed the pride and honour of Albania to his personal ambition.

From Durazzo, I went to San Giovanni di Medua, which was occupied by the Montenegrins, just as I had found Santi Quaranta in the south occupied by the Greeks. Going inland from this port (one must use his imagination in calling San Giovanni di Medua a port) by way of Alessio, I reached Scutari, from whose citadel flew the flags of the Powers. In every quarter of this typically and hopelessly Turkish town, one ran across sailors from various nations. Each Power had its quarter, and had named the streets with some curious results. The Via Garibaldi ran into the Platz Radetzky. On the Catholic cathedral was a sign informing you that you were in the Rue Ernest Renan.

This accidental naming of streets was a prophecy of the hopelessness of trying to reconcile the conflicting aims and ideals of the Powers whose bands were playing side by side in the public garden. In the dining-room of the hotel, when I saw Austrians, Italians, Germans, British, and French officers eating together at the long tables, instead of rejoicing at this seeming spirit of European harmony, I had the presentiment of the inevitable result of the struggle between Slav and Teuton, to prevent which these men were there. Just a year later, I stood in front of the Gare du Montparnasse in Paris reading the order for General Mobilization. There came back to me as in a dream the public garden at Scutari, and the mingled strains of national anthems, with officers standing rigidly in salute beside their half-filled glasses.

In the palatial home of a British nobleman who had loved the Albanians and had lived long in Scutari, Admiral Burney established his headquarters. I talked with him there one afternoon concerning the present and the future of Albania, and the relationship of the problem which he had before him with the peace of Europe. Never have I found a man more intelligently apprehensive of the possible outcome of the drama in which he was playing a part, and at the same time more determinedly hopeful to use all his ability and power to save the peace of Europe by welding together the Albanians into a nation worthy of the independence that has been given to them by the European concert. Such men as Admiral Burney are more than the glory of a nation: they are the making of a nation. The greatness of Britain is due to the men who serve her. High ideals, self-sacrifice, ability, and energy are the corner-stones of the British overseas Empire.

There was little, however, that Admiral Burney, or anyone in fact, could do for Albania. No nation can exist in modern times, when national life is in the will of the people rather than in the unifying qualities of a ruler, if there are no common ideals and the determination to attain them. Albania is without a national spirit and a national past. It is, therefore, no unit, capable of being welded into a state. The creation by the Ambassadors of the Powers in London may have been thought by them to be a necessity. But it was really a makeshift. If the Albanians had done their part, and had shown the possibility of union, the makeshift might have developed into a new European state. As things have turned out, it has stayed what it was in the beginning,—a fiasco.

Among the many candidates put forward for the new throne, Prince William of Wied was finally decided upon. He was a Protestant, and could occupy a position of neutrality among his Moslem, Orthodox, and Catholic subjects. He was a German, and could not be suspected of Slavic sympathies. He was a relative of the King of Rumania, and could expect powerful support in the councils of the Balkan Powers.

It would be wearisome to go into the story of Prince William's short and unhappy reign. At Durazzo, which was chosen for the capital, he quickly showed himself incapable of the rôle which a genius among rulers might have failed to play successfully. Lost in a maze of bewildering intrigues, foreign and domestic, the ruler of Albania saw his prestige, and then his dignity, disappear. He never had any real authority. He had been forced upon the Albanians. They did not want him. The Powers who had placed him upon the throne did not support him. In the spring, the usual April heading, "Albania in Arms," appeared once more in the newspapers of the world. Up to the outbreak of the European war, when Albania was "lost in the shuffle," almost daily telegrams detailed the march of the insurgents upon Durazzo, the useless and fatal heroism of the Dutch officers of the *gendarmerie*, the incursions of the Epirote bands in the south, and the embarrassing position of the international forces still occupying Scutari. What the Albanians really wanted, none could guess, much less they themselves!

The European war, in August, 1914, enabled the Powers to withdraw gracefully from the Albanian fiasco. Their contingents hurriedly abandoned Scutari, and sailed for home. The French did not have time to do this, so they went to Montenegro. Since the catastrophe, to prevent which they had created Albania, had fallen upon Europe, what further need was there for the Powers to bother about the fortunes of Prince William and his subjects? Italy alone was left with hands free, and her interests were not at stake, so long as Greece kept out of the fray. For Prince William of Wied, Italy felt no obligation whatever.

Without support and without money, there was nothing left to Prince William but to get out. He did not have the good sense to make his withdrawal from Albania a dignified proceeding. The palace was left under seals. The Prince issued a proclamation which would lead the Albanians to believe that it was his intention to return. It may be that he thought the triumph of the German and Austrian armies in the European war would mean his re-establishment to Durazzo. But after he was once again safely home at Neu-Wied, he did what he ought to have done many months before. A high-sounding manifesto announced his abdication, and wished the Albanians Godspeed in the future. After this formality had been accomplished, the former Mpret of Albania rejoined his regiment in the German army, and went out to fight against the French.

With Prince William of Wied and the international corps of occupation gone, the Albanians were left to themselves. At Durazzo, a body of notables, calling themselves the Senate, adopted resolutions restoring the Ottoman flag and the suzerainty of the Sultan, invited Prince Burhaneddin effendi, a son of Abdul Hamid, to become their ruler, and solemnly decreed that hereafter the Turkish language should be restored to its former position as the official language of the country.

But Essad pasha thought otherwise. The psychological moment, for which he had been waiting ever since his surrender of Scutari to the Montenegrins, had come. In the first week of October, he hurried to Durazzo with his followers, had himself elected head of a new provisional government by the Albanian Senate, and announced openly that his policy would be to look to Italy instead of to Austria for support. After rendering homage to the Sultan as Khalif, asking the people to celebrate the happy spirit of harmony which now reigned throughout Albania, and prophesying a new era of peace and prosperity for Europe's latest-born independent state, the former *gendarme* of Abdul Hamid entered the palace, broke the seals of the international commission, and went to sleep in the bed of Prince William of Wied.

One wonders whether the new ruler of Albania will have more restful slumbers than his predecessor. In spite of all protests, Greece is still secretly encouraging the Epirotes in their endeavour to push northward the frontier of the Hellenic kingdom. Italy has two army corps at Brindisi waiting for a favourable moment to occupy Valona. The Montenegrins and

Servians are planning once more to reach the Adriatic through the valleys of the Boyana and Drin, after they have driven the Austro-Hungarian armies from Bosnia and Herzegovina. Only an Austrian triumph could now save Albania from her outside enemies. But could anything save her from her inside enemies? When I read of Essad Pasha in Durazzo, self-chosen Moses of his people, there comes back to me a conversation with the leading Moslem chieftain of Scutari, whose guest I had the privilege of being, in his home in the summer of 1913. When I mentioned Essad pasha, he rose to his feet before the fire, waved his arms, and cried out: "When I see Essad, I shall shoot him like a dog!"

CHAPTER XIX
THE AUSTRO-HUNGARIAN
ULTIMATUM TO SERVIA

In discussing the relations of the Austrians and Hungarians with their south Slavic subjects, and the rivalries of races in Macedonia the general causes behind the hostile attitude of Austria-Hungary to the development of Servia have been explained. Specific treatment of the Servian attitude towards the annexation of Bosnia and Herzegovina was reserved for this chapter, because the events of the summer of 1914 are the direct sequence of the events of the winter of 1908-1909.

On October 3, 1908, Marquis Pallavicini, Austro-Hungarian Ambassador at Constantinople, notified verbally the Sublime Porte that Austria-Hungary had annexed the Turkish provinces of Bosnia and Herzegovina, whose administration was entrusted to her by the Treaty of Berlin just thirty years before. Austria-Hungary was willing to renounce the right given her by the Treaty of Berlin to the military occupation of the *sandjak* of Novi Bazar (a strip of Turkish territory between Servia and Montenegro), if Turkey would renounce her sovereignty of the annexed provinces.

This violation of the Treaty of Berlin by Austria-Hungary aroused a strong protest not only in Servia and in Turkey, but also among the other Powers who had signed at Berlin the conditions of the maintenance of the integrity of the Ottoman Empire. The protest was especially strong in London and Petrograd. But Austria-Hungary had the backing of Germany, whose Ambassador at Petrograd, Count de Pourtales, did not hesitate several times during the winter to exercise pressure *that went almost to the point of being a threat* upon the Russian Foreign Office to refrain from encouraging the intractable attitude of Servia towards the annexation.

With Germany's support, Austria-Hungary did not have much difficulty in silencing the protests of all the Great Powers. She had a free hand, thanks to Germany, in forcing Turkey and Servia to accept the *fait accompli* of the annexation.

Turkish protests took the form of the boycott of which we have spoken elsewhere. On November 22d, Austria-Hungary threatened to put the whole status of European Turkey into question by convoking the European congress to revise the Treaty of Berlin. This is exactly what Austria-Hungary herself did not want. But neither did Turkey. Both governments had a common interest in preventing outside intervention in the Balkan

Peninsula. The boycott, as evidencing anti-Austrian feeling, was rather a sop to public opinion of Young Turkey, and a blind to the Powers to hide the perfect accord that existed between Germany and Turkey at the moment, than the expression of hostility to Austria-Hungary. After several months of *pourparlers* an agreement was made between Constantinople and Vienna on February 26, 1909. Turkey agreed to recognize the annexation in return for financial compensation. The negotiations at Constantinople concerning Bosnia and Herzegovina are a monument to the diplomatic finesse and skill of the late Baron Marschall von Bieberstein and of Marquis Pallavicini.

To lose something that you know you can no longer keep is far different from losing the hope of possession. It is always more cruel to be deprived of an anticipation than of a reality. Turkey gave up Bosnia and Herzegovina with her usual fatalistic indifference. Her sovereignty had been only a fiction after all. But Servia saw in the action of Austria-Hungary a fatal blow to her national aspirations. The inhabitants of the two Turkish provinces on her west were Servian: Bosnia-Herzegovina formed the centre of the Servian race. Montenegro on the south was Servian. Dalmatia on the west was Servian. Croatia on the north was Servian. Everything was Servian to the Adriatic Sea. And yet Servia was land-locked. The Servians determined they would not accept this annexation. They appealed to the signatory Powers of Berlin, and succeeded in arousing a sentiment in Europe favourable to a European conference. They threatened to make Austrian and Hungarian sovereignty intolerable, not only in Bosnia and Herzegovina, but also in Croatia and Dalmatia.

Austria-Hungary was more than irritated; she was alarmed. She appealed to her ally, and pictured the danger to the *Drang nach Osten*. The powerful intervention of the German ambassadors in the various European capitals succeeded in isolating Belgrade. Russian support of Servia would have meant a European war. Rather than risk this, France begged Russia to yield. Russia, not yet recovered from the Manchurian disaster, ordered Servia to yield. Austria-Hungary was allowed to force Servia into submission.

Friendless in the face of her too powerful adversary, Servia directed her Minister at Vienna on March 31, 1909, to make the following formal declaration to the Austro-Hungarian Ministry of Foreign Affairs:

"Servia declares that she is not affected in her rights by the situation established in Bosnia, and that she will therefore adapt herself to the decisions at which the Powers are going to arrive in reference to Art. 25 of the Berlin Treaty. By following the councils of the Powers, Servia binds herself to cease the attitude of protest and resistance which she has assumed since last October, relative to the annexation, and she binds herself further to change the direction of her present policies towards Austria-Hungary, and, in the future, to live with the latter in friendly and neighbourly relations."

The crisis passed. Servia's humiliation was the price of European peace. Germany had shown her determination to stand squarely behind Austria-Hungary in her dealings with Servia. It was a lesson for the future. Five years later history repeated itself—except that Russia did not back down!

We have already told the story of Austria-Hungary's dealings with Servia after the first victorious month of the Balkan War with Turkey: how Servia was compelled, owing to lack of support from Russia, to give satisfaction to Austria-Hungary in the Prochaska incident, to withdraw her troops from Durazzo and from before Scutari; and how the Powers saved the peace of Europe in May, 1913, by compelling Montenegro to abandon Scutari.

Ever since the Treaty of Bukarest, Austria-Hungary watched Servia keenly for an opportunity to pick a quarrel with her. It is marvellous how the Servians, elated as they naturally were by their military successes against Turkey and Bulgaria, avoided knocking the chip off the shoulder of their jealous and purposely sensitive neighbour.

It was one thing to be able to keep a perfectly correct official attitude towards the Austro-Hungarian Government. This the Servian Government had promised to do in the note wrung from it on March 31, 1909. This it *did* do. But it was a totally different thing to expect the authorities at Belgrade to stifle the national aspirations of twelve million Servians, the majority of whom were outside of her jurisdiction. Even if it had been the wiser course for her to pursue—and this is doubtful,—could Servia have been able to repress the thoroughly awakened and triumphant nationalism of her own subjects who had borne so successfully and so heroically the sufferings and sacrifices of two wars within one year?

Individual Servians, living within the kingdom of Servia, were irredentists, but without official sanction. They were undoubtedly in connection with the revolutionaries created by Austrian and Hungarian methods in the Servian provinces of the Dual Monarchy. There was undoubtedly a dream of Greater Servia, and a strong hope in the hearts of nationalists on both sides of the frontiers that the day would dawn *by their efforts* when Greater Servia would be a reality. No government could have continued to exist in Servia which tried to suppress the *Narodna Obrana*. I make this statement without hesitation. King Peter did not intend to become another Charles Albert.

Ought the Vienna and Berlin statesmen to have expected Servia to do so? What answer would Switzerland or Holland or Belgium or Brazil receive, were their ministers to present a note at Wilhelmstrasse or Ballplatz, calling attention to the menace to their independence of the Pan-Germanic movement, citing speeches delivered by eminent professors in universities, books written by officials of the imperial Governments, and asking that certain societies be suppressed and certain geographies be removed from use in German schools? Their cause would have been as just, and their right as clear, *for exactly the same reasons*, as that of the Austrian Government in its attitude towards Servia. The only difference between Pan-Servianism and Pan-Germanism—and you must remember that the latter is not only encouraged, but also subsidized, by the Berlin and Vienna governments—is that the former is the aspiration of twelve millions while the latter is the aspiration of ninety millions. Is not the answer the old Bismarckian formula that might makes right?

During the winter following the Treaty of Bukarest the Austro-Hungarian agents and police continued their careful surveillance of the *Narodna Obrana*, and followed all its dealings with Servians of Austro-Hungarian nationality. But it could find no *casus belli*. The attitude of the Servian Government was perfectly correct at all times. Traps were laid, but Servian officials did not fall into them. The occasion for striking Servia came in a most tragic way.

It seems like tempting Providence to have sent the Archduke Franz Ferdinand and his wife to Sarajevo on the anniversary of the battle of Kossova. Things had been going from bad to worse in Bosnia. Flags of the Dual Monarchy had been burned in Sarajevo and Mostar, and the garrisons called upon to intervene to restore order. The Constitution of 1910 had been modified in 1912, so that the military Governor was invested with civil power. The local Bosnian Diet had been twice prorogued. In May, 1913, the constitution was suspended, and a state of siege declared in Bosnia-Herzegovina. Throughout the winter of 1913-1914, incipient rebellions had to be checked by force in many places. It was known to the police that Servian secret societies were active, and that the provinces were in a state of danger and insecurity. The Servian Government was apprehensive concerning the announced visit of the heir to the Austro-Hungarian throne. In fact, so greatly was it feared that some attempt might be made against the life of Franz Ferdinand, and that this would be used as an excuse for an attack upon Servia, that the Servian Minister at Vienna, a week before the date announced for the visit, informed the Government that there was reason to fear a plot to assassinate the Archduke.

On June 28, 1914, the Archduke Franz Ferdinand and his wife, the Duchess of Hohenberg, were assassinated in the streets of Sarajevo. Austria-Hungary realized that her moment had come. Germany was sounded, and found to be ready to prevent outside interference in whatever measures Vienna might see fit to take with Belgrade.

In the spring of 1914, the Pasitch Cabinet had almost succumbed in the struggle between civil and military elements. Premier Pasitch retained his power by agreeing to a dissolution of Parliament, and binding himself to the necessity of following the leadership of the military part. So far were the chiefs of the military party from being in a mood to consider the susceptibilities of Austria-Hungary that they were actually, according to a telegram from a well-informed source in Agram on June 26, 1914, debating the means of uniting Servia and Montenegro. The difficult question of dynasties was in the way of being solved, and, despite Premier Pasitch's misgivings, the *ballon d'essai* of the project of union had been launched in Europe. It was at this critical and delicate moment for the Belgrade Cabinet that the storm broke.

I was surprised by the spirit of optimism which seemed to pervade the French press during the period immediately following the assassination of Franz Ferdinand. For three weeks the telegrams from Vienna repeated over and over again the statement that the ultimatum which Austria-Hungary intended to present at Belgrade as a result of the Sarajevo assassination would be so worded that Russia could not take offence. This optimistic opinion, which seems to have been given almost official sanction by the Ballplatz, was shared by the French Government. France is a country in which the inmost thoughts of her statesmen are voiced freely in the daily newspapers of Paris. If there had been any serious misgivings, the protocol for the visit of President Poincaré to Petrograd and to the Scandinavian capitals would certainly have been modified.

The President of France sailed for the Baltic on July 15th. At six o'clock in the evening of the 23d, the note of the Austro-Hungarian Government concerning the events of the assassination of Sarajevo was given to the Servian Government. It commenced by reproducing the text of the Servian declaration of March 31, 1909, which we have quoted above. Servia was accused of not having fulfilled the promise made in this declaration, and of permitting the Pan-Servian propaganda in the newspapers and public schools of the kingdom. The assassination of the Archduke Franz Ferdinand was stated to be the direct result of Servian failure to live up to her declaration of March 31, 1909. Austria-Hungary claimed that the assassination of the heir to her throne had been investigated, and that ample proof had been found of the connivance of two Servians, one an army officer and the other a functionary who belonged to the *Narodna Obrana*; that the assassins had received their arms and their bombs from these two men, and had been knowingly allowed to pass into Bosnia by the Servian authorities on the Serbo-Bosnian frontier. Being unable to endure longer the Pan-Servian agitation, of which Belgrade was the *foyer* and the crime of Sarajevo a direct result, the Austro-Hungarian Government found itself compelled to demand of the Servian Government the formal assurance that it condemned this propaganda, which was dangerous to the existence of the Dual Monarchy, because its final end was to detach from Austria-Hungary large portions of her territory and attach them to Servia.

After this preamble, the note went on to demand that on the first page of the *Journal Officiel* of July 26th the Servian Government publish a new declaration, the text of which is so important that we quote it in full.

"The Royal Servian Government condemns the propaganda directed against Austria-Hungary, *i.e.*, the entirety of those machinations whose aim it is to separate from the Austro-Hungarian Monarchy territories belonging thereto, and she regrets sincerely the ghastly consequences of these criminal actions.

"The Royal Servian Government regrets that Servian officers and officials have participated in the propaganda cited above, and have thus threatened the friendly and neighbourly relations which the Royal Government was solemnly bound to cultivate by its declaration of March 31, 1909.

"The Royal Government, which disapproves and rejects every thought or every attempt at influencing the destinies of the inhabitants of any part of Austria-Hungary, considers it its duty to call most emphatically to the attention of its officers and officials, and of the entire population of the kingdom, that it will hereafter proceed with the utmost severity against any persons guilty of similar actions, to prevent and suppress which it will make every effort."

Simultaneously with the publication in the *Journal Officiel*, Austria-Hungary demanded that the declaration be brought to the knowledge of the Servian army by an order of the day of King Peter, and be published in the official organ of the army. The Servian Government was also asked to make ten promises:

1. To suppress any publication which fosters hatred of, and contempt for, the Austro-Hungarian Monarchy, and whose general tendency is directed against the latter's territorial integrity;

2. To proceed at once with the dissolution of the society *Narodna Obrana*, to confiscate its entire means of propaganda, and to proceed in the same manner against the other societies and associations in Servia which occupy themselves with the propaganda against Austria-Hungary, and to take the necessary measures that the dissolved societies may not continue their activities under another name or in another form;

3. To eliminate without delay from the public instruction in Servia, so far as the teaching staff as well as the curriculum is concerned, whatever serves or may serve to foster the propaganda against Austria-Hungary;

4. To remove from military service and public office in general all officers and officials who are guilty of propaganda against Austria-Hungary and whose names, with a communication of the evidence which the Imperial and Royal Government possesses against them, the Imperial and Royal Government reserves the right to communicate to the Royal Government;

5. To accept the collaboration in Servia of members of the official machinery (*organes*) of the Imperial and Royal Government in the suppression of the movement directed against Austro-Hungarian territorial integrity;

6. To commence a judicial investigation (*enquête judiciaire*) against the participants of the conspiracy of June 28th, who are on Servian territory— members of the official machinery (*organes*) delegated by the Austro-Hungarian Government will take part in the researches (*recherches*) relative thereto;

7. To proceed immediately to arrest Major Vorja Tankositch and a certain Milan Ciganovitch, a functionary of the Servian State, who have been compromised by the result of the preliminary investigation at Sarajevo;

8. To prevent, by effective measures, the participation of the Servian authorities in the smuggling of arms and explosives across the frontier, to dismiss and punish severely the functionaries at the frontier at Shabatz and at Loznica, guilty of having aided the authors of the crime of Sarajevo by facilitating their crossing of the frontier;

9. To give to the Austro-Hungarian Government explanations concerning the unjustifiable remarks of high Servian functionaries, in Servia and abroad, who, in spite of their official position have not hesitated, after the crime of June 28th, to express themselves in interviews in a hostile manner against the Austro-Hungarian Monarchy;

10. To notify without delay to the Austro-Hungarian Government the execution of the measures included in the preceding points.

Annexed to the note was a memorandum which declared that the investigation of the police, after the assassination of the Archduke and his wife, had established that the plot had been formed at Belgrade by the assassins with the help of a commandant in the Servian army, that the six bombs and four Browning pistols with their ammunition had been given at Belgrade to the assassins by the Servian functionary and the Servian army officer whose names were cited in the note, that the bombs were hand grenades which came from the Servian army headquarters at Kragujevac, that the assassins were given instruction in the use of the arms by Servian officers, and that the introduction into Bosnia and Herzegovina of the assassins and their arms was facilitated by the connivance of three frontier captains and a customs official.

The wording of this note seemed to have been entirely unexpected. The intention of the ultimatum was clear. It was understood that Russia would not accept an attack upon the integrity of Servia. Six years had passed since 1908, and two since 1912. Russia had recuperated from the Japanese War, and her Persian accord with Great Britain had borne much fruit. She was sure of France. Was this not a deliberate provocation to Russia?

Forty-eight hours had been given to Servia to respond. Russia and France had both counselled Servia to give an answer that would be a *general* acceptance of the Austro-Hungarian ultimatum. Neither France nor Russia wanted war. So anxious were they to avoid giving Austria-Hungary the opportunity to precipitate the crisis before they were ready for it that *for the third time in six years* Servia was asked to swallow her pride and submit. On the night of July 24th, a memorable council was held in Belgrade. The Premier and the leaders of the opposition, together with some members of the *Narodna Obrana* were shown clearly what course they must follow, if they expected the loyal support of Russia. The answer to the ultimatum must be worded in such a way that Austria-Hungary would have no ground upon which to stand in forcing immediately the war. Servia must once more "eat humble pie." But this time the promise of Russian support was given *to defend the territorial integrity and the independence of Servia.*

The Servian answer was far more conciliatory than was expected. The allegations of the Austro-Hungarian preamble were denied, but the publication of the declaration in the *Journal Officiel* and in the army bulletin, and its incorporation in an order of the day to the army, were promised. But there were to be two changes in the text of the declaration. Instead of "the Royal Servian Government condemns *the propaganda against* Austria-Hungary," the Servians agreed to declare that "the Royal Servian Government condemns *every propaganda which should be directed against* Austria-Hungary," and instead of "the Royal Government regrets *that Servian officers and officials* ... have participated in the propaganda cited above," the Servian King could say no more than "the Royal Government regrets *that according to a communication of the Imperial and Royal Government certain officers and functionaries* ... *etc.*"

The German *White Book* makes a special point of the bad faith of Servia in altering the text of the declaration in this way. But what government could be expected to admit what was only a supposition, and what king worthy of the name would denounce as a regicide openly before his army one of his officers upon the unsupported statement of a political document? The Austro-Hungarian ultimatum had given no proof of its charges against the man named in its note, and forty-eight hours was too short a time for the Servian Government to investigate the charges to its own satisfaction.

In order to make clear just what was the nature of the demands which Austria-Hungary made upon Servia, I have cited the ten articles in full.

One can readily see that the demands of Articles 1, 2, and 3, in their entirety, meant the extinction of the Pan-Servian movement and Servian nationalism. Austria-Hungary was asking of Servia something that neither member of the Dual Monarchy had succeeded in accomplishing in its own territories! The German *White Book* attempts to sustain the justice of the demands of its ally in striking at the press, the nationalist societies, and the schools. The methods of arousing a nationalistic spirit in the Servian people through the press, through the formation of societies, and through the teaching of irredentism by school-books, were borrowed from Germany. But Servia agreed to make her press laws more severe, to dissolve the *Narodna Obrana* and other societies; and "to eliminate from the public instruction in Servia anything which might further the propaganda directed against Austria-Hungary, provided the Imperial and Royal Government furnishes actual proofs."

Article 4 was agreed to only so far as it could be actually proved that the officers and officials in question had been "guilty of actions against the territorial integrity of the monarchy." To promise to remove all who were "guilty of propaganda against Austria-Hungary" would have meant the disbanding of the Servian army and the Servian Government! Is there any man with red blood in his veins who can be prevented from having hopes and dislikes, and expressing them? Could Servia prevent Servians from stating how they felt about the political *status* of their race in Croatia and in Bosnia? Did Austria-Hungary ever make a similar request to her ally, Italy, about irredentist literature and speeches?

Articles 5 and 6 are open to discussion. There is no doubt that the newspapers of nations hostile to Austria-Hungary and Germany have been unfair in their interpretation and in their translation of these two articles. The Servian answer deliberately gives a false meaning to the Austrian request here, and represents it as an attack upon the independence of her courts. Servia had enough good grounds for resistance to the ultimatum without equivocating on this point. In her answer she refused what had not been actually demanded, a co-operation in the *enquête judiciaire* of

Austro-Hungarian *organes*. What Austria-Hungary demanded was the co-operation of her police officials in the *recherches*.

Articles 7 to 10 were accepted by Servia *in toto*. As a proof of her good faith, the Servian answer declared that Major Tankositch had been arrested on the evening of the day on which the ultimatum was received.

In conclusion, Servia offered, if her response to the ultimatum were found insufficient, to place her case in the hands of the Hague Tribunal and of the different Powers at whose suggestion she had signed the declaration of March 31, 1909, after the excitement over the Austro-Hungarian annexation of Bosnia and Herzegovina.

The answer to the ultimatum was taken by Premier Pasitch in person to the Minister of Austria-Hungary at Belgrade before six o'clock on the evening of July 25th. Without referring the response to his Government, the Austro-Hungarian Minister, acting on previous instructions that *no answer other than an acceptance in every particular of the ultimatum would be admissible*, replied that the response was not satisfactory. At half-past six, he left Belgrade with all members of the legation.

While the European chancelleries were trying to find some means to heal the breach, Austria-Hungary formally declared war on Servia on the morning of July 28th. The same evening, the bombardment of Belgrade from Semlin and from the Danube was begun. The Servian Government retired to Nish.

Only the intervention of Germany could now prevent the European cataclysm.

CHAPTER XX
GERMANY FORCES WAR UPON RUSSIA AND FRANCE

The title of this chapter seems to indicate that I have the intention of taking sides in what many people believe to be an open question. But this is not the case. The German contention, that Russia caused the war, must be clearly distinguished from the contention, that Russia forced the war. There is a great deal of reason in the first contention. No impartial student, who has written with sympathy concerning Great Britain's attitude in the Crimean War, can fail to give Germany just as strong justification for declaring war on Russia in 1914 as Great Britain had in 1854. But, when we come down to the narrower question of responsibility for launching the war in which almost all of Europe is now engaged, there can be no doubt that it was deliberately willed by the German Government, and that the chain of circumstances which brought it about was carefully woven by the officials of Wilhelmstrasse and Ballplatz. There may be honest difference of opinion as to whether Germany was justified in forcing the war. But the facts allow no difference of opinion as to whether Germany *did* force the war.

A war to crush France and Russia has for many years been accepted as a necessary eventuality in the evolution of Germany's foreign policy. That when this war came, Great Britain would take the opportunity of joining in order to strike at German commerce, which had begun to be looked upon by British merchants as a formidable rival in the markets of the world, was thought probable. The leading men of Germany, especially since the passing of Morocco and Persia, have felt that this war was vital to the existence of the German Empire. During recent years the questions, "Ought there to be a war?" and "Will there be a war?" ceased to be debated in Germany. One heard only, "Under what circumstances could *the* war be most favourably declared?" and "How soon will *the* war come?"

Germany has believed that the events of the past decade have shown the unalterable determination of Great Britain and France to make impossible the political development of the *Weltpolitik*, without which her commercial development would always be insecure. This determination has been consistently revealed in the hostility of her western rivals to her colonial expansion in Africa and Asia. The world equilibrium, already decidedly disadvantageous to the overseas future of Germans at the time they began their career as a united people, has been disturbed more and more during the past forty years.

The Balkan wars, resulting as they did in the aggrandizement of Servia, threatened the equilibrium of the Near East, where lay Germany's most vital and most promising external activities. We must remember, when we are considering the reasons for the consistent backing given to Austria-Hungary by Germany in her treatment of Servian aspirations, the words of Wirth: "*To render powerful the Servian people would be the suicide of Germany.*"

Germany has had as much reason, in the development of the present crisis, for regarding Servia as the outpost of Russia as had Great Britain for awarding this rôle to Bulgaria in 1876. Germany has had as much reason for declaring war on Russia to prevent the Russians from securing the inheritance of the Ottoman Empire as had Great Britain and France to take exactly the same step in 1854. The extension, in 1914, of Russian influence in what was until recently European Turkey would be just as disastrous to the interests of Germany and Austria-Hungary—far more so—than it would have been to Great Britain and France sixty years ago. What she has in Asia-Minor to-day is as great a stake for Germany to fight for as what Great Britain had in India in the middle of the nineteenth century.

There is, however, this important difference. Germany, in supporting the Austro-Hungarian ultimatum, was not responding to the overt act of an enemy. She calculated carefully the cost, waited for a favourable moment, and, when she decided that the favourable moment had come, deliberately provoked the war.

Germany, looking for the opportunity to strike her two powerful neighbours on the east and west, believed that the propitious moment had come in the summer of 1914. Her rivals were facing serious internal crises. Russia was embarrassed by the menace of a widely-spread industrial strike. But Russia did not count for much in the German calculations. *It was the situation in France that induced the German statesmen to take advantage of the assassination of Franz Ferdinand.* The spring elections had revealed a tremendous sentiment against the law recently voted extending military service for three years. The French Parliament had just overthrown the admirable Ribot Cabinet for no other reason than purely personal considerations of a bitter party strife. An eminent Parliamentarian had exposed publicly from the tribune the alarming unpreparedness of France for war. The trial for murder of the wife of the former Premier Caillaux bade fair to complicate further internal Parliamentary strife.

These were the favourable circumstances of the end of June and the beginning of July.

But the decision had wider grounds than the advantages of the moment. The German Government was finding it more and more difficult every year to secure the credits necessary for the maintenance and increase of her naval and military establishments. Socialism and anti-militarism were making alarming progress in the German *Reichstag*. On the other hand, the Russian military reorganization, commenced after the Japanese War, was beginning to show surprising fruits. And was France to be allowed time for the spending of the eight hundred and five million francs just borrowed by her in June to correct the weak spots in her fortifications and war material, and for the application of the *loi des trois ans* to increase her standing army?

Furthermore, would Great Britain be able to intervene on behalf of France and Russia? The crisis over the Home Rule Bill seemed to have developed so seriously that civil war was feared. Sir Edward Carson, leader of the Protestant irreconcilables in the north of Ireland, had formed an army that was being drilled in open defiance of the Government.

The assassination of the Archduke Franz Ferdinand and the Duchess of Hohenberg came at this advantageous moment. A *casus belli* against Servia, so provokingly lacking, had at last been given. Austria-Hungary was only too ready for the chance to crush Servia. If there were any misgivings about the risk of doing this, they were immediately allayed by Germany, who assured Austria-Hungary that she would not allow Russia even to mobilize. Austria-Hungary was given by Germany *carte blanche* in the matter of her dealings with Servia. It is possible, as the German Ambassador at Petrograd declared to M. Sasonow, that the text of the Austro-Hungarian ultimatum had not been submitted beforehand for the approval of Wilhelmstrasse. But the general tenor of the ultimatum had certainly been agreed upon. Germany knew well that the ultimatum would be so worded as to be a challenge to Russia. Either Russia would accept once more the humiliation of a diplomatic defeat and see Servia crushed, or she would intervene to save Servia. In the latter contingency, Germany could declare war upon Russia on the ground that her ally, Austria-Hungary, had been attacked. The Franco-Russian Alliance would then be put to the test, as well as whatever understanding there might be between Great Britain and France.

Subsequent events proved that Germany left no means, other than complete submission to her will, to France and Russia for avoiding war. Negotiations were so carried on that there would be no loop-hole for escape either to Servia, or to the Great Powers that were her champions. She did not even wait for Russia to attack Austria-Hungary, or for France to aid Russia. As for Great Britain, it is not yet clear whether Germany really thought that she was making an honest effort to keep her out of the war.

From the very beginning of the Servian crisis, Germany associated herself "for better or for worse with Austria-Hungary." On the day that the ultimatum to Servia was delivered, Chancellor von Bethmann-Hollweg wrote to the German Ambassadors at London, Paris, and Petrograd, requesting them to call upon the Foreign Ministers of the governments to which they were accredited and point out that the ultimatum was necessary for the "safety and integrity" of Austria-Hungary, and to state with special "emphasis" that "*in this question there is concerned an affair which should be settled absolutely between Austria-Hungary and Servia, the limitation to which it must be the earnest endeavour of the Powers to ensure. We* anxiously desire *the localization of the conflict*, because any intercession by another Power would precipitate, on account of the various alliances, inconceivable consequences."

The position of Germany is admirably stated in these instructions, which I quote from Exhibit I of the German official *White Book*. To this position, Chancellor von Bethmann-Hollweg consistently held throughout the last week of July. In the four words "*localization of the conflict*" the intention of Germany was summed up. There was to be a conflict between Austria-Hungary and Servia. That could not be avoided. The only thing that could be avoided was the intervention of Russia to prevent the approaching attack of Austria-Hungary upon Servia. If the Powers friendly to Russia did not prevail upon the Czar to refrain from interfering, there would be, "*on account of the various alliances, inconceivable consequences.*"

The next day, July 24th, a telegram from the German Ambassador at Petrograd to the Chancellor stated that M. Sasonow was very much agitated, and had "declared most positively that Russia could not permit under any circumstances that the Servo-Austrian difficulty be settled alone between the parties concerned."

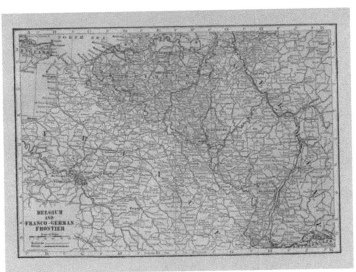

Map—Belgium and the Franco-German Frontier

There was still time for Germany, warned by the attitude taken by Russia, to counsel her ally to accept whatever conciliatory response Servia might give. But this was not done. As we have already seen in the previous chapter, the Austro-Hungarian Minister at Belgrade, without communicating with his Government, declared the Servian response unsatisfactory, even though it gave an opening for further negotiations, and withdrew from Belgrade with all the members of the legation staff.

This precipitate, and, in view of the gravity of the international situation, unreasonable action could have been avoided, had Chancellor von Bethmann-Hollweg telegraphed the word to Vienna.

Not only was the Austro-Hungarian Minister allowed to leave Belgrade in this way, but, *after three days had elapsed*, Austria-Hungary took the irrevocable step of declaring war on Servia.

During these three days, Sir Edward Grey requested the British Ambassadors at Rome and Vienna and Berlin to make every possible effort to find ground for negotiation. On the morning of July 27th, Sir Maurice de Bunsen, British Ambassador at Vienna, submitted to Count Berchtold the proposition of Sir Edward Grey, which was made simultaneously at Petrograd, that the question at issue be adjusted in a conference held at London. In the meantime, after a conversation with Sir Rennell Rodd, the Marquis di San Giuliano, the Italian Minister of Foreign Affairs, telegraphed to Berlin, suggesting that Germany, France, Great Britain, and Italy mediate between Austria-Hungary and Russia. In sharp contrast to the efforts being made by the British Ambassadors, the German Ambassador at Paris, in an interview with Premier Viviani, insisted upon the impossibility of a conference of mediation, and announced categorically that *the only possible solution of the difficulty was a common French and German intervention at Petrograd.* In other words, France could avoid war by assisting her enemy in humiliating her ally!

On July 28th, the German position was: "That Austria-Hungary must be left a free hand in her dealings with Servia, and that it must be pointed out to Russia, if France and Great Britain really wanted to save the peace of Europe, that she should not mobilize against Austria-Hungary." Diplomatic intervention, then, could do nothing except attempt to force Russia to refrain from interfering between Austria-Hungary and Servia. Germany would aid the other Powers in coercing Russia, but she would not urge herself, or aid them in urging, upon Austria-Hungary, *who had started the trouble,* the advisability of modifying her attitude towards Servia, and postponing hostilities that were bound to lead to a European war.

Germany had refused all intervention at Vienna. She agreed, however, to prove her good-will by letting it be known that Austria-Hungary was willing to make the promise to seek no territorial aggrandizement in her war with Servia, but to limit herself to a "punitive expedition." *But this suggestion did not come until Russia had already committed herself to defend Servia against invasion.*

There was another way in which the peace of Europe could have been saved, and that was by a declaration on the part of Germany that she would allow Russia and Austria-Hungary to fight out the question of hegemony in south-eastern Europe. But there was no proposition from Germany to France suggesting a mutual neutrality. On the other hand, Germany let it be known that she would stand by Austria-Hungary if Russia attacked her, and, in the same breath, warned France against the danger of being loyal to the Russian alliance!

On July 29th, it was announced from Petrograd that a partial mobilization had been ordered in the south and south-east. The German Ambassador in Petrograd, in an interview with M. Sasonow, pointed out "very solemnly that the entire Austro-Servian affair was eclipsed by the danger of a general European conflagration, and endeavoured to present to the Secretary the magnitude of this danger. It was impossible to dissuade Sasonow from the idea that Servia could now be deserted by Russia." On the same day, Ambassador von Schoen at Paris was directed by the German Chancellor to "call the attention of the French Government to the fact that preparation for war in France would call forth counter-measures in Germany." An exchange of telegrams on the 29th and 30th between the Kaiser and the Czar showed the irreconcilability between the Russian and German points of view. The idea of the Kaiser was that the Czar should give Austria-Hungary a free hand. The idea of the Czar was that the attack by Austria-Hungary upon Servia absolutely demanded a Russian mobilization "directed solely against Austria-Hungary."

On July 31st, the German Ambassador at Petrograd was ordered to notify Russia that mobilization against Austria-Hungary must be stopped within twelve hours, or Germany would mobilize against Russia. At the same time a telegram was sent to the German Ambassador at Paris, ordering him to "ask the French Government whether it intends to remain neutral in a Russo-German war."

On August 1st, at 7.30 P.M., the German Ambassador at Petrograd handed the following declaration of war to Russia:

"The Imperial Government has tried its best from the beginning of the crisis to bring it to a peaceful solution. Yielding to a desire which had been expressed to Him by His Majesty the Emperor of Russia, His Majesty the Emperor of Germany, in accord with England, was engaged in accomplishing the rôle of mediator between the Cabinets of Vienna and of Petrograd, when Russia, without awaiting the result of this mediation, proceeded to the mobilization of its forces by land and sea.

"As a result of this threatening measure, which was actuated by no military preparation on the part of Germany, the German Empire found itself facing a grave and imminent danger. If the Imperial Government had failed to ward off this danger, it would compromise the security and very existence of Germany. Consequently the German Government saw itself forced to address itself to the Government of His Majesty, the Emperor of all the Russias, insisting upon the cessation of the said military acts. Russia having refused to accede, and having manifested by this refusal that this action was directed against Germany, I have the honour of making known to Your Excellency the following order from my Government:

"His Majesty, the Emperor, my august Sovereign, in the name of the Empire, accepts the challenge, and considers himself in the state of war with Russia."

The same afternoon, President Poincaré ordered a general mobilization in France. What Ambassador von Schoen tried to get from Premier Viviani, and what he *did* get was expressed in his telegram sent from Paris three hours before the call to mobilization was issued:

"Upon the repeated definite enquiry whether France would remain neutral in the case of a Russo-German War, the Premier declared that France would do that which her interests dictated."

Germany violated the neutrality of Luxemburg on August 2d, and of Belgium on August 3d, after vainly endeavouring to secure permission from Belgium for the free passage of her troops to the French frontier. On Sunday morning, August 2d, French soil was invaded. But Ambassador von Schoen stayed in Paris until Monday evening "waiting for instructions." Then he called at the Quai d'Orsay, and handed the following note to Premier Viviani, who was acting also as Minister of Foreign Affairs:

"The German civil and military authorities have reported a certain number of definite acts of hostility committed on German territory by French military aviators. Several of these have clearly violated the neutrality of Belgium in flying over the territory of this country. One of them tried to destroy structures near Wesel; others have been seen in the region of Eiffel, another has thrown bombs on the railway near Karlsruhe and Nürnberg.

"I am charged, and I have the honour to make known to Your Excellency that, in the presence of these aggressions, the German Empire considers itself in state of war with France by the act of this latter Power.

"I have at the same time the honour to bring to the knowledge of Your Excellency that the German authorities will detain the French merchant ships in German ports, but that they will release them if in forty-eight hours complete reciprocity is assured.

"My diplomatic mission having come to an end, there remains to me no more than to beg Your Excellency to be willing to give me my passports and to take what measures you may judge necessary to assure my return to Germany with the staff of the embassy, as well as with the staff of the legation of Bavaria and of the German Consulate-General at Paris."

In communicating this declaration of war to the Chamber of Deputies on the following morning, August 4th, Premier Viviani declared formally that "at no moment has a French aviator penetrated into Belgium; no French aviator has committed either in Bavaria or in any part of the German Empire any act of hostility."

CHAPTER XXI
GREAT BRITAIN ENTERS THE WAR

The balance of power in European diplomacy led inevitably to a *rapprochement* between France and Russia and Great Britain to offset the Triple Alliance of Germany and Austria-Hungary and Italy.

The Triple Alliance, however, while purely *defensive*, was still an alliance. It had endured or over thirty years, and the three Powers generally sustained each other in diplomatic moves. Their military and naval strategists were in constant communication, and ready at any time to bring all their forces into play in a European war.

France and Russia had also entered into a defensive alliance. This had not been accomplished without great difficulty. Were it not for the constant menace to France from Germany, the French Parliament would not have ratified the alliance in the first place, nor would it have stood the strain of increasing Radicalism in French sentiment during the last decade. While there is much intellectual and temperamental affinity between Gaul and Slav, there is no political affinity between democratic France and autocratic Russia.

The commercial rivalry of Great Britain and Germany led to a rivalry of armaments. The struggle of German industry for the control of the world markets is the real cause of the creation and rapid development of the German navy to threaten the British mastery of the seas. It is possible that the statesmen of Great Britain, by a liberal policy in regard to German colonial expansion in Africa and Asia and in regard to German ambitions in Asiatic Turkey, might have diverted German energy from bending all its efforts to destroy British commerce. It is possible that such a policy might have enabled the German democracy to gain the power to prevent Prussian militarism from dominating the Confederation. But that would have been expecting too much of human nature. Nations are like individuals. There never has been any exception to this rule. What we have we want to keep. We want more than we have, and we try to get it by taking it away from our neighbour. Thus the world is in constant struggle. Until we have the millennium, and by the millennium I mean the change of human nature from selfishness to altruism, we shall have war. Then, too, the British have seen in themselves so striking an illustration of the proverb that the appetite grows with eating that they could hardly expect anything else of the Germans, were they to allow them voluntarily "a place in the sun."

The rapid growth of Germany along the lines similar to the development of Great Britain has made the two nations rivals. As a result of this rivalry, Great Britain has been forced to prepare for the eventuality of a conflict between herself and Germany by giving up the policy of "splendid isolation," and seeking to enter into friendly relationship with those European Powers that were the enemies of her rival. The first decade of the twentieth century saw British diplomacy compounding colonial rivalry with France in Africa and with Russia in Asia. The African accord of 1904 and the Asiatic accord of 1907 marked a new era in British foreign relations. Since their conclusion, Great Britain has drawn gradually nearer to France and Russia.

But British statesmen have had to reckon with the development of Radical tendencies in the British electorate. These tendencies have become more and more marked during the very period in which British foreign policy found that its interests coincided with those of Russia and France. British democracy had the same antipathy to a Russian alliance as had French democracy. But the menace of Germany, which threw France into the arms of Russia, has not seemed as real to the British electorate. There was also the sentiment against militarism, which has made it difficult for the Liberal Cabinet to secure from Parliament sufficient sums for the maintenance of an adequate naval establishment, and has blocked every effort to provide even a modified form of compulsory military service and military training in Great Britain and Ireland.

When one considers all that Sir Edward Grey has had to contend with during the years that he has held the portfolio of Foreign Affairs in the British Cabinet admiration for his achievements knows no limits. It is never safe to make comparisons or form judgments in the appreciation of contemporary figures in history. But I cannot refrain from stating my belief that British foreign policy has never passed through a more trying and critical period, and British interests have never been more ably served, than during the years since the conference of Algeciras.

The menace of a war between Great Britain and Germany has disturbed Europe several times during the past decade. There has not been, however, a direct crisis, involving the interests of the two rival nations, to make an appeal to arms inevitable, or even probable. But, although British public sentiment might have been slow in supporting the intervention of the Cabinet in favour of France, had Germany attacked France in 1905, in 1908, or in 1911, to have stayed out of the war would have been suicidal folly, and Great Britain would soon have awakened to this fact.

The crisis over the ultimatum of Austria-Hungary to Servia became acute after the terms of the ultimatum were known. Sir Edward Grey, seconded by as skilful and forceful ambassadors as have ever represented British interests on the continent of Europe, honestly tried to prevent the outbreak of war. It was not to the interests of Great Britain that this war should be fought. All sentimental considerations to one side, the moment was peculiarly unfavourable on purely material grounds. The British Parliament was facing one of the most serious problems of its history. The confidence of the country in the wisdom of the measures in Ireland that the Government seemed determined to carry out was severely shaken. The interest of the British public in the troubles between Austria-Hungary and Servia was not great enough to make the war popular. The efforts of Lord Haldane had done much to improve the relationship between Great Britain and Germany. Sympathy with Russia had been alienated by the increasingly reactionary policy of the Czar's government towards the Poles, the Finns, and the Jews. The British press was disgusted by the overthrow of the Ribot Ministry and by the revelations of the Caillaux trial.

As there was no actual alliance between Great Britain and France, and no understanding of any nature whatever with Russia, French public opinion was far from being certain that British aid would be given in the approaching war, *and British public opinion was far from being certain as to whether it would be necessary to give this aid, or whether it wanted to do so.* I am speaking here of the feeling among the electorate, which, accurately represented by Parliament, is the final court of appeal in Great Britain. There was no doubt about the opinion of Sir Edward Grey and the majority of his colleagues in the Cabinet, as well as of the leaders of the Opposition. There was, however, very serious doubt as to the attitude of Parliament. Would it sustain France and Russia over the question of Servia, at a time when there was so serious a division in the nation concerning the Home Rule Bill— even the open menace of civil war?

When Germany decided to declare war on Russia, and it was seen that France would be drawn into the struggle, Chancellor von Bethmann-Hollweg declared to Sir Edward Goschen, British Ambassador to Germany, that "the neutrality of Great Britain once guaranteed, every assurance would be given to the Cabinet at London that the Imperial Government did not have in view territorial acquisitions at the expense of France." Sir Edward questioned the Chancellor about the French colonies, "the portions of territories and possessions of France situated outside of the continent of Europe." Herr von Bethmann-Hollweg answered that it was not within his power to make any promise on that subject.

There was no hesitation or equivocation in the response of the British Secretary of State for Foreign Affairs to this proposition. He said that neutrality under such conditions was impossible, and that Great Britain could not stand by and see France crushed, even if she were left her

European territory intact, for she would be reduced to the position of a satellite of Germany. To make a bargain with Germany at the expense of France would be a disgrace from which Great Britain would never recover. It was pointed out to the Chancellor that the only means of maintaining good relations between Great Britain and Germany would be for the two Powers to continue to work together to safeguard the peace of Europe. Sir Edward Grey promised that all his personal efforts would be directed towards guaranteeing Germany and her Allies against any aggression on the part of Russia and France, and hoped that, if Germany showed her good faith in the present crisis, more friendly relations between Great Britain and Germany would ensue than had been the case up to that moment.

This dignified and manly response could have left no doubt in the minds of German statesmen as to the stand which the British Cabinet intended to take. Did they believe that Parliament and the people would not support Sir Edward Grey?

The position of Great Britain was explicitly put before the House of Commons on the evening of August 3d. Because of her naval agreement with France, by which the French navy was concentrated in the Mediterranean in order that the British Admiralty might keep its full forces in home waters, Great Britain was bound in honour to prevent an attack of a hostile fleet upon the Atlantic seacoast of France. If Germany were to make such an attack, Great Britain would be drawn into the war without any further question. There had also been since November, 1912, an understanding between the British and French military and naval authorities concerning common action on land and sea "against an enemy." But, at the time this understanding was made, it was put in writing that it was merely a measure of prudence, and did not bind Great Britain in any way whatever to act with France either in a defensive or offensive war.

Great Britain was drawn into the war by the German violation of the neutrality of Belgium.

On Sunday evening, August 2d, at seven o'clock, Germany gave the following ultimatum to Belgium:

"The German Government has received sure news, according to which the French forces have the intention of marching on the Meuse by way of Givet and Namur; this news leaves no doubt of the intention of France to march against Germany by way of Belgian territory. The Imperial German Government cannot help fearing that Belgium, in spite of its very good will, will not be able to repulse, without help, a forward march of French troops which promises so large a development.

"In this fact we find sufficient certitude of a threat directed against Germany; it is an imperious duty for self-preservation for Germany to forestall this attack of the enemy.

"The German Government would regret exceedingly should Belgium regard as an act of hostility against it the fact that the enemies of Germany oblige her to violate, on her side, the territory of Belgium. In order to dissipate every misunderstanding, the German Government declares as follows:

"1. Germany has in view no act of hostility against Belgium, if Belgium consents, in the war which is going to commence, to adopt an attitude of benevolent neutrality in regard to Germany. The German Government, on its side, promises, at the moment of peace, to guarantee the kingdom and its possessions in their entire extent. 2. Germany promises to evacuate Belgian territory, under the condition above pronounced, immediately peace is concluded. 3. If Belgium observes a friendly attitude, Germany is ready, in accord with the authorities of the Belgian Government, to buy, paying cash, all that would be necessary for her troops, and to indemnify the losses caused to Belgium. 4. If Belgium conducts herself in a hostile manner against the German troops and makes in particular difficulties for their forward march by an opposition of the fortifications of the Meuse or by the destruction of roads, railways, tunnels, or other constructions, Germany will be obliged to consider Belgium as an enemy.

"In this case, Germany will make no promise in regard to the kingdom, but will leave the subsequent adjustment of the relations of the two states one toward the other to the decision of arms.

"The German Government has the hope with reason that this eventuality will not take place, and that the Belgian Government will know how to take the necessary measures suitable for preventing it from taking place.

"In this case, the relations of friendship which unite the two neighbouring states will become narrower and more lasting."

Belgium did not hesitate to respond promptly as follows:

"By its note of August 2, 1914, the German Government has made known that according to sure news the French forces have the intention of marching on the Meuse by way of Givet and Namur, and that Belgium, in spite of her very good will, would not be able to repulse without help the forward march of the French troops.

"The German Government would believe itself under the obligation of forestalling this attack and of violating the Belgian territory. In these conditions, Germany proposes to the Government of the King to adopt in regard to her a friendly attitude, and she promises at the moment of the peace to guarantee the integrity of the kingdom and of its possessions in their entire extent.

"The note adds that if Belgium makes difficulty for the forward march of the German troops, Germany will be obliged to consider her as an enemy but will leave the subsequent adjustment of the relations of the two states one towards the other by the decision of arms.

"This note has aroused in the Government of the King a deep and grievous astonishment. The intentions that it attributes to France are in contradiction with the formal declarations which have been made to us on August 1st, in the name of the Government of the Republic.

"However, if in opposition to our expectation a violation of the Belgian neutrality is going to be committed by France, Belgium would fulfil all her international duties, and her army would oppose itself to the invader with the most vigorous resistance. The treaties of 1839, confirmed by the treaties of 1870, make sacred the independence and the neutrality of Belgium under the guarantee of the Powers and notably of the Government of His Majesty the King of Prussia.

"Belgium has always been faithful to her international obligations; she has accomplished her duties in a spirit of loyal impartiality, she has neglected no effort to maintain and to make respected her neutrality. The attack upon her independence with which the German Government menaces her would constitute a flagrant violation of international law.

"No strategic interest justifies the violation of international law. The Belgian Government in accepting the propositions of which it has received notice would sacrifice the honour of the nation at the same time as it would betray its duties toward Europe. Conscious of the rôle that Belgium has played for more than eighty years in the civilization of the world, it does not allow itself to believe that the independence of Belgium can be preserved only at the price of the violation of her neutrality. If this hope is deceived, the Belgian Government is firmly decided to repulse by every means in its power every attack upon its rights."

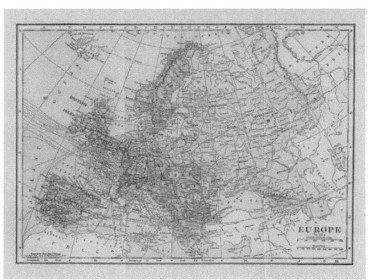

Map—Europe in 1914

As I record these two statements, there is before me a cartoon from a recent issue of *Punch*. The Kaiser, with a leer on his face, is leaning over the shoulder of King Albert, who is looking out with folded arms upon the smoking ruins of his country, and the long defile of refugees. The Kaiser says, "See, you have lost all." King Albert answers, "Not my soul."

To be just to Germany, is necessary for us to quote the explanation of this action made by Chancellor von Bethmann-Hollweg to the *Reichstag*, on August 4th, when Germany had commenced to carry into execution her threat:

"Here is the truth. We are in necessity, and necessity knows no law.

"Our troops have occupied Luxemburg, and have perhaps already put their foot upon Belgium territory.

"It is against the law of nations. The French Government has, it is true, declared at Brussels that it would respect the neutrality of Belgium, so long as the enemy respected it. We knew, however, that France was ready for the aggression. France could wait; we, no. A French attack upon our flank in the Lower Rhine might have been fatal to us. So we have been forced to pass beyond the well-founded protestations of Luxemburg and the Belgian Government. We shall recompense them for the wrong that we have thus caused them as soon as we shall have attained our military end.

"When one is as threatened as we are and when one fights for that which is most sacred to him, one can think only of one thing, that is, to attain his end, cost what it may."

"I repeat the words of the Emperor; 'It is with pure conscience that Germany goes to the combat.'"

On the afternoon of August 3d, as Sir Edward Grey was leaving for Parliament to make his *exposé* of Great Britain's position in the European crisis, he received from the King a telegram that had just arrived from King Albert of Belgium:

"Remembering the numerous proofs of friendship of Your Majesty and of Your predecessor, and the friendly attitude of Great Britain in 1870, as well as of the new gage of friendship that she has just given me, I address a supreme appeal to the diplomatic intervention of Your Majesty to safeguard the integrity of Belgium."

Sir Edward Grey read this telegram to Parliament, and explained that the diplomatic intervention asked for had already been made both at Paris and Berlin, for this eventuality had been foreseen. To the questions of the British Ambassadors concerning their intentions towards Belgium, *to respect and maintain the neutrality of which each of these Powers was equally bound with Great Britain by the treaty of 1839*, France responded by telegraph received August 1st:

"French Government are resolved to respect the neutrality of Belgium, and it would only be in the event of some other Power violating that neutrality that France might find herself under the necessity, in order to assure defense of her own security, to act otherwise."

Germany answered the same day through Sir E. Goschen;

"I have seen the Secretary of State, who informs me that he must consult the Emperor and the Chancellor before he could possibly answer."

When Sir Edward Goschen expressed the hope that the answer would not be delayed, Herr von Jagow gave him clearly to understand that he doubted whether he could respond, "for any response on his part would not fail, in case of war, to have the regrettable effect of divulging a part of the German plan of campaign!"

There was no doubt about the sentiment of Parliament. The Cabinet saw that party lines had been obliterated, and that the country was behind them. The following day, August 4th, Great Britain presented an ultimatum to Germany, demanding an assurance that the neutrality of Belgium should be respected. Germany gave no answer. Her army had already invaded Belgium. A few hours after the reception of the British ultimatum, the advance on Liège was ordered. After waiting until evening, Great Britain declared war on Germany.

It is probable that Germany counted the cost before she invaded Belgium. Whatever may have been said at Berlin, the intervention of Great Britain was not the surprise that it has been represented to be. In deciding to violate Belgian neutrality, in spite of the British ultimatum, the German argument was: It is morally certain that Great Britain will intervene if we enter Belgium. But what will this intervention mean? She has no army worth the name. Her navy can do practically nothing to harm us while we are crushing France and Russia. The participation of Great Britain in the war is a certainty a few weeks later. By precipitating her intervention, we are less harmed than we would be by refusing to avail ourselves of the advantage of attacking France through Belgium.

In believing that the eventual participation of Great Britain was certain, even if there were no Belgian question, Germany was right. The violation of the neutrality of Belgium was not the cause, but the occasion, of Great Britain's entry into the war. It was, however, a most fortunate opportunity for the British Cabinet to secure popular sympathy and support in declaring war upon Germany. For it is certain that Great Britain ought not to have delayed entering the war. The nation might have awakened too late to the fact that the triumph of Germany in Europe would menace her national existence. There is no room in the world for the amicable dwelling side by side of Anglo-Saxon idealism and German militarism. One or the other must perish.

In August, 1914, the only way to have avoided the catastrophe of a general European war would have been to allow Germany to make, according to her own desires and ambitions, the new map of Europe.

Lightning Source UK Ltd.
Milton Keynes UK
UKHW010743271222
414464UK00004B/366